IMAGES
*of America*

# PRESTON

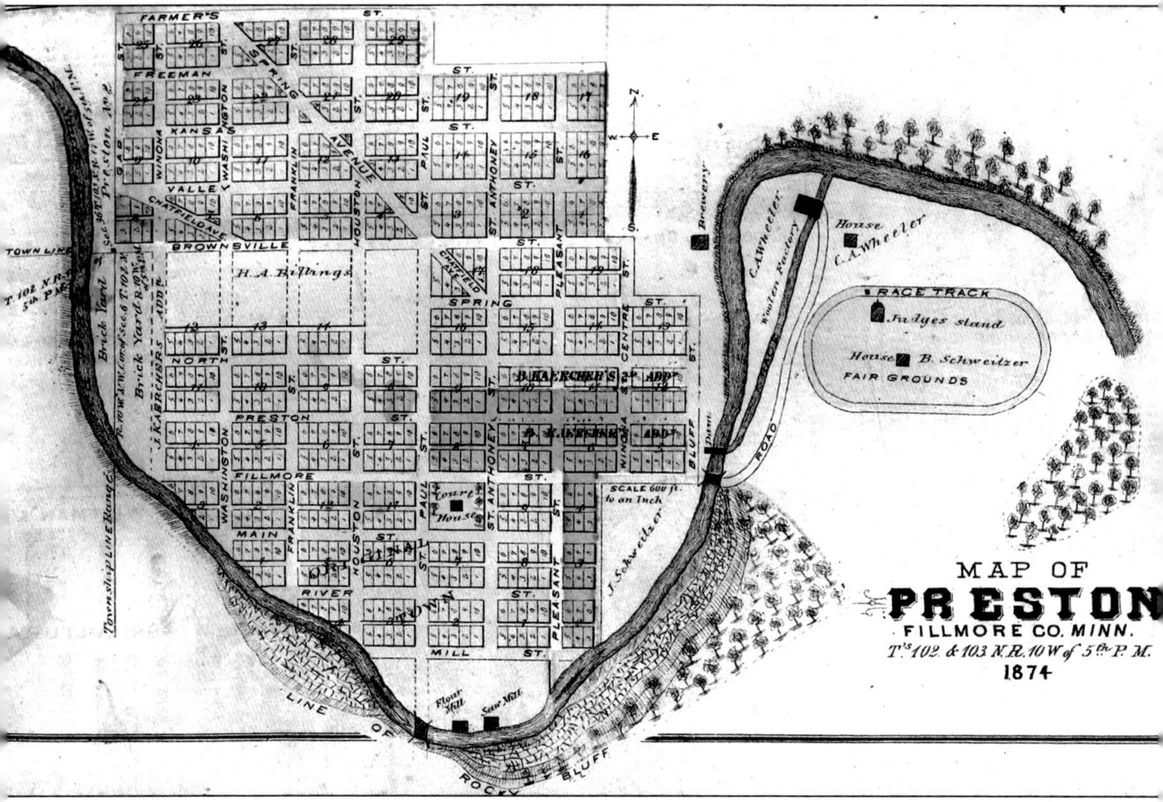
MAP OF
PRESTON
FILLMORE CO. MINN.
T's 102 & 103 N. R. 10 W of 5th P. M.
1874

IMAGES
*of America*

# PRESTON

Al Mathison

ARCADIA

ISBN 0-7385-3236-3

Published by Arcadia Publishing
Charleston SC, Chicago IL, Portsmouth NH, San Francisco CA

Printed in Great Britain

Library of Congress Catalog Card Number: 2004108651

For all general information contact Arcadia Publishing at:
Telephone 843-853-2070
Fax 843-853-0044
E-mail sales@arcadiapublishing.com
For customer service and orders:
Toll-Free 1-888-313-2665

Visit us on the internet at http://www.arcadiapublishing.com

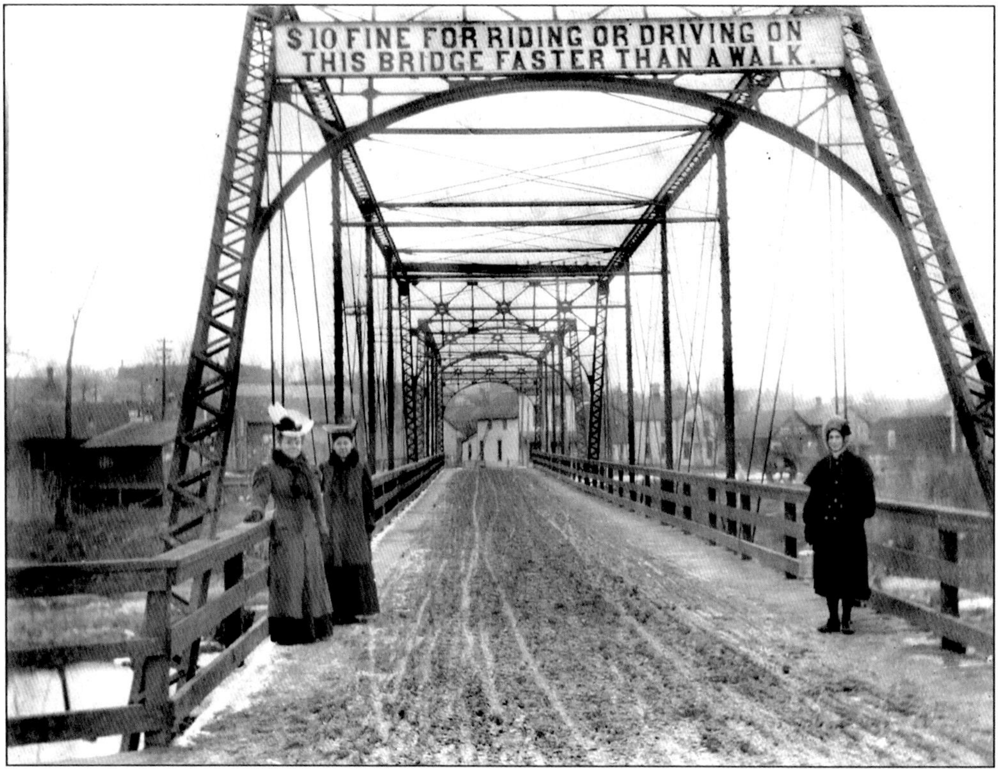

# Contents

# ACKNOWLEDGMENTS

I would like to acknowledge and thank the many people who were instrumental in making the publication of this book possible. This venture would never have gotten far off the ground without the assistance and vast knowledge of Jerry Henke, the director of the Fillmore County History Center in Fountain. His humor and insight helped keep the project on course.

Thanks also to Alma Syvertson of the History Center, and to research volunteer Howard Sanborn for being gracious and accommodating during my many lengthy visits. The Fillmore County History Center is a tremendous resource for anyone interested in the rich history of the area.

Equally important were the staff and resources provided by John and Pat Torgrimson of the *Fillmore County Journal*. Many special thanks to Shari Jones for her expertise and prompt scanning of all the photographs, and for her lively interest in the development of this book. I would also like to thank Damita Crouse and Hallie Snyder for their assistance and encouragement.

The information contained in the 1980 book, *Coming Home*, provided many of the details that ensured that this book would be historically accurate. A celebration of Preston's 125th anniversary, *Coming Home* was produced through the diligent labor of numerous volunteers, many of whom still live in the Preston area. I tip my hat to them.

While many of the following images came from the collection of the Fillmore County History Center, numerous individuals contributed pictures from their private collections, as well. I would like thank the following: Lois Hoag, Garaine Wildgrube, Esther Dreier, Dr. John Nehring, Don Ward, Norma Vogt, Gary Feine, Charlotte Hampel, Maxine and Jerome Simonson, Gerrie Daley, Margaret Gross, Merrill Pickett, Loyal Woellert, Marshall Ebert, Marsha Ebert Brouillet, Kristi Anderson, Jon Haugen, Steven Schlick, Bob Linden, Jim Pickett, Frankie Riehl, Vern Runningen, Diane Ruud, Scott Soffa, Lyle Miller, Rosalie Bjorkman, Roger McKenzie, Shirley Kaase, and Beverly Seibert. The Minnesota Historical Society also contributed several photographs for this book. My apologies to anyone I may have omitted.

Finally, I would like to thank my wife, Linda, and children, Jamie and Alex, for their support, patience, and help while I was immersed in this project.

# INTRODUCTION

The settlement of Preston was part of the great land rush that began with the signing of the 1851 Treaty of Traverse des Sioux. The treaty opened millions of acres to land-hungry settlers and speculators and southeast Minnesota was one of the first regions to be developed.

The first settler to stake a claim in the town that would become Preston was John Vail, of Ohio, who built a cabin at the site of today's Power Plant. The year was 1853 and it was estimated that there were just 14 "white families" living in Fillmore County.

By the fall of 1854, Vail transferred his claim to John Kaercher and his nephew, Theobald Schweitzer. It is Kaercher who is considered the founding father of Preston. He built a gristmill, a sawmill and a hotel, and also oversaw the platting of the town site in 1855. Kaercher named the fledging village after his millwright, Luther Preston.

By 1858 the population of the county was 11,000, and Preston, located at the geographic center, had been named the county seat. New settlers continued arriving in great numbers, lured by promises of cheap fertile land and limitless possibilities. A book published in Chatfield in 1858 went so far as to claim that Fillmore County's winter air was "generally clear, dry and sharp and seldom raw damp or changeable."

In the 1860s W.A. Hotchkiss, editor of the *Preston Republican*, wrote in glowing terms of Preston's future potential: "Preston, the county seat of Fillmore County, the largest and best in the state, is of so much importance . . . that it is attracting the earnest attention of sagacious capitalists. All the elements required in building up a large and rich inland city are here being developed."

Most of the information for writing the captions that appear in this book was gleaned from the marvelous newspapers that Preston has been home to over the past 150 years. The editors of the *Preston Times*, the *Preston Republican*, the *Preston Democrat* and the *National Republican* wrote with clarity and home-spun wisdom in a wonderful literary style that still resonates today.

This book is not meant to be a definitive history of Preston, but rather a photographic journey through some of the stories of its past—back to a time when there were distinct neighborhoods in town with their own nicknames. There were Oak Ridge and Fairview, and on the northeast side of town was Limerick, with its shady streets and stately homes. There was the Columbian Addition, located in the heights above the Root River, which was advertised as a peaceful and tranquil place to call home. Down along the river was Goose Flat, the original platted part of town, where as the legend goes, everybody once kept a goose or two in their backyards.

Outside of town in the rolling farm fields and forests were unincorporated places with exotic Native American names like Oneota, Carimona, and Waukokee. There were other places with descriptive names that never made it on the official maps, including Windy Ridge, Clear Grit, Buffalo Grove, Crystal Springs, and Dutch Hollow. Preston was the commercial hub and social center and the town would fill up on Saturday afternoons as farm families streamed in to shop at the numerous mercantile, dry goods, and grocery stores.

County Fair week was the biggest week of the year and attendance records were smashed in 1938 when 15,000 people attended the fair in a single day. Every day of the week Preston residents heard the whistle calls for the passenger trains that were headed out to Isinours or east to Caledonia. Before movies became the rage, entertainment could be found in the form of Chautauqua shows or local talent fests at the Grand Opera House. At the Tibbetts Skating Rink a person could go roller-skating for 10¢ an hour. During the first five years of the 1900s the Preston Tigers were called the second best indoor baseball team in the country. A thousand spectators packed into the upstairs Grand Opera House to cheer their local heroes on, when they played teams from the big cities of Milwaukee, St. Paul, and Chicago.

Shortly after Preston's stately Carnegie library was built in 1912, a promotional postcard set of scenes from around town was produced. The cover envelope contained a few paragraphs of descriptive and historical tribute that describes the proud little town as follows:

"First settled in 1853, a beautiful thriving village of 1,500 inhabitants situated on the south branch of the Root River, in the geographical center of Fillmore County, and is the county seat. Its railroad facilities are unsurpassed. The county has never known a failure of crops."

The surrounding farm lands are noted for their fertility; stock raising and corn being particularly successful. Preston has a nursery, a brickyard, and a farmer's co-operative creamery. Preston has two banks, two newspapers, two mills, three hotels, numerous stores, iron works, opera house, excellent schools—none better, six churches, no saloons, a fine city hall, and Carnegie library.

Preston is famed for its beautiful elm and maple shade trees, its picturesque location around the courthouse square, its surrounding scenery and trout streams. It invites the capitalist and those in quest of rest and health, or the pleasure bent. It has all the advantages of the city with none of its drawbacks."

Preston, today in the 21st century, is home to 1,500 people and remains the county's crossroads and government center. Its scenic beauty draws visitors from throughout the Midwest, and bicyclists flock to the Root River State Trail, which runs through the town. Fishing, canoeing, biking, or just plain relaxing, Preston has become a destination for all.

# One

# The Early Years

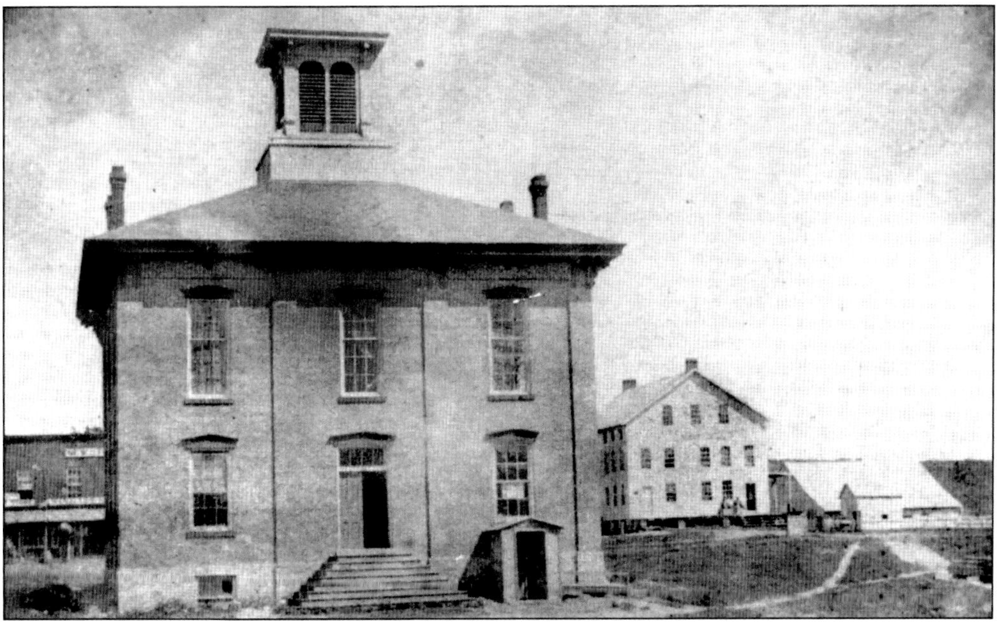

The Fillmore County courthouse stands in the middle of the public square at Preston, with the Stanwix House in the background. Built in 1864, the courthouse was constructed of local brick and limestone. The building measured 51 by $51^1/_2$ feet, and was two stories high. In the full basement there was a boiler room and a coal room. The County Commissioners met in the basement where there was also a general vault for county records and documents. (Photograph courtesy of the Minnesota Historical Society.)

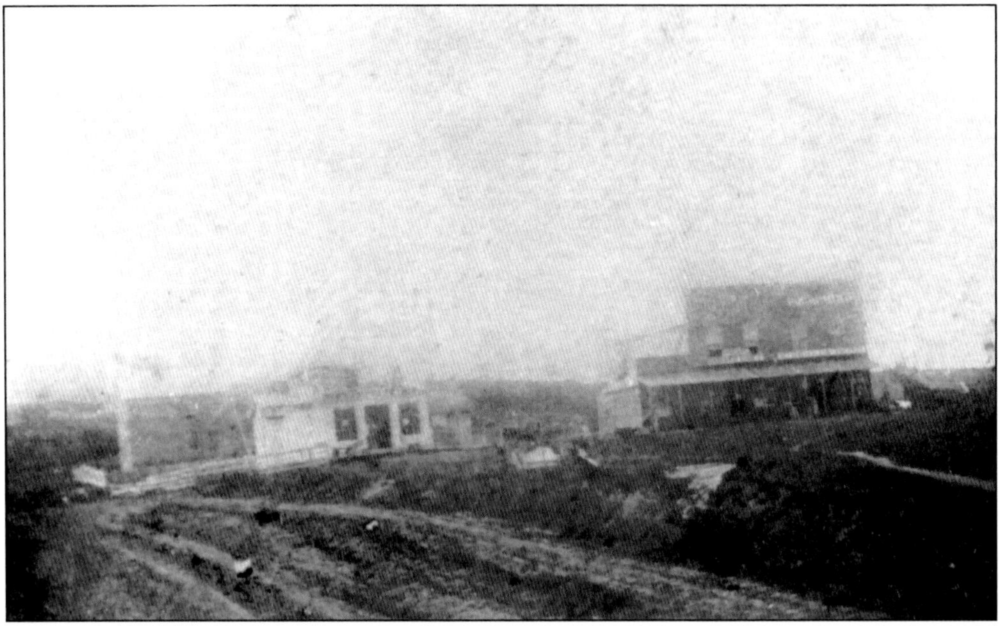

Photography was still in its infancy, as was Preston, when this picture was taken around 1865. Preston appears to be a rugged frontier town in this view up St. Paul Street with the courthouse park on the right. (Photograph courtesy of the Minnesota Historical Society.)

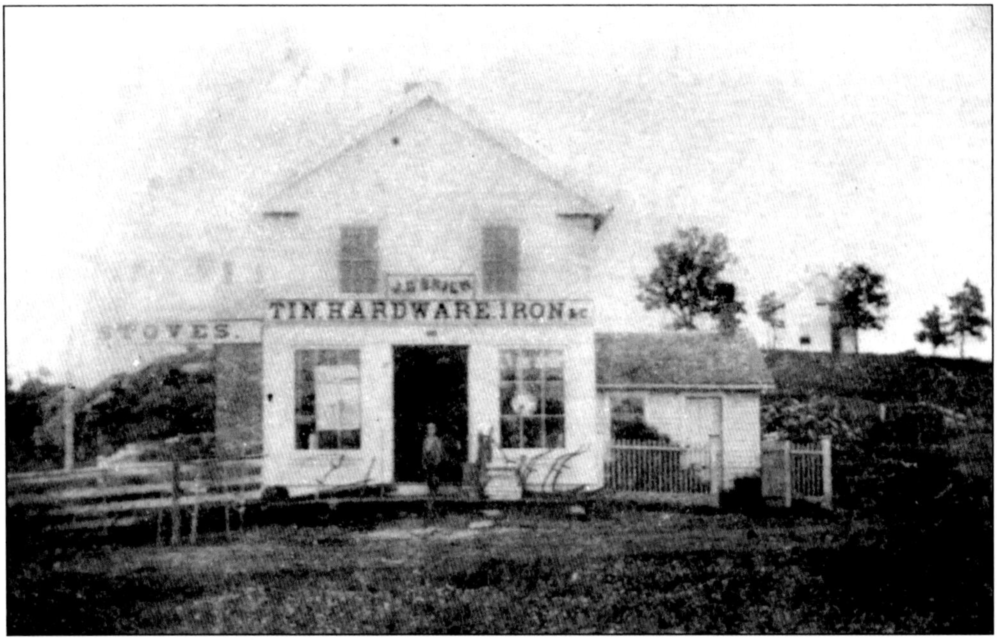


Another picture from 1865 shows the storefront of the J. O'Brien store. An advertisement from that year states that the store dealt in stoves, hardware, and tin and sheet iron ware. It was located near the corner of today's Fillmore Street and St. Paul Street. (Photograph courtesy of the Minnesota Historical Society.)

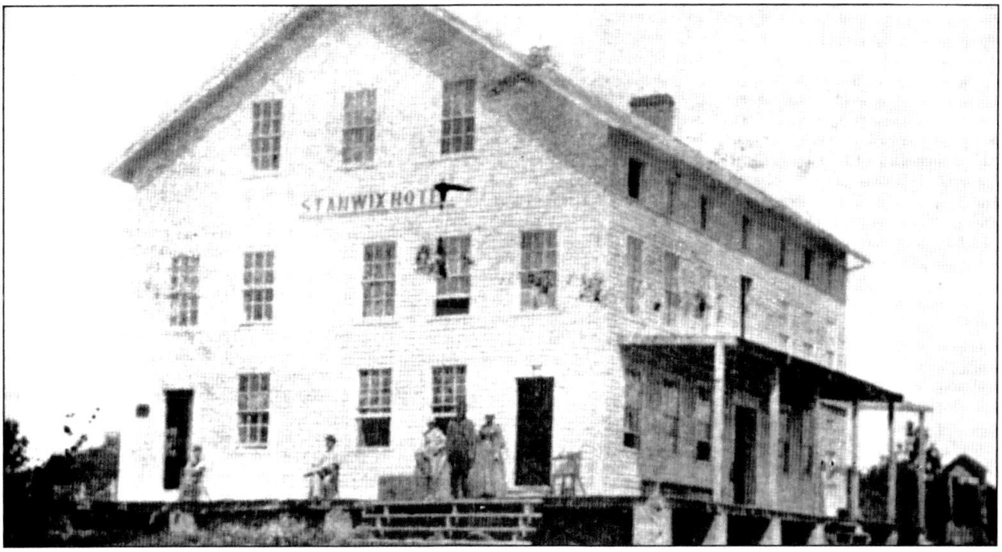

The Stanwix Hotel, later the Tibbetts House, was built by Preston's founder John Kaercher in 1857. The building was 36 by 50 feet and four stories high. Preston had its sights set on a prosperous future as evidenced by the following statement printed in the *Preston Republican* during 1865, the year this photograph was taken: "The prospects of our village are highly encouraging. Our people are intelligent and enterprising. We have always enjoyed prosperity and have had a steady growth. Preston provides an excellent field to those who are seeking a home." (Photograph courtesy of the Minnesota Historical Society.)

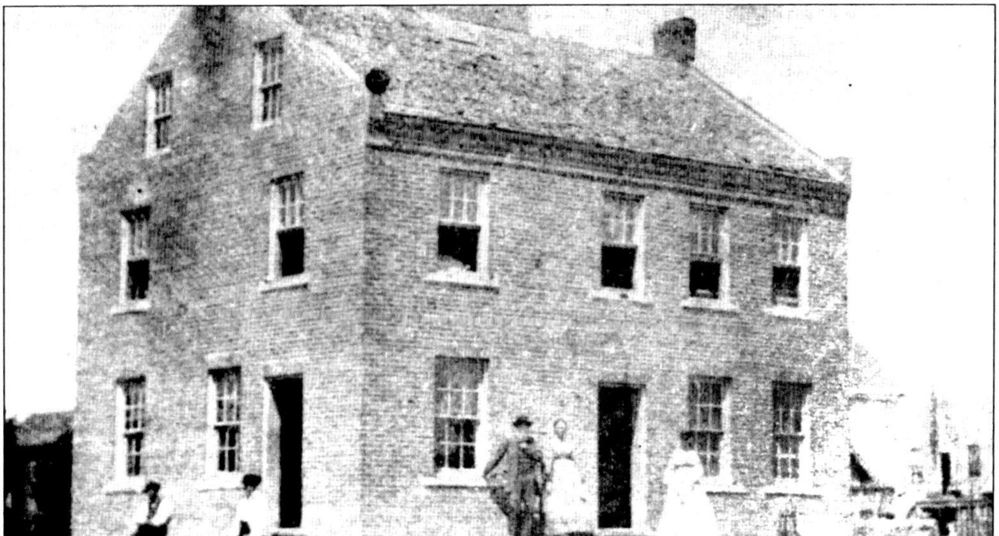

Another c. 1865 photograph shows the Minnesota House that was built by Joseph Ober in 1857. Ober ran the hotel, located on the corner of St. Anthony and River Streets, for many years. It later was used as a private residence. In 1868 a correspondent for the *Rochester Post* wrote after a visit to Preston that its buildings, "are strong and permanent, and the whole place has a look of solidity not often seen in Western towns of that size. As we first saw it with the evening sun shining upon the ripe wheat fields that framed it in gold, it was a pretty, cozy home like sight." (Photograph courtesy of the Minnesota Historical Society.)

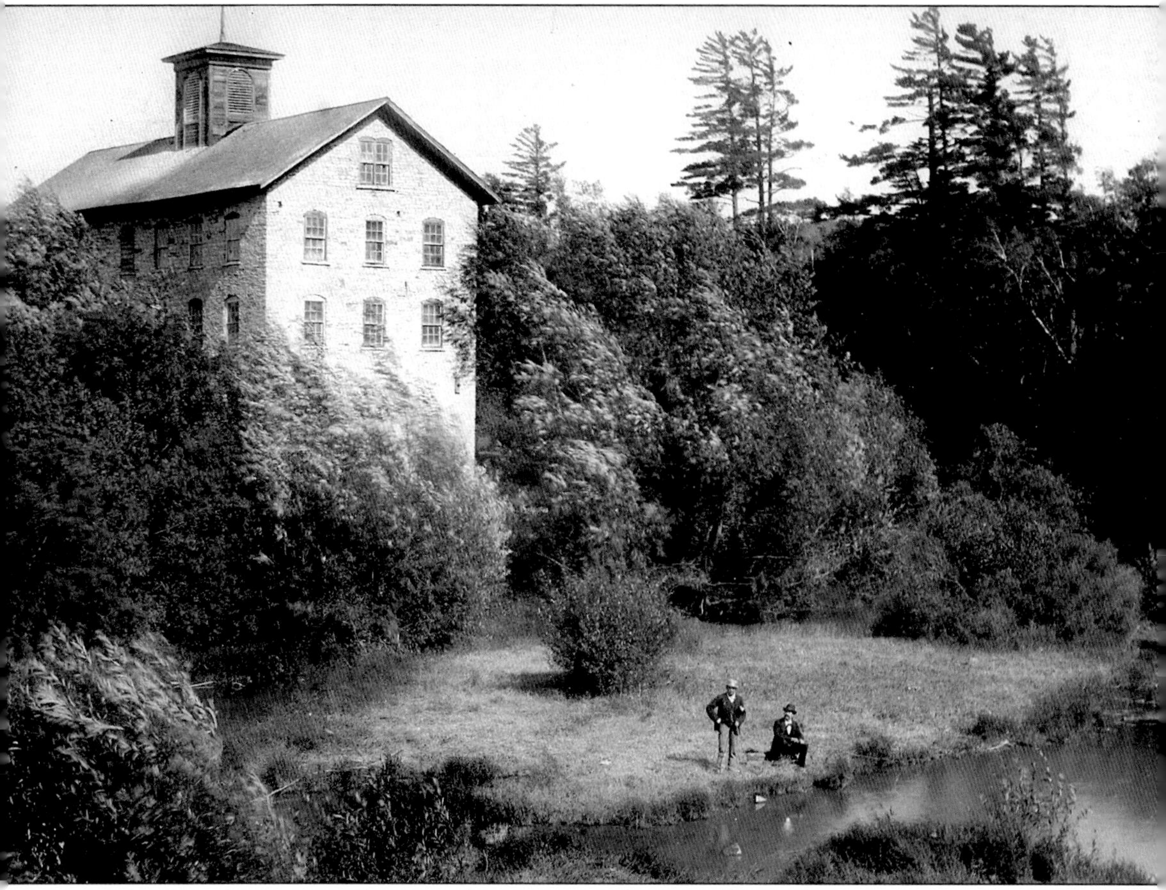

John Kaercher's gristmill was made of stone and was 30 by 40 feet in area. Kaercher hired Luther Preston to be his miller and even named the new village after him. Preston moved into the mill with his family. It had four stories and by 1858 was capable of flouring 500 bushels of wheat in 24 hours. Due to financial difficulties, Kaercher advertised his mill for sale that year with the following ad:

> *Grist Mill and Saw Mill, for sale, cheap, for cash. First and Best in Fillmore County.*
>
> —John Kaercher.

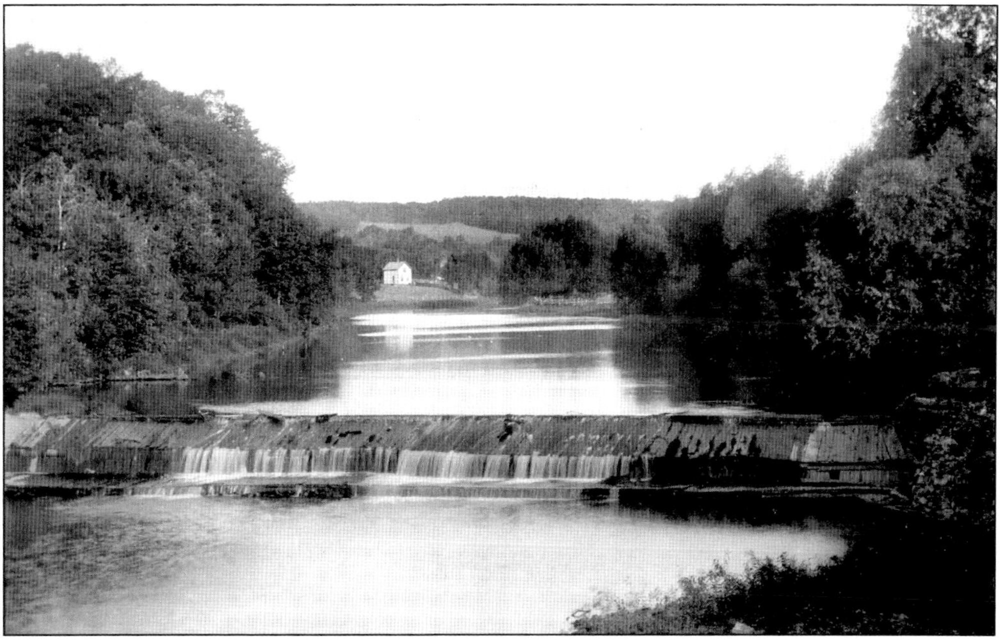

John Kaercher built this dam just west of the present-day south bridge. Its purpose was to provide power for his gristmill. A race was dug to divert the water to the mill, where a wheel provided power to the grinding stones inside the mill.

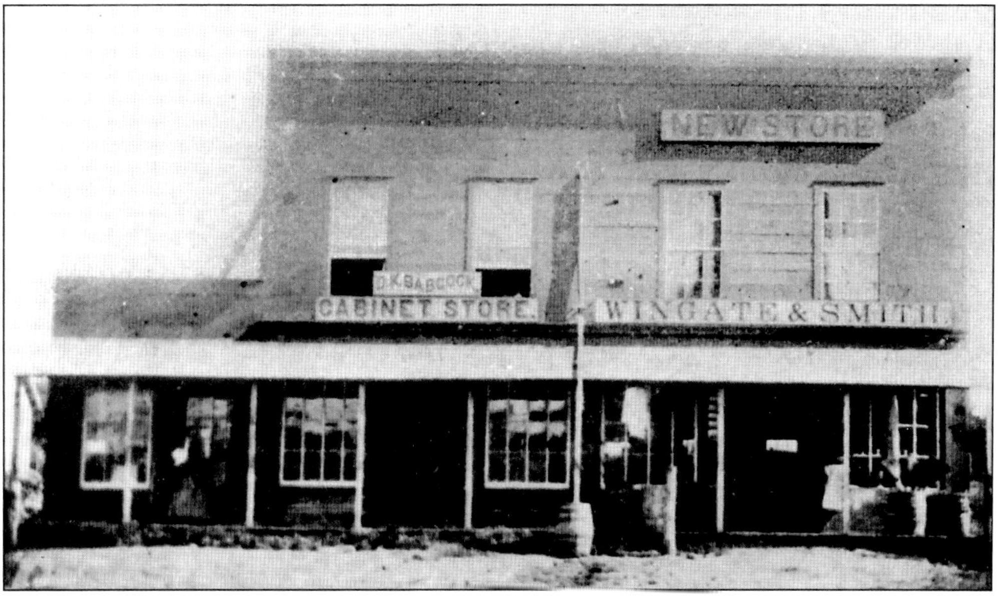


Another early mercantile store was that of Wingate and Smith, located north of the courthouse. The *Preston Democrat* published a report of a shoplifting spree by a family of thieves from Lenora Township in July of 1866. "The raiders numbered five persons, four women and one man—they visited the store of the Conkeys appropriating a number of articles, which as fast as obtained were deposited in their wagon, standing convenient. They then visited the store of Wingate and Smith, where they were detected in their lifting operations and handed over to the law." (Photograph courtesy of the Minnesota Historical Society.)

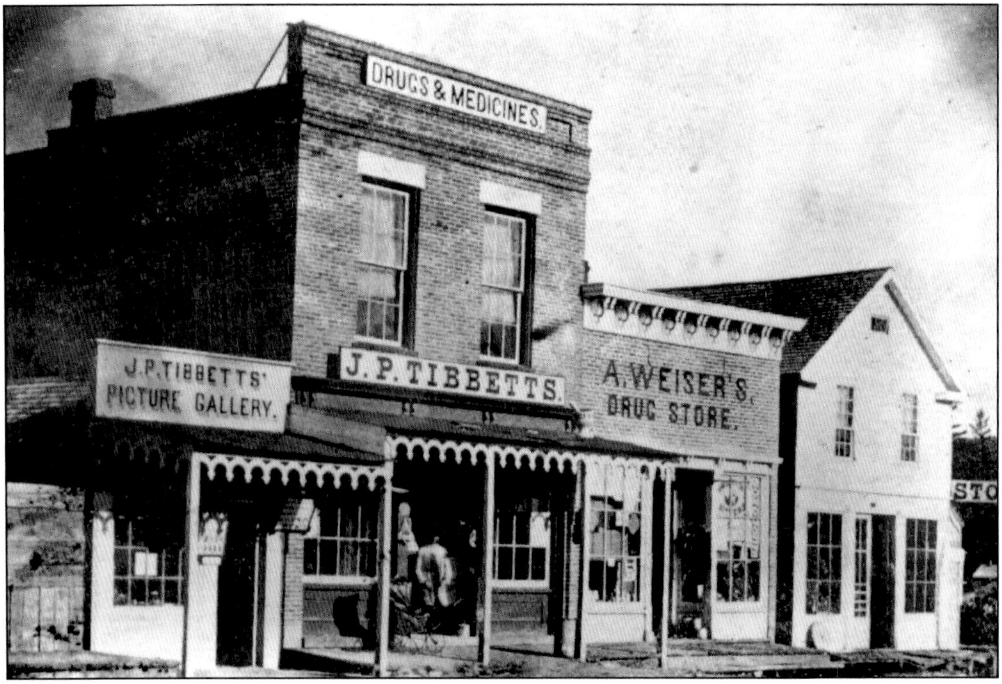


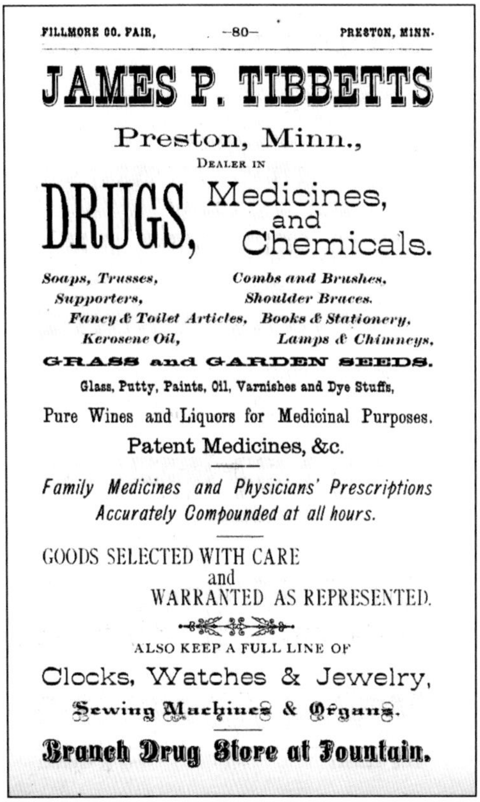


Among the businesses in Preston *c.* 1865 were the Tibbetts Drugstore and his adjacent photo gallery. J.P. Tibbetts (1830–1904) was born in Bangor, Maine, and worked as a traveling photographer and jewelry salesman throughout New England and Canada (then the British Provinces) before heading west. He arrived in Fillmore County in 1856 and began establishing businesses. Not only was he the largest property owner in Preston, but he owned drugstores in Fountain and Lanesboro as well. Tibbetts built the New England House, an early Preston hotel, and in 1879 he purchased the Stanwix Hotel and renamed it the Tibbetts House.

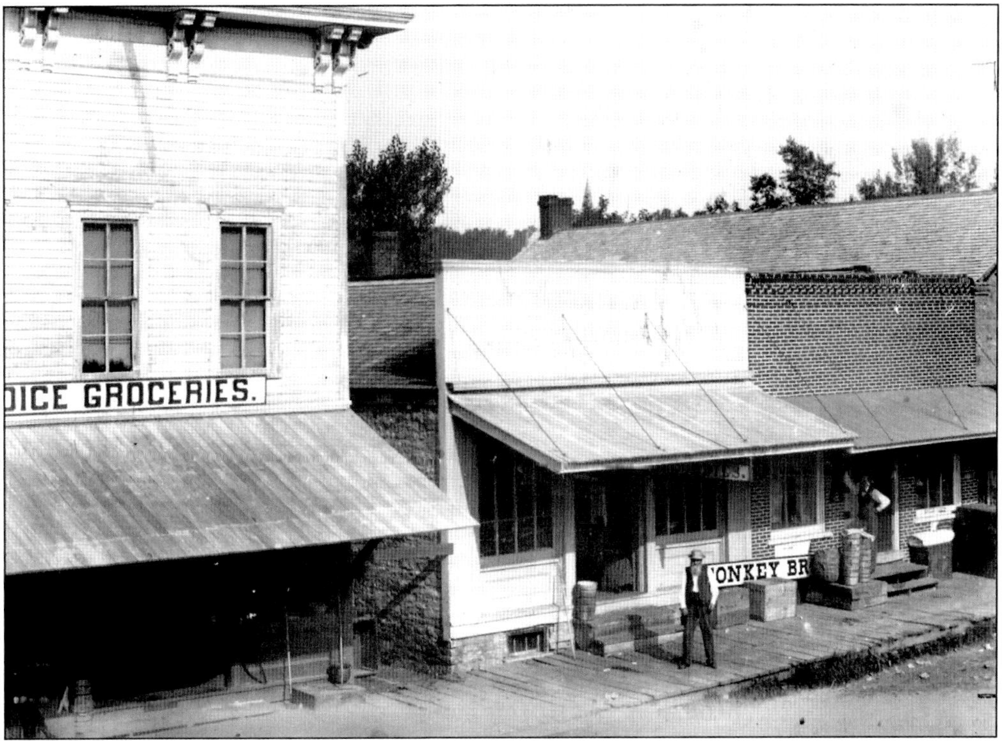


The Conkey Brothers Pioneer Store opened in 1867 on lower St. Paul Street. The advertisement is from the 1883 Fillmore County Fair Book. The editor of the *National Republican*, Major Hotchkiss wrote in 1869: "A few moments spent in the store of Conkey Bros. convinced us of the great value of a reputation for keeping none but the very best articles of merchandise. The success of this firm has been owing to the entire absence of deception in its transactions with customers. Such men always succeed." Besides being a businessman, Charles Conkey (1828–1907) also served as a state senator and mayor of Preston for four terms.

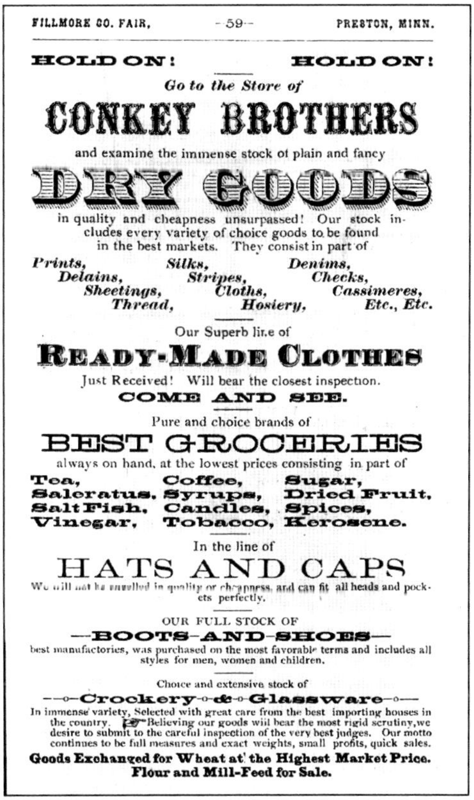
FILLMORE CO. FAIR, -59- PRESTON, MINN.

HOLD ON! HOLD ON!

*Go to the Store of*

**CONKEY BROTHERS**

and examine the immense stock of plain and fancy

**DRY GOODS**

in quality and cheapness unsurpassed! Our stock includes every variety of choice goods to be found in the best markets. They consist in part of

*Prints, Silks, Denims, Delains, Stripes, Checks, Sheetings, Cloths, Cassimeres, Thread, Hosiery, Etc., Etc.*

Our Superb line of

**READY-MADE CLOTHES**

Just Received! Will bear the closest inspection.

**COME AND SEE.**

Pure and choice brands of

**BEST GROCERIES**

always on hand, at the lowest prices consisting in part of

**Tea, Coffee, Sugar, Saleratus, Syrups, Dried Fruit, Salt Fish, Candles, Spices, Vinegar, Tobacco, Kerosene.**

In the line of

**HATS AND CAPS**

We will not be excelled in quality or cheapness, and can fit all heads and pockets perfectly.

OUR FULL STOCK OF

**—BOOTS-AND-SHOES—**

best manufactories, was purchased on the most favorable terms and includes all styles for men, women and children.

Choice and extensive stock of

**—o—Crockery-o-&-o-Glassware-o—**

In immense variety, Selected with great care from the best importing houses in the country. ☞Believing our goods will bear the most rigid scrutiny, we desire to submit to the careful inspection of the very best judges. Our motto continues to be full measures and exact weights, small profits, quick sales.

**Goods Exchanged for Wheat at the Highest Market Price.**
**Flour and Mill-Feed for Sale.**

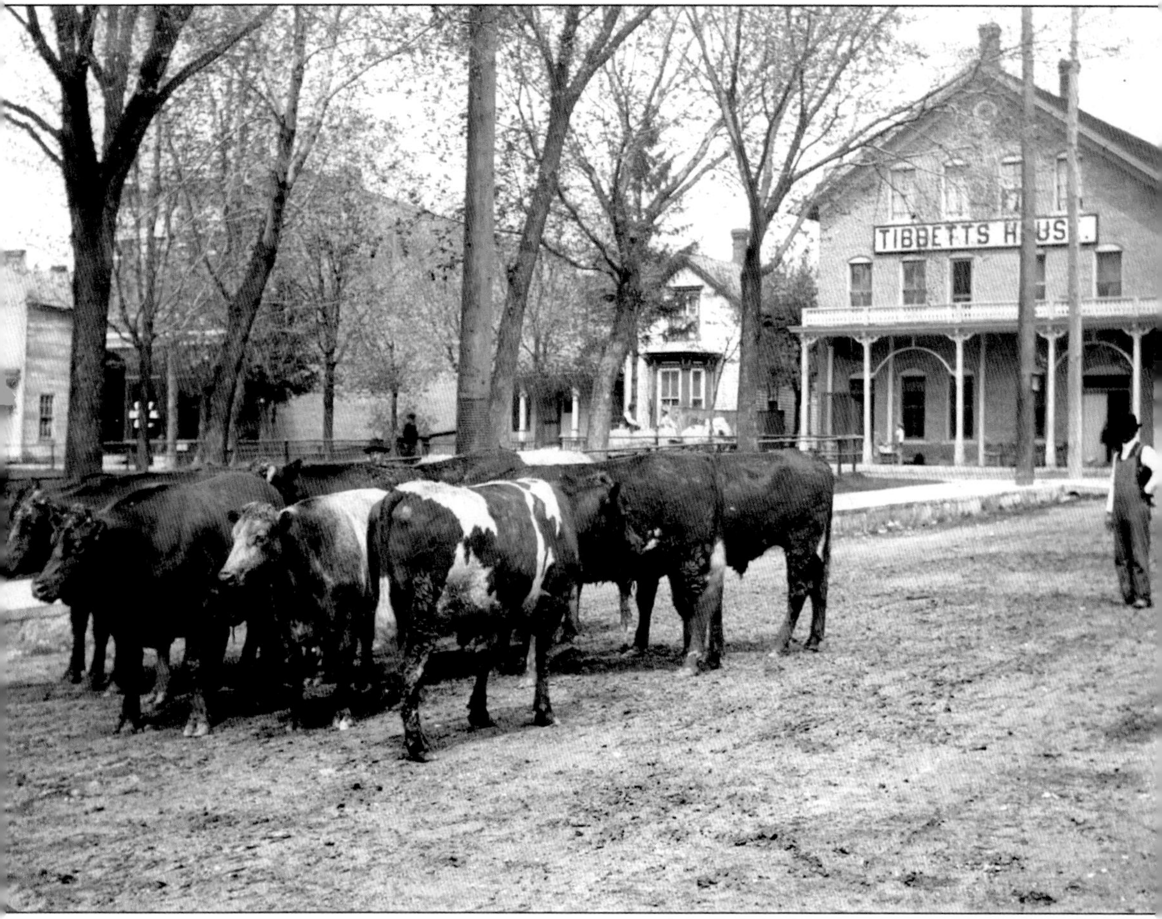


Dairying became Fillmore County's biggest agricultural enterprise during the 1880s, as the county milk cowherd increased from 10,719 to 22,306. With the elegant hotel, the Tibbetts House, in the background, this farmer is driving his cattle down St. Anthony Street in the late 1800s. It is uncertain whether these cattle were being moved to a pasture on the other side of town or were being herded to the railroad station where they would be sent east to a slaughterhouse.

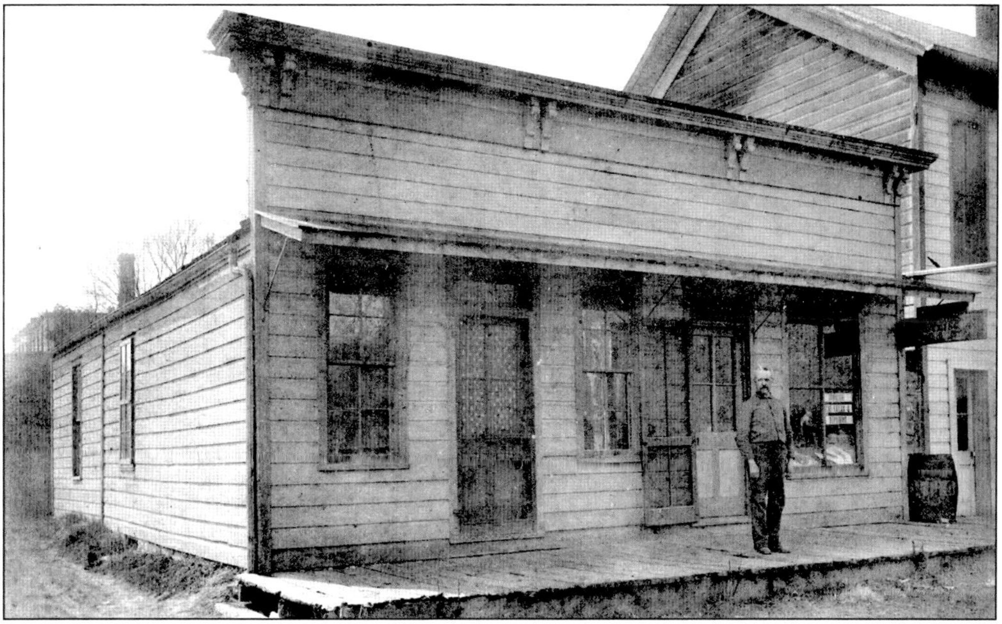

T.H. Johnson was a "merchant tailor" whose business was located just north of the Minnesota House on St. Anthony Street. In 1883 he advertised that his suits were "well and honestly made at a fair price. A Fine Suit, A Nobby Suit, A Strong and Durable Suit, at a Fair Price, Just call on me, for I can SUIT you sure, and please do not allow this hard tact to vanish from your memory."

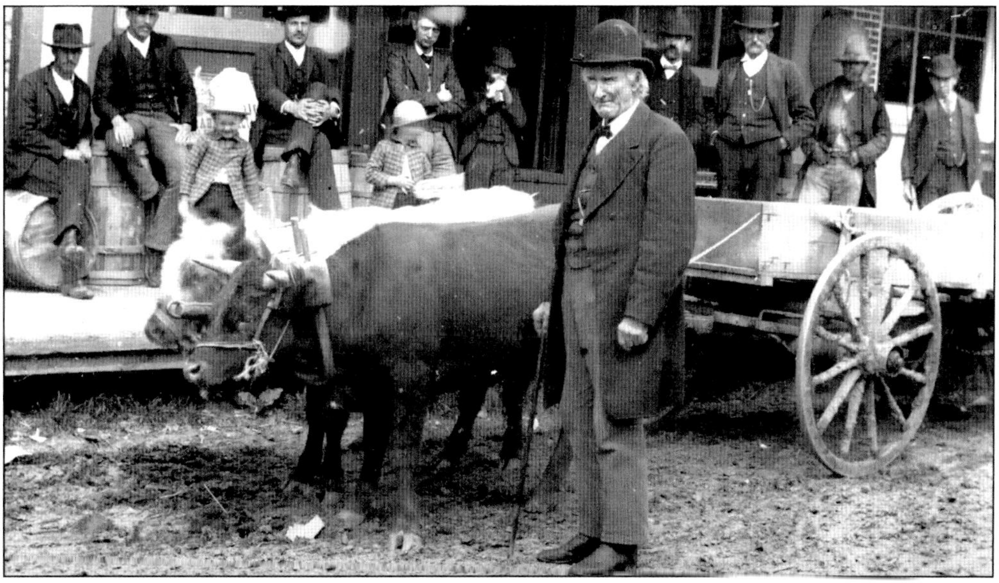

An elderly fellow identified as "Grandpa" McNeely stands next to an oxen cart on the streets of Preston during the early days. Standing in the doorway is George Mann. The little boys are the Peterson twins. Others pictured are Al Smith, Fred Garham, Julius Johnson (fourth from left), Matt McKindley, and Henry Mann. The pioneers relied upon the power of oxen to break the new soil in the area. In 1869 a census showed that there were 2,035 oxen in Fillmore County and ten years later there were a mere 159 left. In the same ten-year span, the number of horses in the county increased from 6,558 to 13,781.

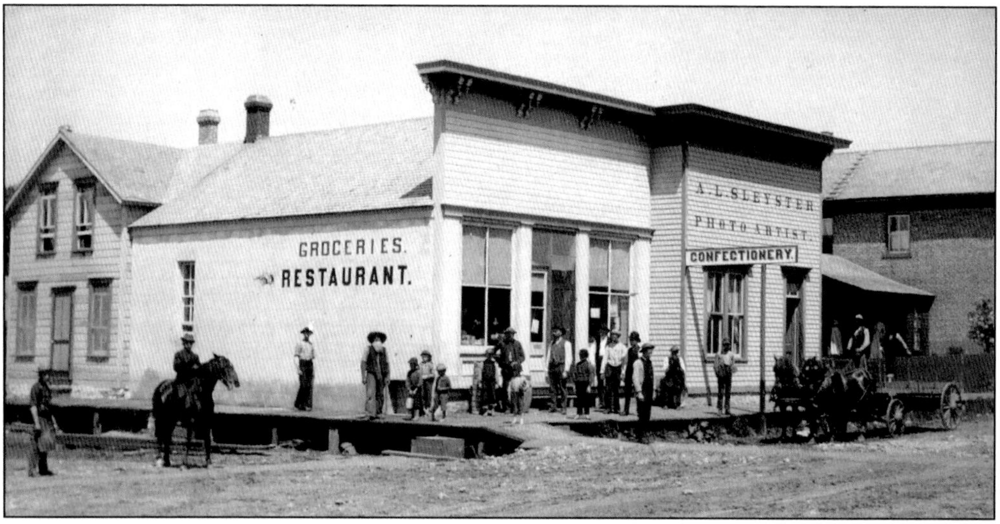


An 1883 newspaper advertisement read: "Aaron L Sleyster, Photo Artist, Produces Portraits in Oil, India Ink, and Water Colors. Studio over Tibbetts' Drug Store." By 1890 when this picture was taken, Sleyster had his own building across the street near the northwest corner of St. Paul and River Streets.

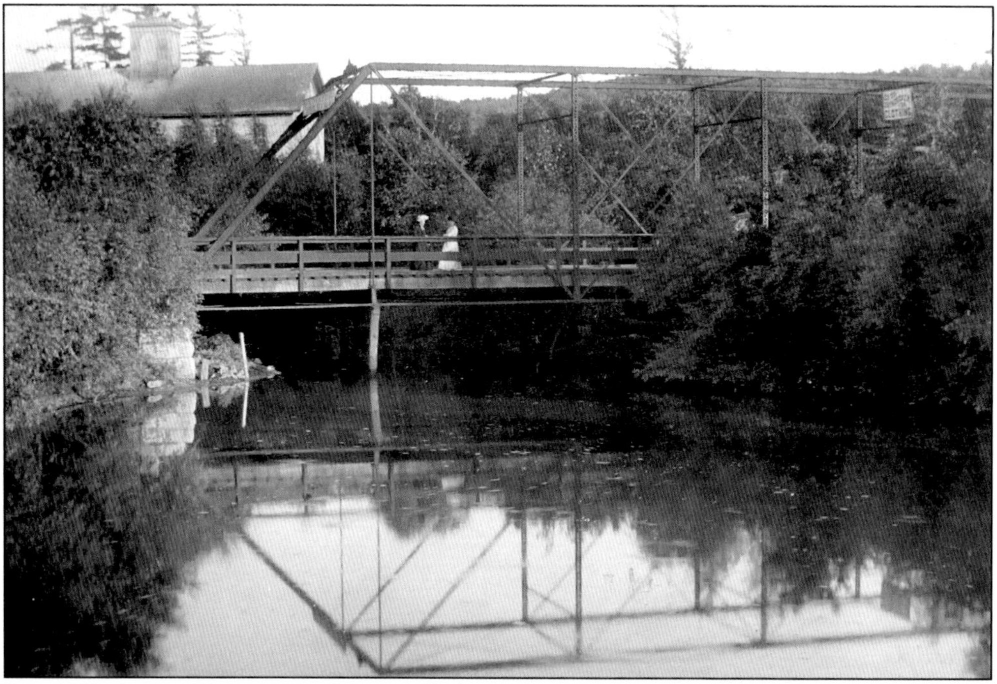

By 1893, Aaron Sleyster was being called Preston's "poet laureate" in the local press. He published a book of poetry called *Hours of Pleasure*, which was immensely popular. Included with the poems are several photographs of Preston and its surroundings. One of the poems is called "River Root," which ends with these melancholic lines: "When my daily toil is ended, / And the sun begins to wane, / Oft' I seek this grand old river / To dispel my care and pain. // River Root, when I am sleeping / Calmly on the other shore, / Purer hearts than mine will love thee, / Purer lives thy banks adore."

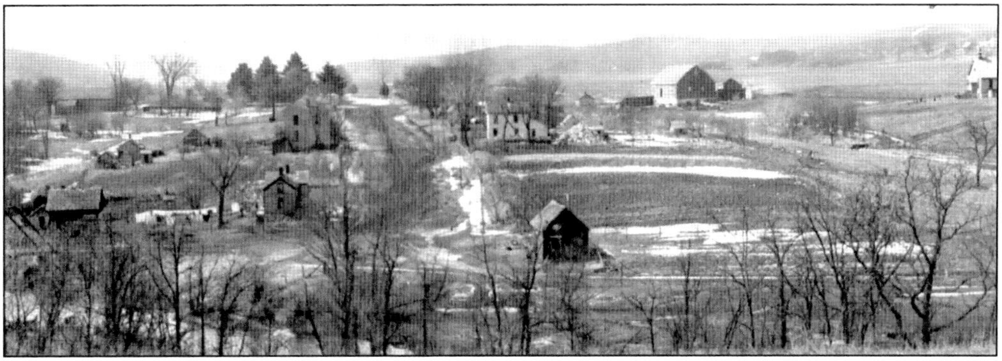

Named for Chief Carimona of the Winnebago, Carimona was located just four miles west of Preston on the South Branch of the Root River. During the mid-1850s it was a thriving village and an important stage stop on the road from St. Paul to Dubuque. The town had a hotel, a jail, two churches, and a newspaper called the *Carimona Pioneer*. There was a sawmill, a gristmill, and blacksmith and hardware shops. Carimona was named the county seat in 1855 and the county records were kept on the upper floor of the hotel. In April 1856, a county election was held to vote upon one of three locations for the county seat—Forestville, Carimona, or Preston. Preston won! In the late 1860s, when the railroad refused to put a track through Carimona, the once-thriving village became doomed.

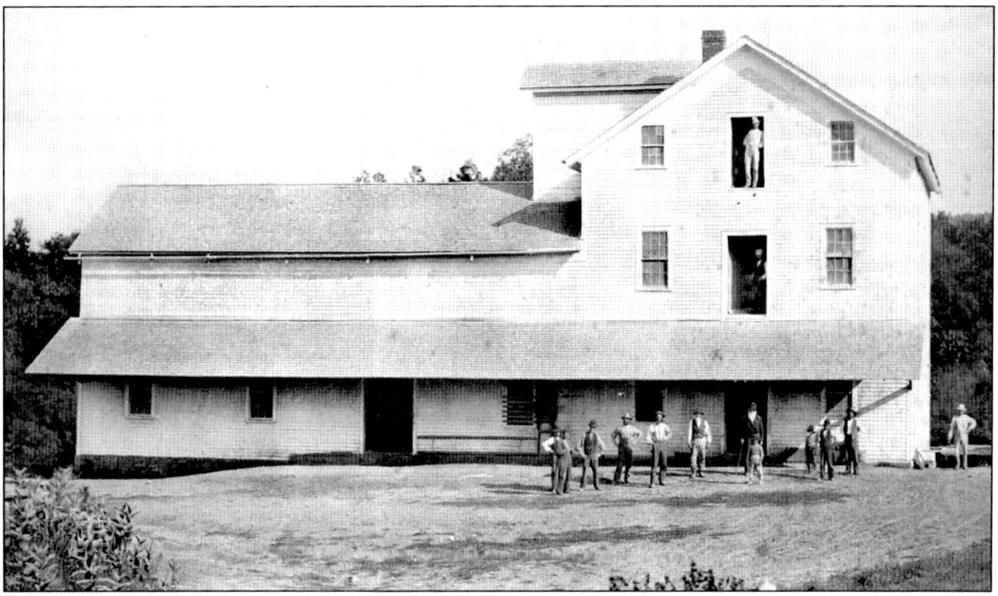

The Carimona Flour Mill was owned by Henry Spies Sr. (standing far right on ground). This mill burned to the ground on December 23, 1883. The *National Republican* reported: "Nothing was saved, not even the books. No insurance. This is a heavy loss to a good enterprising citizen. He had in the building 3,000 bushels of wheat and a car load of flour ready for shipment which was burned. The burning of this mill will be a great misfortune to many farmers residing near and west of Carimona."

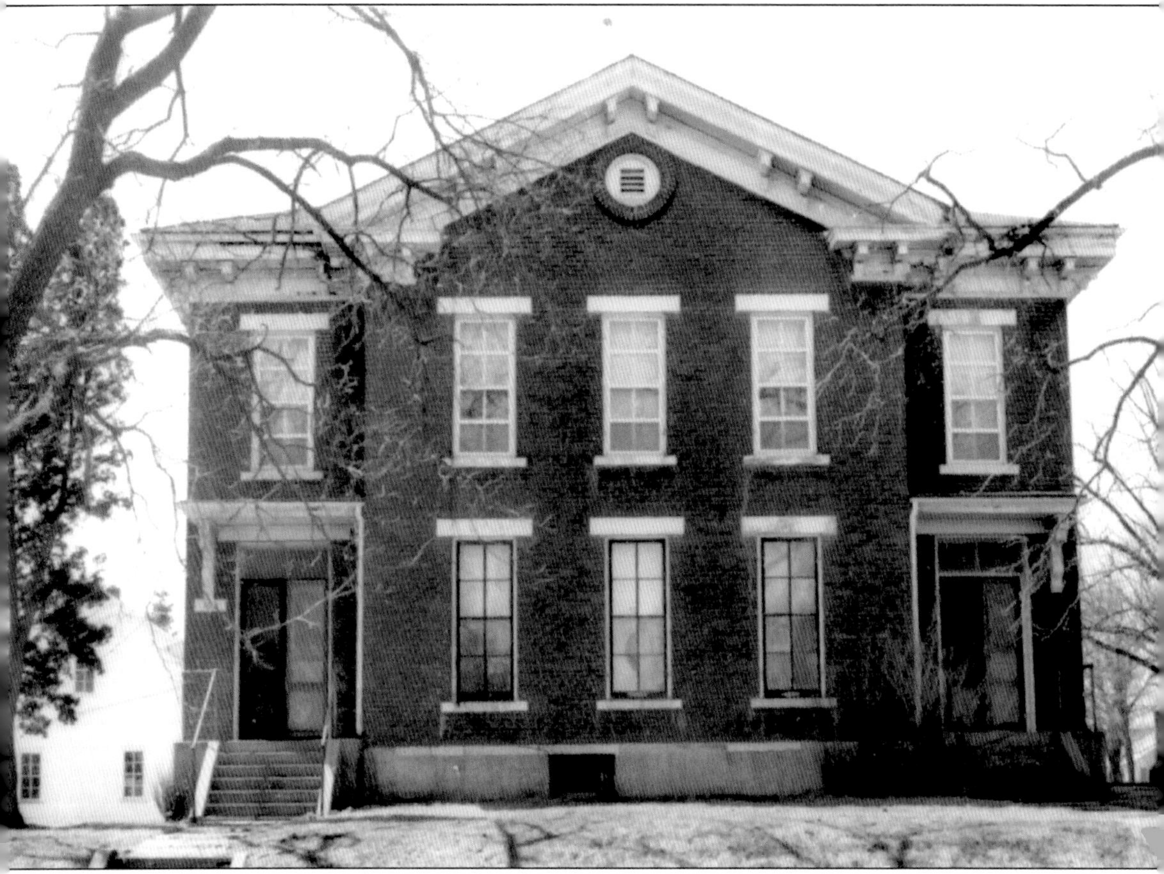

The Fillmore County Jail was completed in 1870 at a cost of around $12,000. Using local stone, brick and wood, the design was called "Italianate," a style popular in the latter half of the 19th century. The front part of the jail was the sheriff's residence and the back part had the prisoners' cellblocks. In 1900 the jail was condemned by the state of Minnesota. It was reported that the facility had "bad sanitation, defective plumbing, an entire absence of proper ventilation, and conditions that were conducive to the spread of disease." The lockups were not strong enough to hold prisoners and escapes had been frequent. The county commissioners voted to renovate the jail instead of building a new one. The old jail continued to be used until a modern jail was built in 1971.

During the 1862 Sioux Indian Uprising, three Preston-area soldiers were killed and seven wounded in the western part of the state. Among the dead was Captain Josiah F. Marsh (right) of Preston, who was the commander of Fort Ridgely. Marsh, along with a troop of 45 men, was caught in an ambush while crossing the Minnesota River on August 18, 1862.

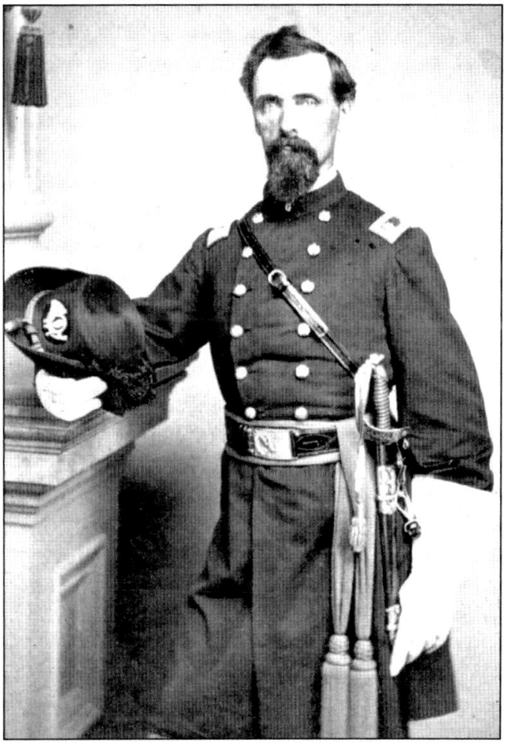

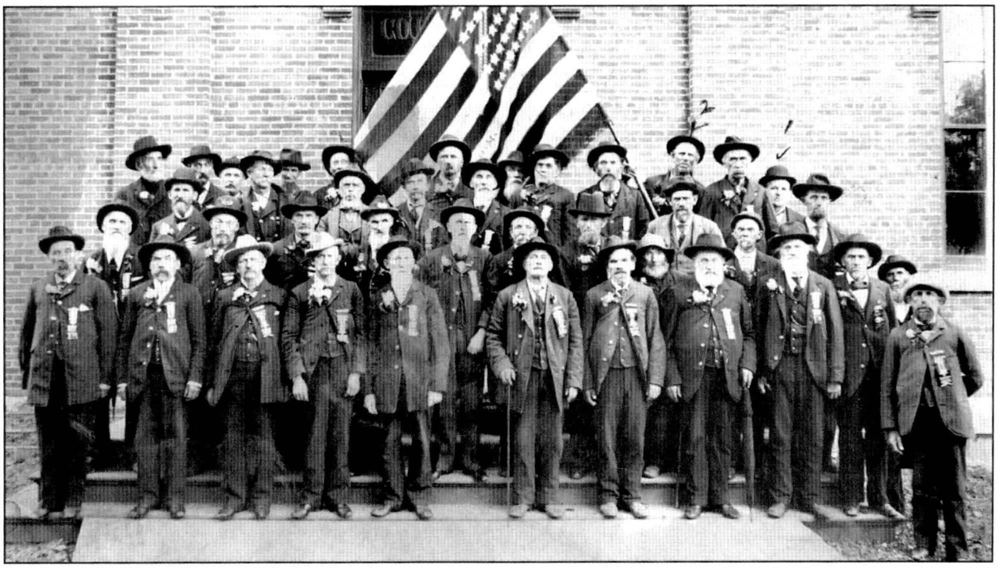

Preston's Civil War veterans organized to form the Underwood Post in 1884. The post was named in honor of Sgt. Joel Underwood, of the 5th Minnesota Infantry, who died in Tennessee during the Civil War. There are only two identifiable men in this photograph taken in front of the courthouse. In the back row on the right (marked #1) is Dr. Henry Jones, who was a physician in Preston for many years and later a dentist. The other (marked #2) is William "Dad" Hutchinson, who fought in both the Sioux Indian wars and later against the Confederates throughout the South. In total, Hutchinson participated in 42 battles during his soldiering career. He died in 1933, and at that time was heralded as "Preston's Last Civil War Veteran."

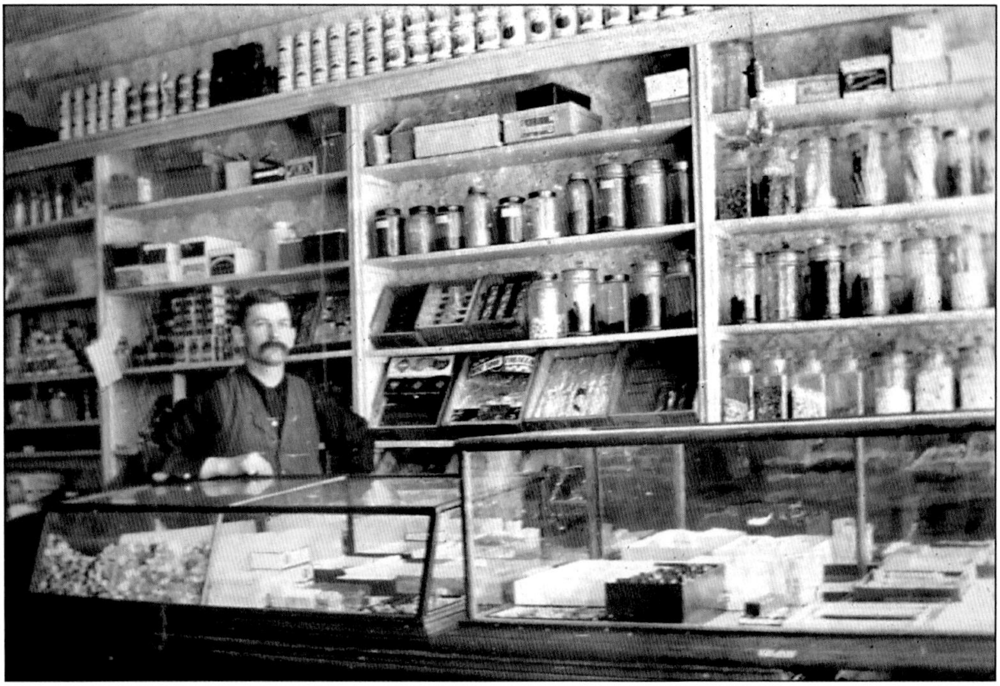

Romen Grebin stands in his confectionery, which was located on lower St. Paul Street. Grebin started business in Preston in 1894 and also operated a billiard parlor, pictured below. In a taped interview in 1978, Romen's son, Tim Grebin, said that his father specialized in milk shakes. "He had an ice shaver and he'd get the ice from the river. Then he'd put some chocolate in the bottom, some milk and the river ice and he'd shake it up. Ten cents for a milk shake."

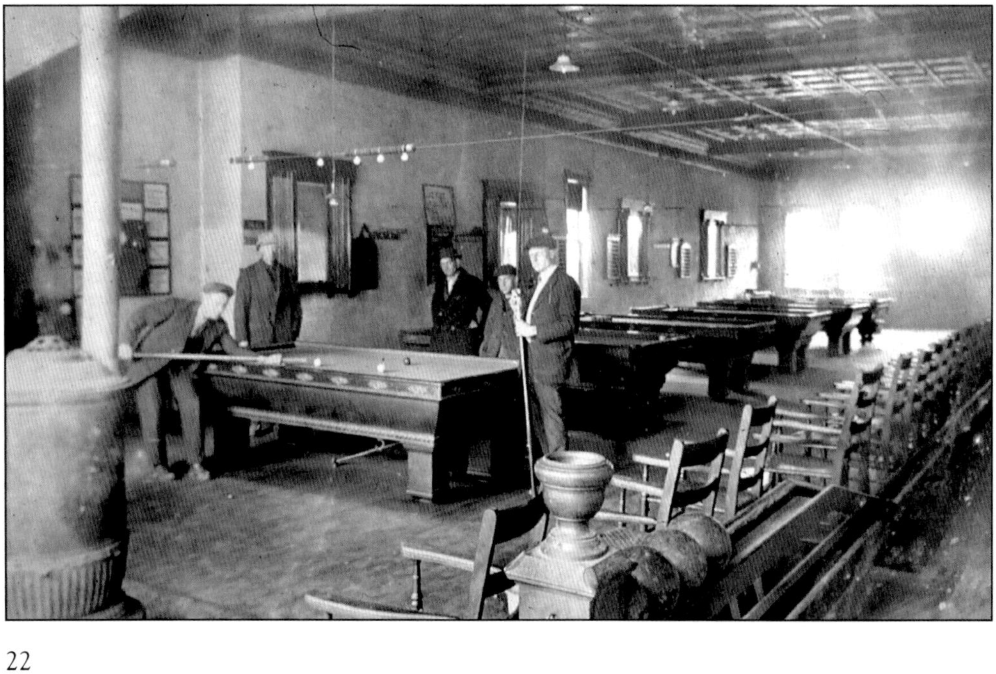

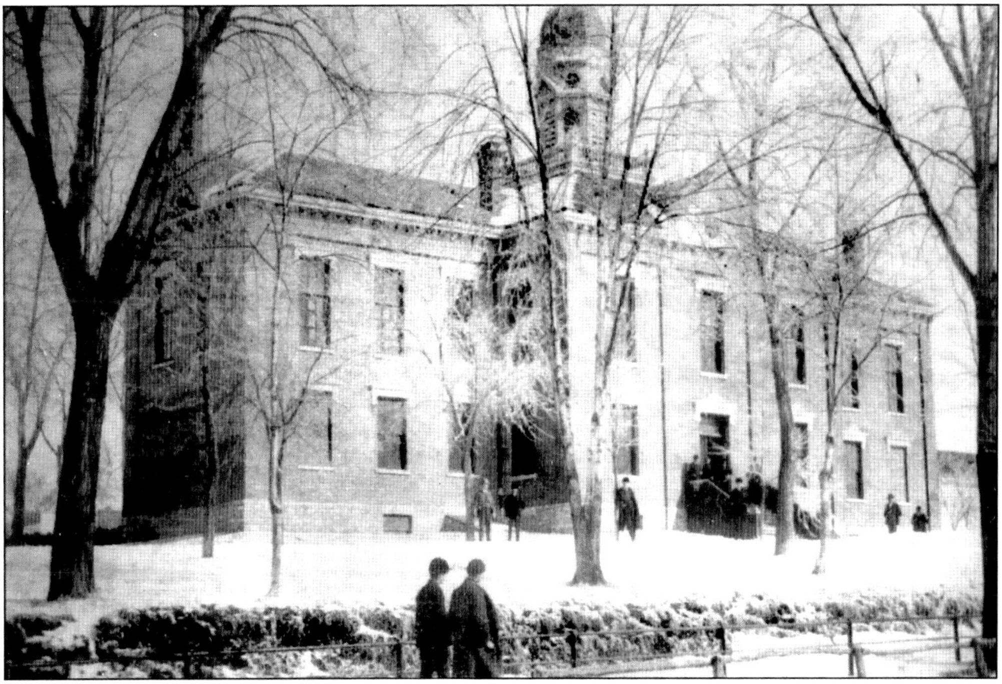

This 1885 photograph shows the wings recently added to the courthouse. The wings measured $27^{1}/_{2}$ feet in length. The courtroom took up most of the second floor, with the wings containing the offices of the various county officials. It wasn't until 1903 that the porticos were added on the south side.

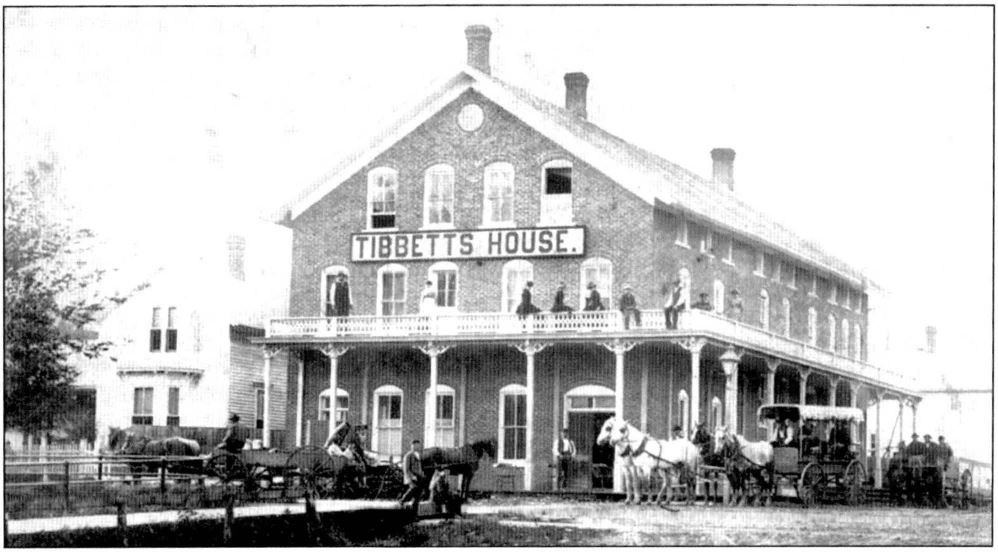


When J.P. Tibbetts bought the Stanwix Hotel in 1879 he renamed it the Tibbetts House and made many improvements, making it Preston's most exclusive hotel. The *National Republican* reported in 1885: "Twenty-three traveling men (salesmen) at the Tibbetts' House yesterday and still there was room and plenty to eat for as many more." Here the stage from Chatfield is sitting out front. The trip to Rochester in the early years was a two-day affair. First a traveler had to take the stage to Chatfield, spending the night, and then board the train the next morning for Rochester.

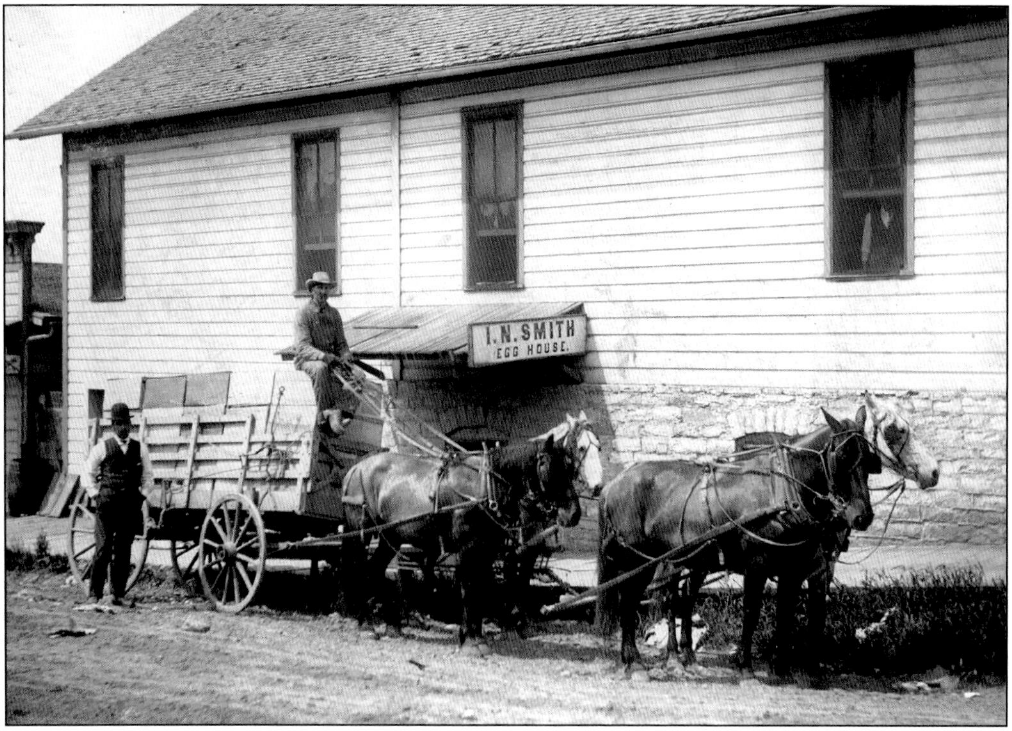


The I.N. Smith Poultry and Egg House was located on the corner of Main and St. Anthony Street. In 1905 the *Preston Times* wrote that "the highest market price is always paid for eggs and poultry by Mr. Smith at all seasons of the year. This institution gives employment to 4 to 6 hands in the summer season and in winter during chicken dressing season from 12 to 15."

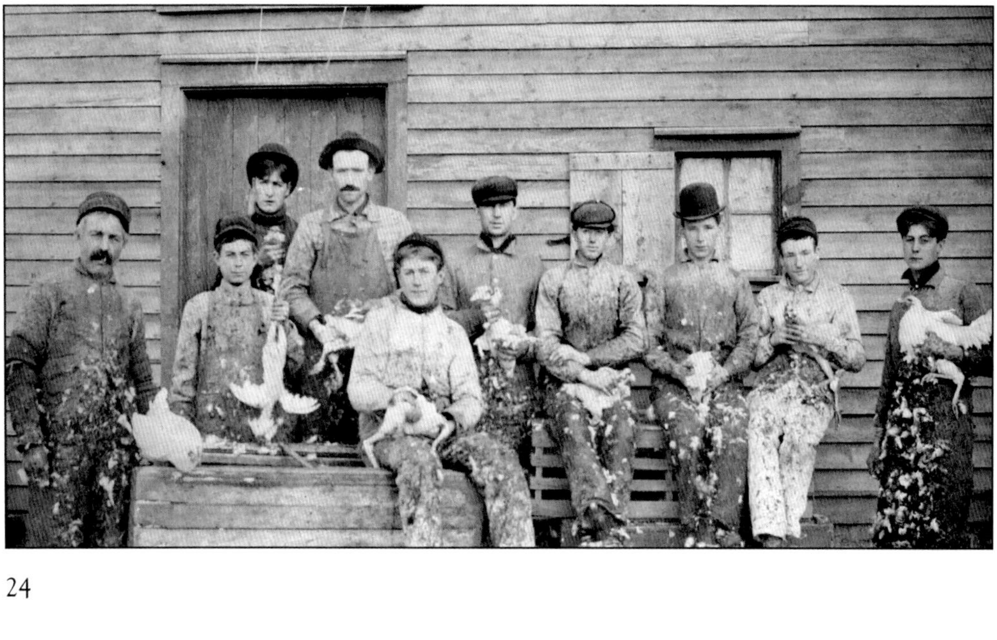

# *Two*

# PRESTON COMES OF AGE

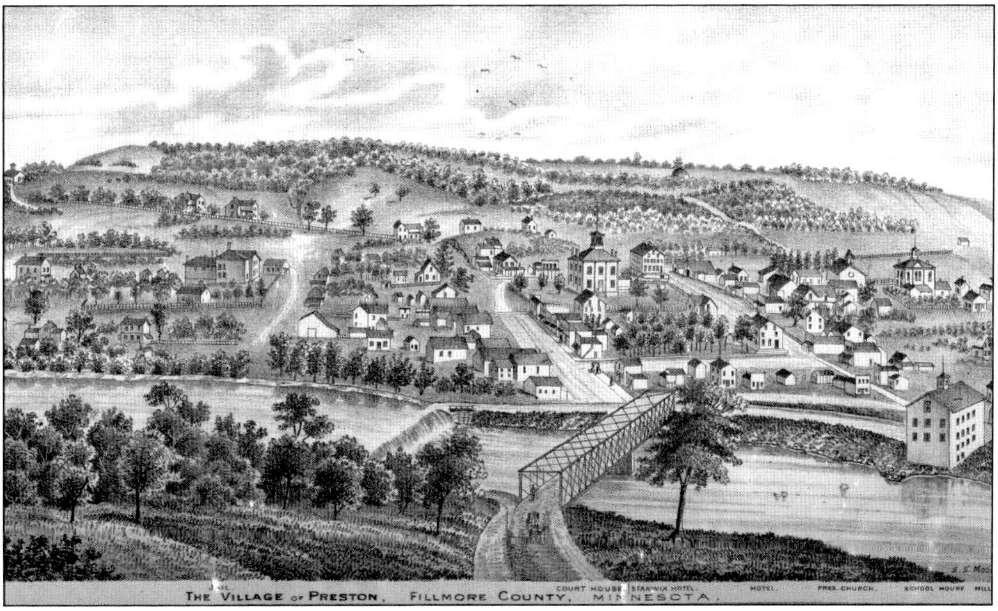


This illustrated map of Preston from the 1874 Minnesota State Atlas shows the small village centered mainly around the courthouse square. The county jail building, just four years old at the time, can be seen at left center while the village school house is on the right center. The race on the north side of the dam is clearly illustrated, where the water was diverted to provide power for the Kaercher gristmill located at the bottom right of the map.

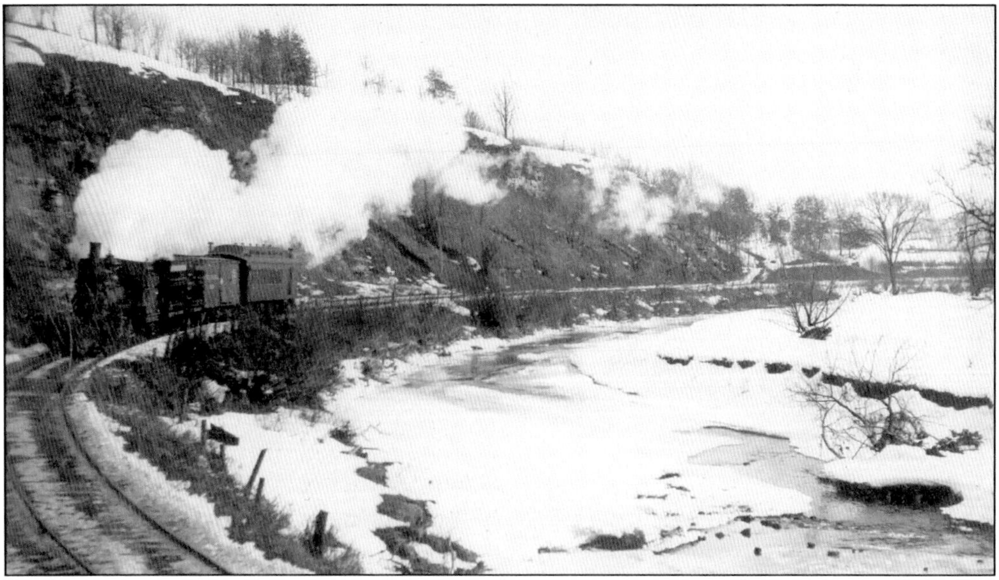

Nothing influenced a small town's chance for business growth and prosperity more than the arrival of the railroad. Calling Preston a place of "glorious destiny," the *Preston Republican* wrote in June of 1869 that "The day is not distant however when Preston will have a depot into which and from which will come and go richly laden trains." When the track was laid west out of Lanesboro, it climbed the steep Fountain hill instead of following the valley over to Preston.

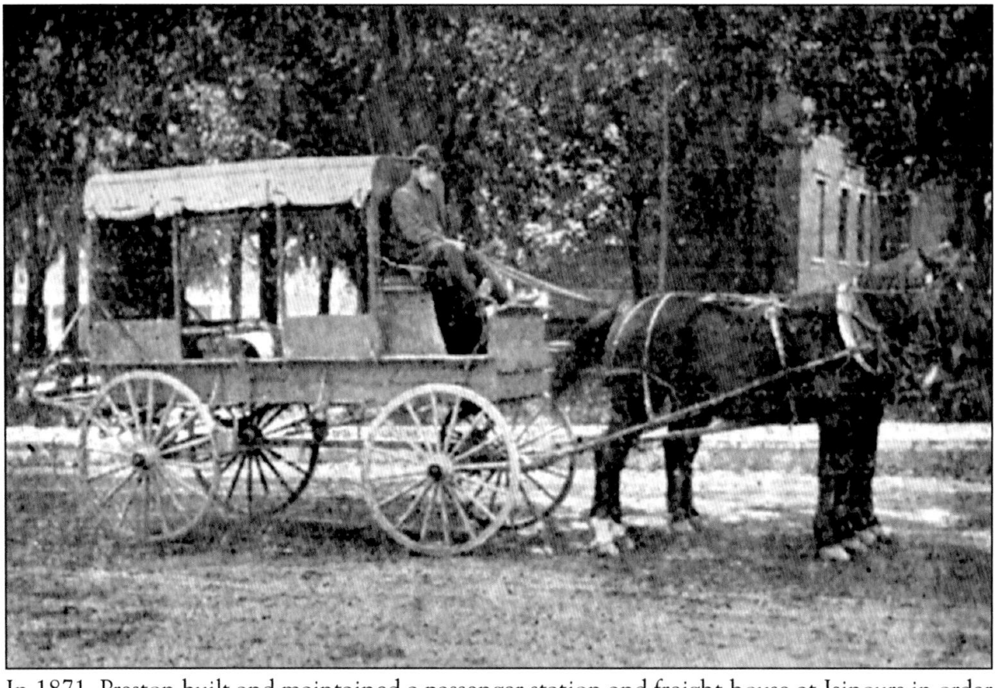

In 1871, Preston built and maintained a passenger station and freight house at Isinours in order to have access to the railroad line that had passed them by. Stage and freight lines were established to take passengers and freight back and forth from Preston to the Isinours station. Pictured is the stage in the 1890s with its driver, Billy Young.

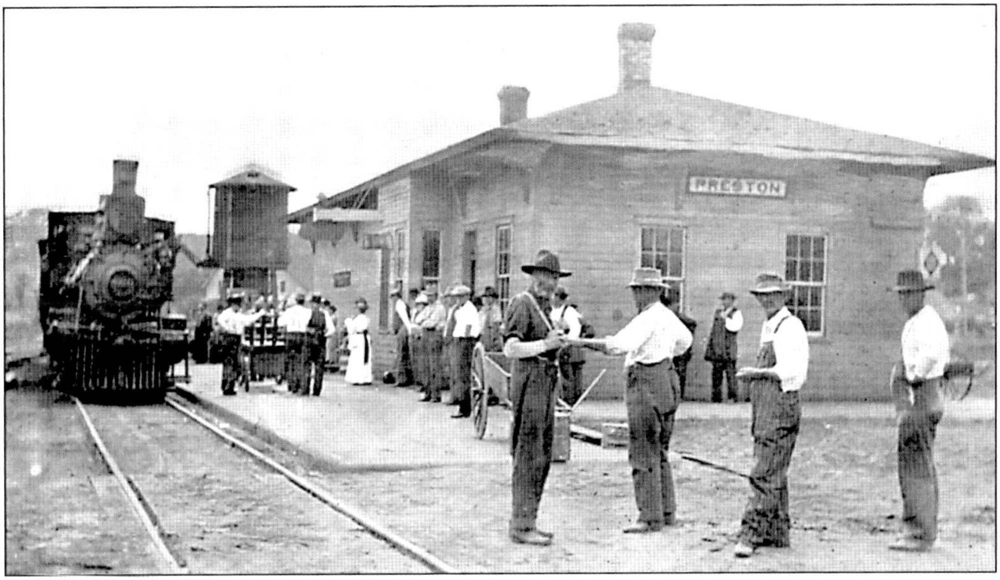


A steam locomotive is shown filling with water at the Preston station. It wasn't until December 26, 1879 that the first train arrived in Preston. The Caledonia, Mississippi and Western Company built a narrow gauge track from Reno to Preston. The *Preston Times* wrote about the narrow gauge at the time: "The cars were tiny affairs and the road bed narrow, but it was better than hauling freight from Isinours and our people rejoiced greatly."

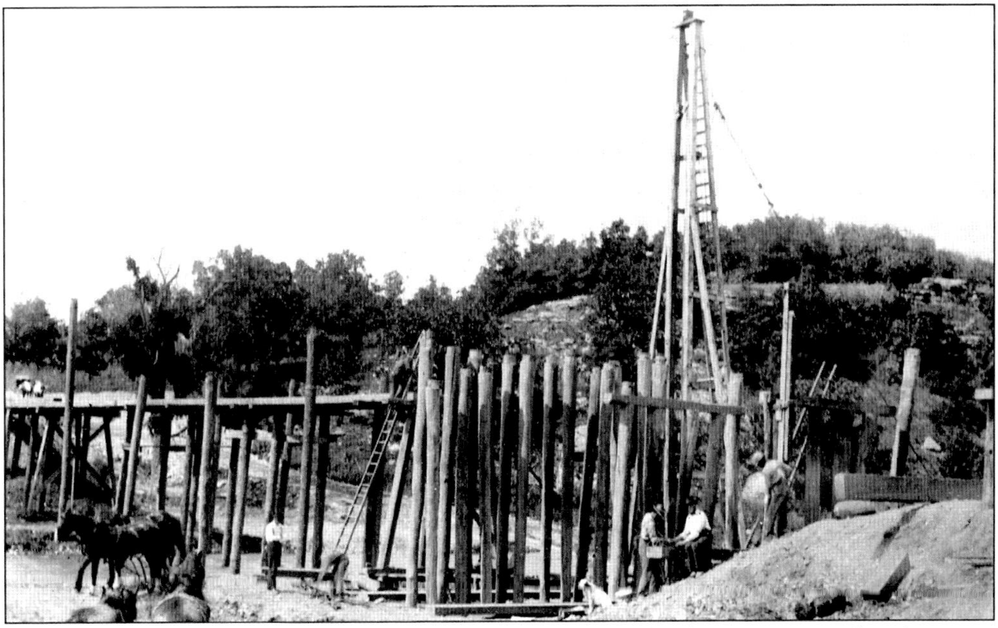

By 1901 the narrow gauge track to Caledonia was replaced with a broad gauge track and Preston once again rejoiced, with the *Times* writing, "We are broad gauge at last and woe be to him who shall henceforth refer to Preston or the sister towns east of us as 'narrow gauge towns.' " In 1903 a spur track was built to the Isinours station and Preston was finally hooked up with the towns on the Chicago Milwaukee & Saint Paul line. After discontinuing passenger service, the railroad came to Preston as a freight hauler until the mid-1970s when the tracks were abandoned.

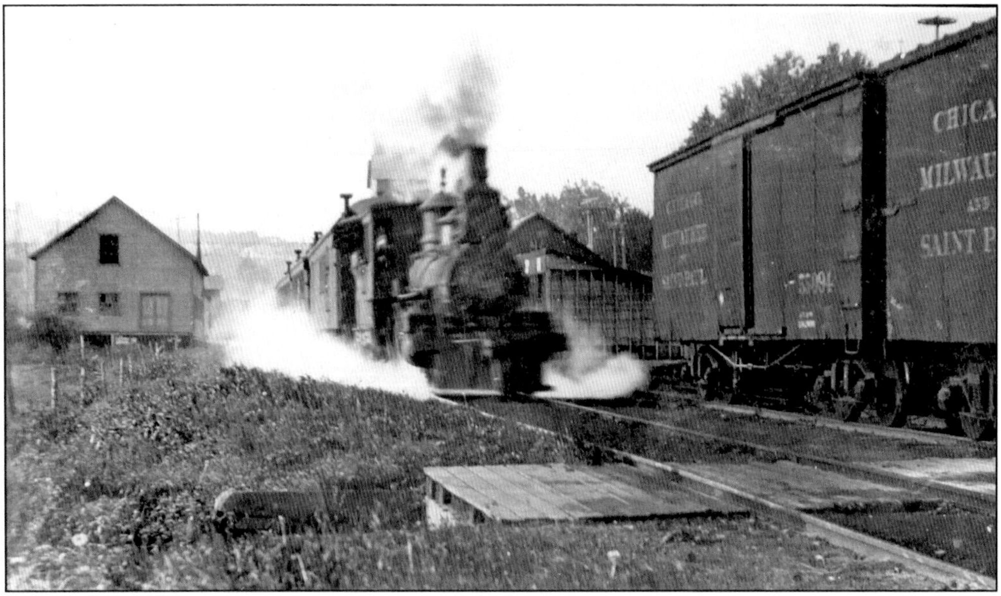


Shown above is a wide gauge locomotive speeding through Preston in the early 1900s. Shown below is a railroad bridge just outside of Preston. The earliest locomotives burned wood for fuel. The wood would be cut to specific lengths and placed along the tracks at regular intervals. Later, coal was introduced. The railroad tracks were a particularly dangerous place as is indicated by an 1876 accident report of the Southern Minnesota Railroad Company. The report states that six people were killed on the tracks and seven injured, "all by want of caution or through their own misconduct." The company also paid out $5,295 for livestock killed by trains.

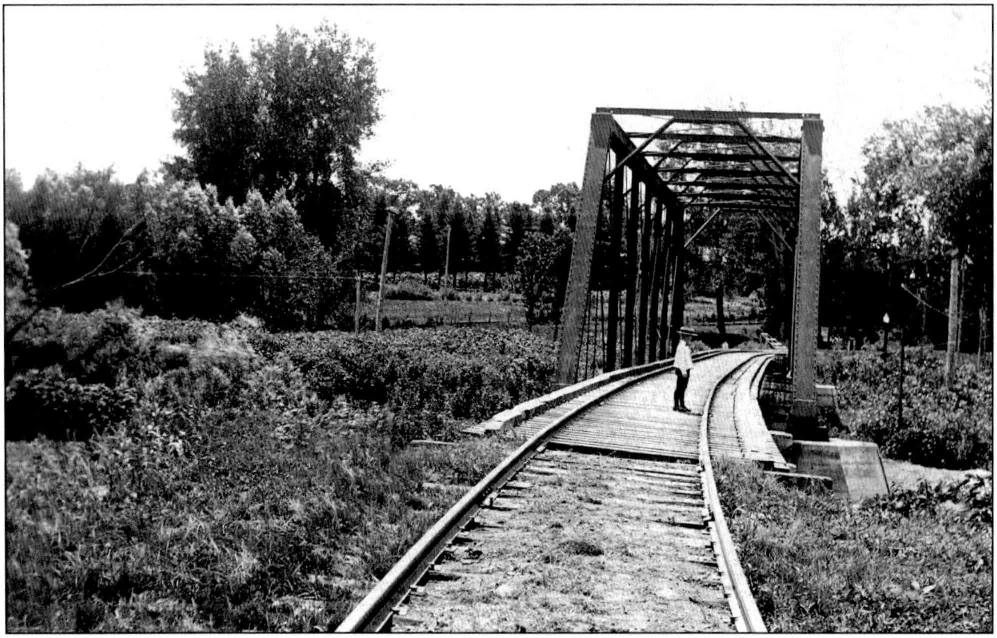

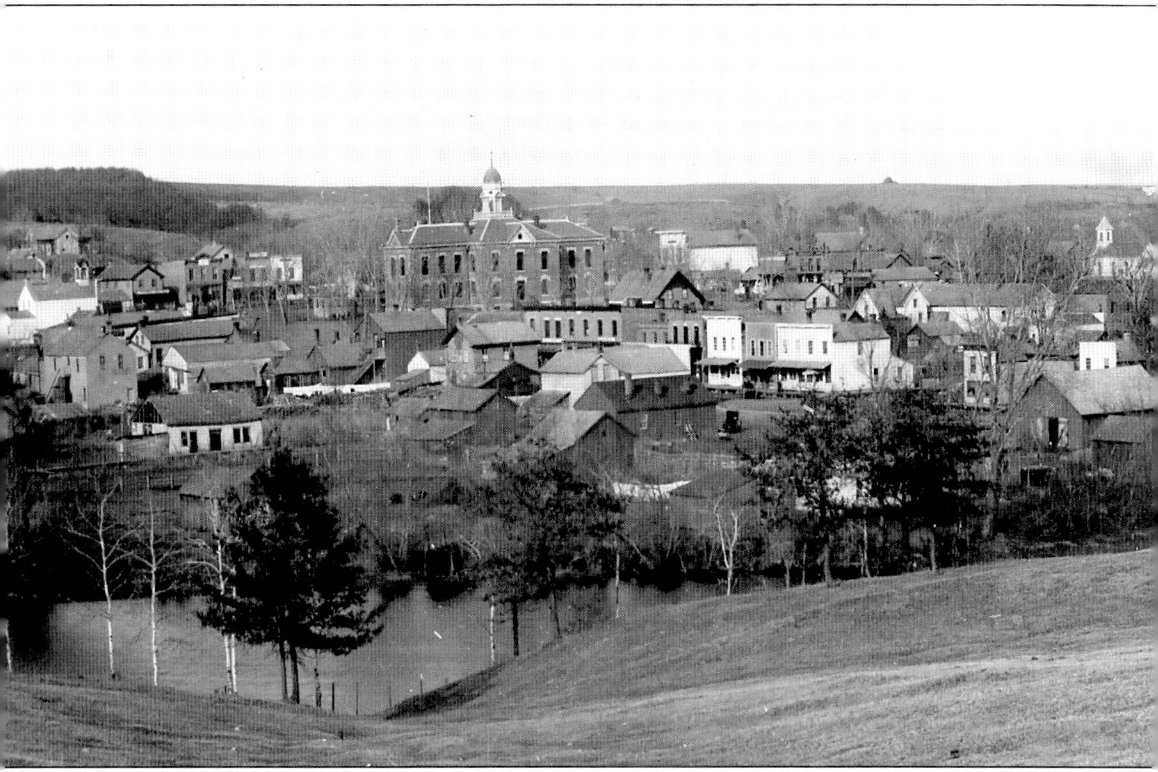

This bird's-eye view taken by A.L. Sleyster shows a sweeping view of the growing town. In 1894 the *Preston Times* reported, "We understand that sidewalks will be laid and building soon commenced in the O'Brien Columbian Addition (the swimming pool hill) to Preston. We do not see why that portion of the town wouldn't make desirable residence property. You will be close by a beautiful spring besides being wafted to sleep every night by the rippling sound of the water over the dam. All in all we should think it a desirable place to live."

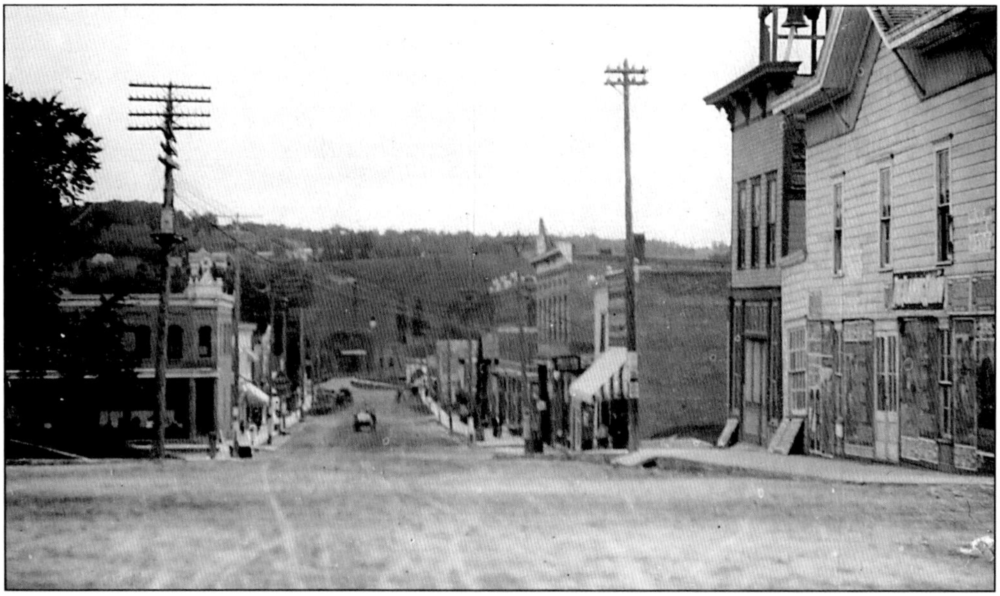

Seen here are two views of St. Paul Street in the first decade of the 20th century before the library and town hall were built. Yet another Tibbetts building was the Tibbetts Opera House, which doubled as the Tibbetts Rink, located on the corner where the Public Library now stands. The Opera House featured vaudeville-type acts and traveling medicine shows. Other nights it served the town as a roller skating rink, with the Hamre Brass Band playing for the skaters. In 1895 the price for gentlemen skaters was 25¢, 20¢ cents for lady skaters, and 10¢ for spectators. Just south of the Tibbetts Opera House was the Town Hall.

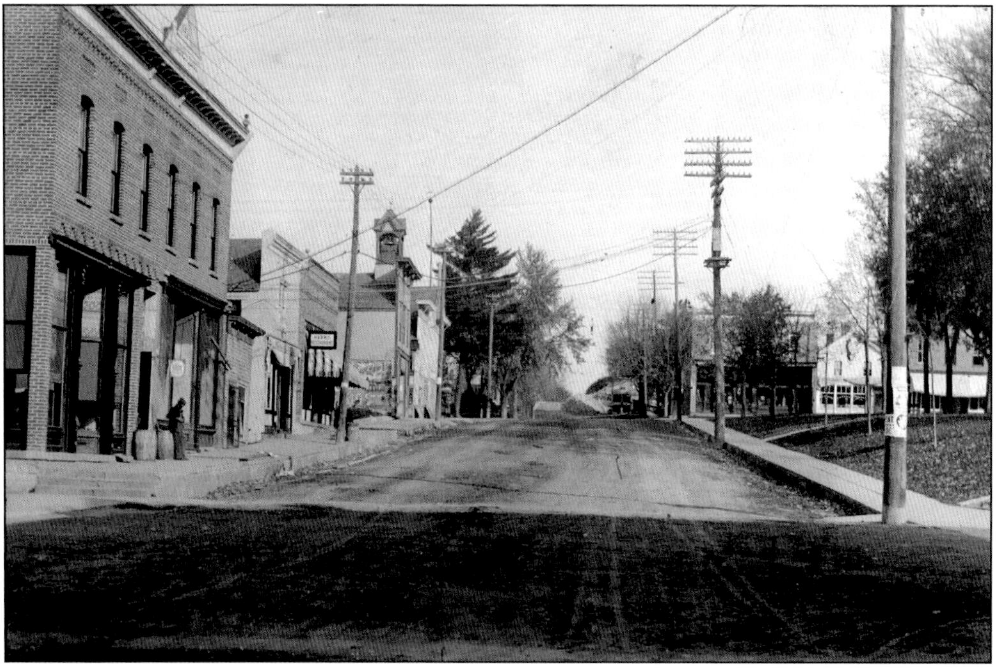

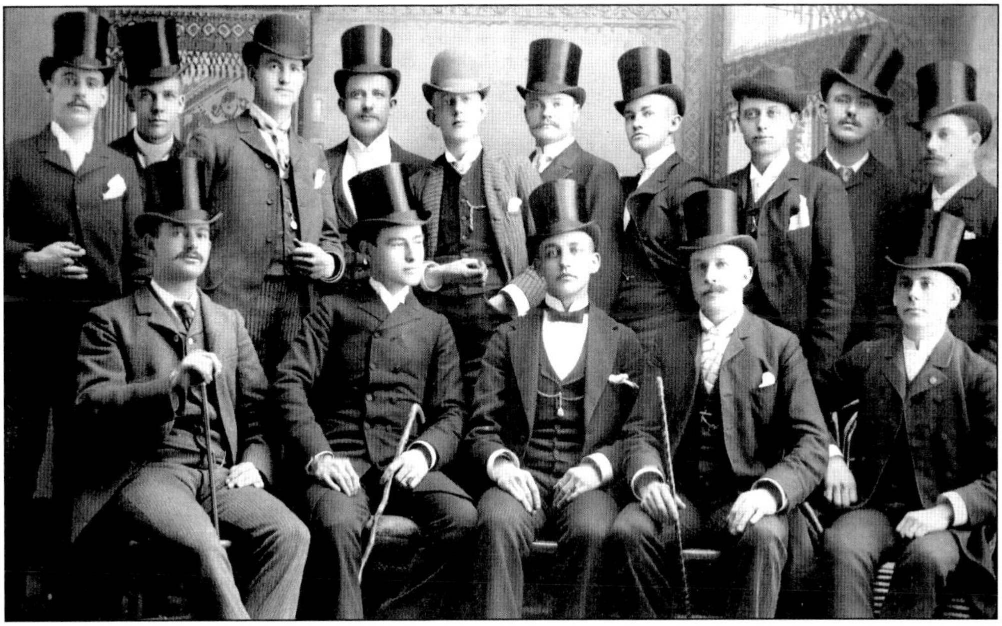

This photograph resurfaced in 1954 when Harold Hopp was going through some old family photo albums. It shows a group of what were then called Preston's "gay blades" in a picture taken in March of 1889. Many of the names listed indicate that these were the sons of Preston's earliest business and professional men. Pictured from left to right are as follows: (front row) Ed Conkey, John Hopp, Les Loomis, Decker, and W. Kruppenbacher; (back row) Chas. Foote, Henry Hayes, O. Clark, Ned Maloney, John Hamre (leader of Hamre's Brass Band), ? Day, H. Wells, J. Johnson, Harry Conkey, and W. Hay.

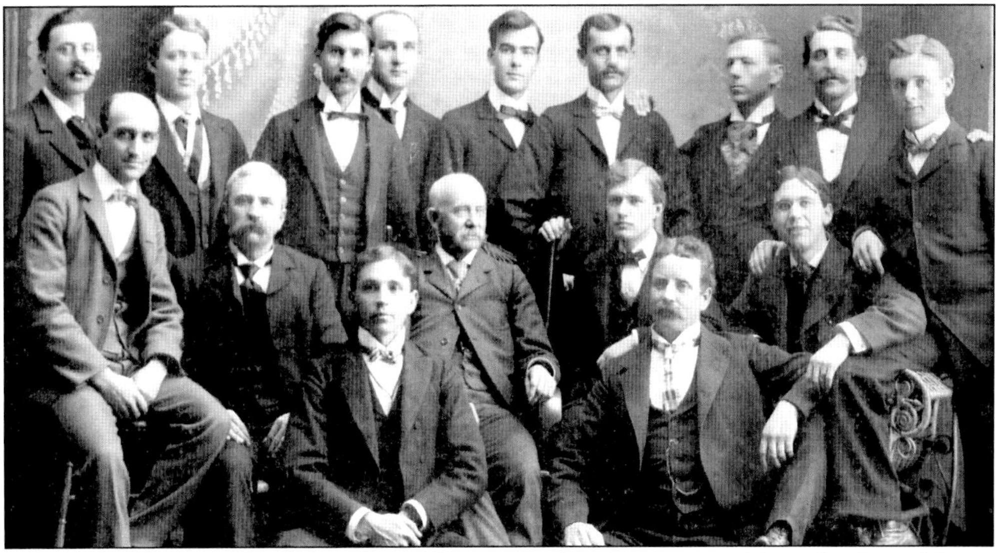

A group of Preston businessmen got together on Sunday, January 10, 1904 at the Opera House. Pictured from left to right are the following: (front row) Ben Fowler and Holly Bartlett; (second row) George Fifield, Rob Lynch, Perry Engle, Roy Wells, and John Pulham; (third row) James Broderick, Victor Clark, Bert Strand, Ed Read, Will Read, Charlie Schoenbaum, Will Kuethe, Dr. U.E. Richardson, and Frank Broderick.

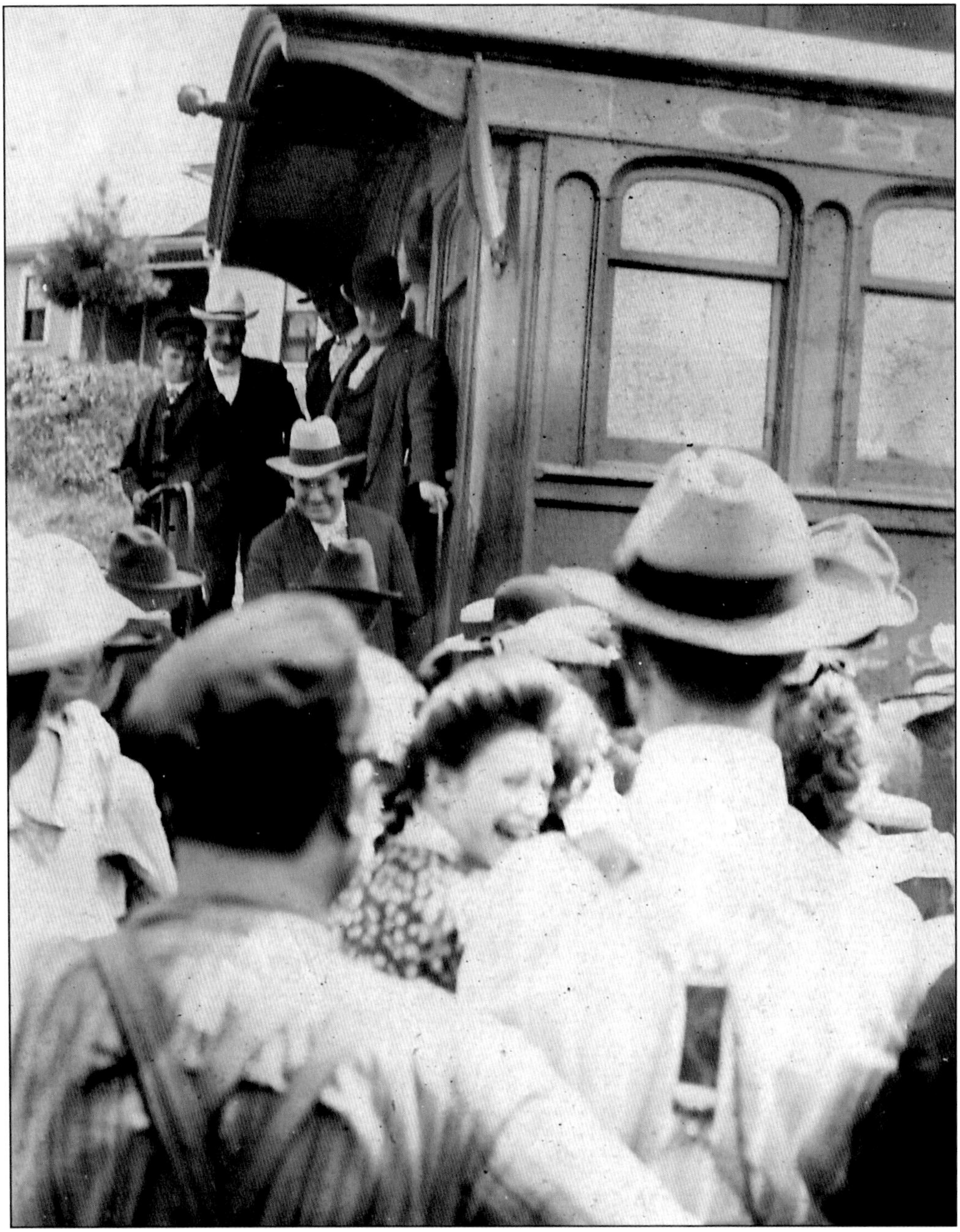

In 1903, William Jennings Bryan (1860–1925, shown stepping off the train) came to Preston and gave a speech at the Tibbetts Rink entitled "The Value of an Ideal." Nicknamed "The Great Commoner," Bryan was known for his populist politics and oratory skills. He ran for President of the United States three times and was later Woodrow Wilson's Secretary of State. The promoters considered his appearance in Preston a disappointment due to the fact that only 300 people showed up to see him. The *Preston Times* wrote, "We should have been glad to have an audience of 5,000 instead of 300." The small turnout was attributed to the fact that the area's farmers were busy putting up their hay before an approaching front of threatening weather. Still, Bryan's speech was reported to be "elevating, ennobling and replete with Christian sentiments."

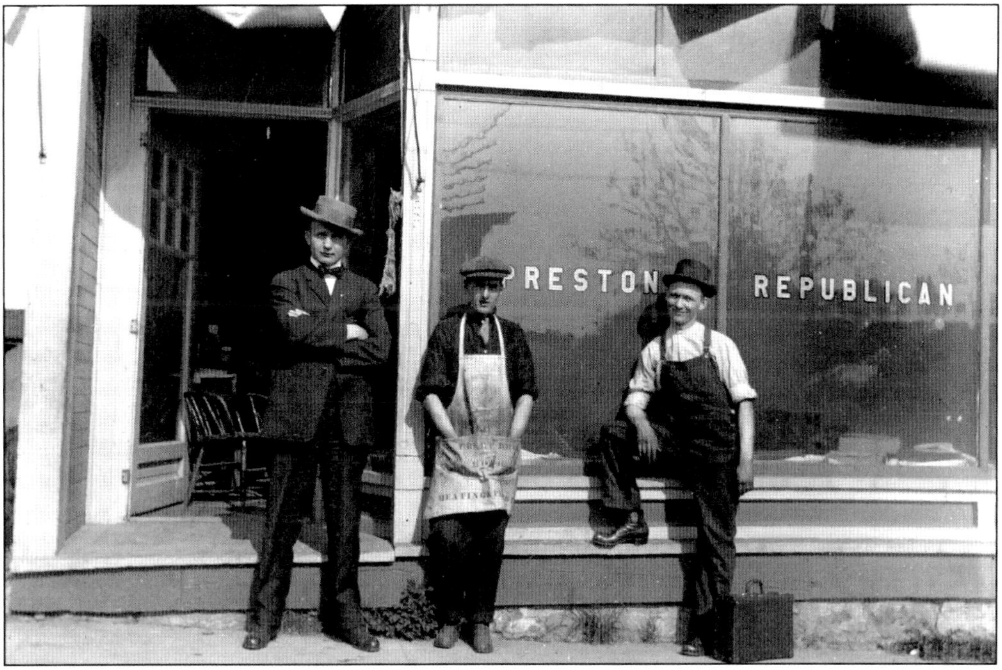


The *Preston Republican* was owned by Frank Ibach (standing left, above) who purchased the *National Republican* from Major Hotchkiss in 1903. The man standing next to Ibach is Anona Ingall. The photo below shows an interior shot of the building. At the time, *Republican*'s office was located just south of the Ebert Hardware Store on lower St. Anthony Street, less than a block from their fierce competitor and rival weekly paper, the *Preston Times*. Other newspapers that have been published from Preston are: The *Preston Courier*, the *Preston Democrat*, the *Fillmore County Republican*, and the *National Republican*.

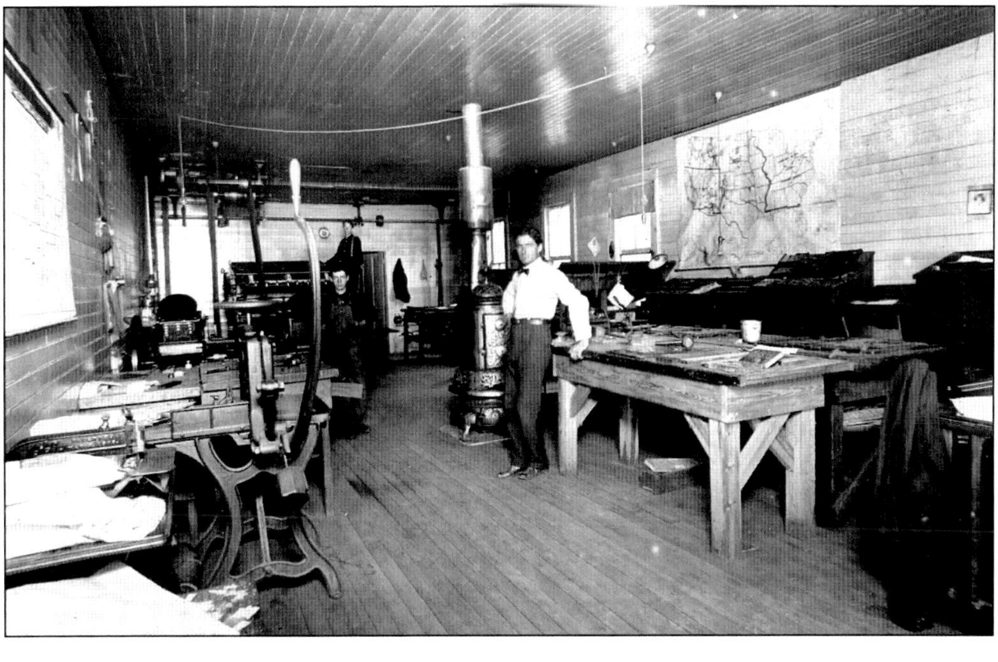

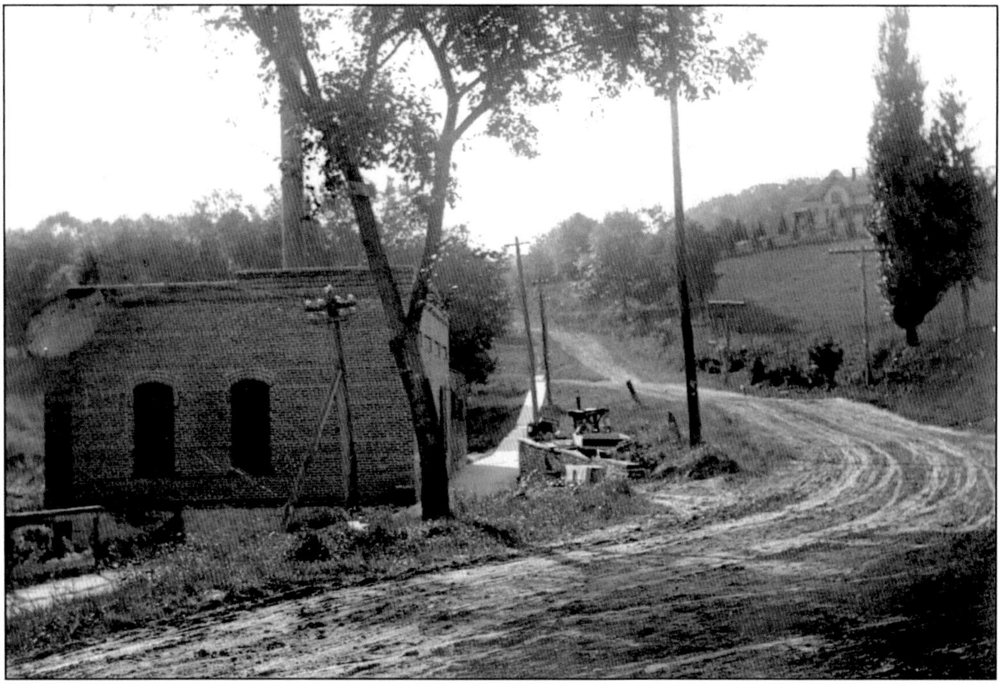

Preston finally got electric lights in the fall of 1896, when the village built its first power plant. For power a "direct-connected multipooler 50 kilowatt dynamo was purchased from Chicago for $636." The plant didn't start generating electricity until dusk and then only continued until midnight. In the event of a dance in town, the lights would stay on until 1 a.m.

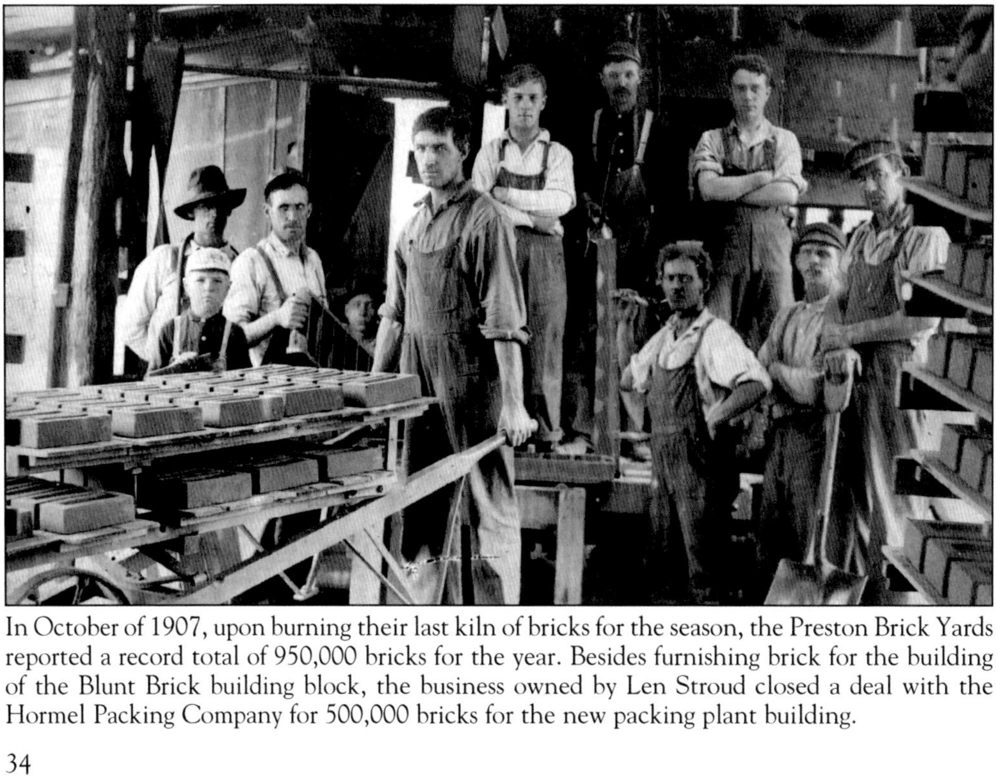

In October of 1907, upon burning their last kiln of bricks for the season, the Preston Brick Yards reported a record total of 950,000 bricks for the year. Besides furnishing brick for the building of the Blunt Brick building block, the business owned by Len Stroud closed a deal with the Hormel Packing Company for 500,000 bricks for the new packing plant building.

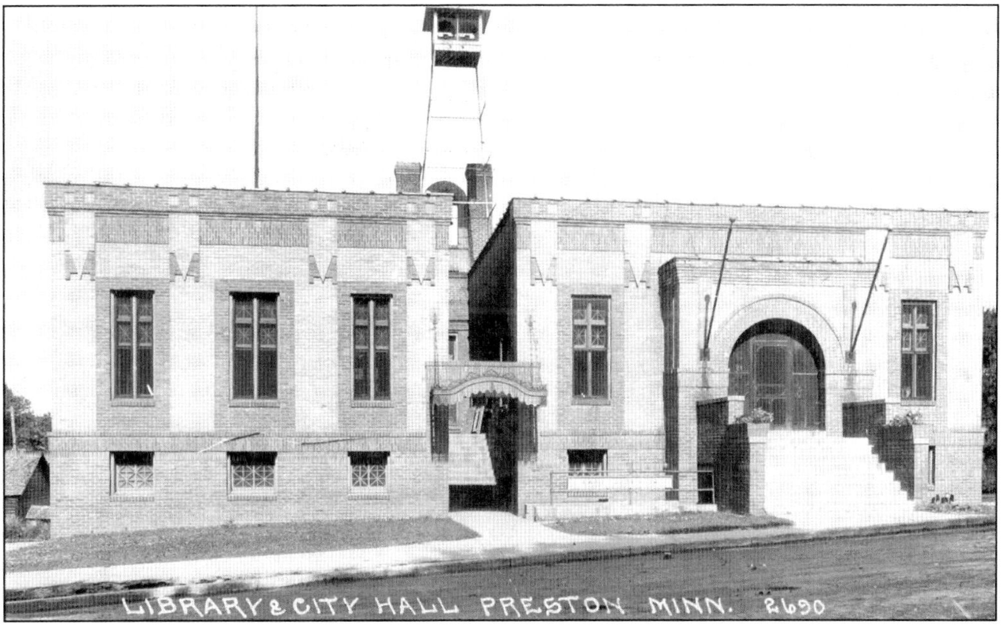


The Browning Club, a literary reading group, was formed in 1898 and began to loan books to the community. In 1905 the Browning Club sent a letter to the Eastern industrialist Andrew Carnegie soliciting a grant to construct a library building. Carnegie eventually donated $8,000. A disagreement arose between Preston and the Carnegie Foundation over the design of the building. Preston eventually spent $11,000 on the building and asked Carnegie for an additional $3,000 which he refused to donate. The library along with the adjoining town hall was completed in 1913.

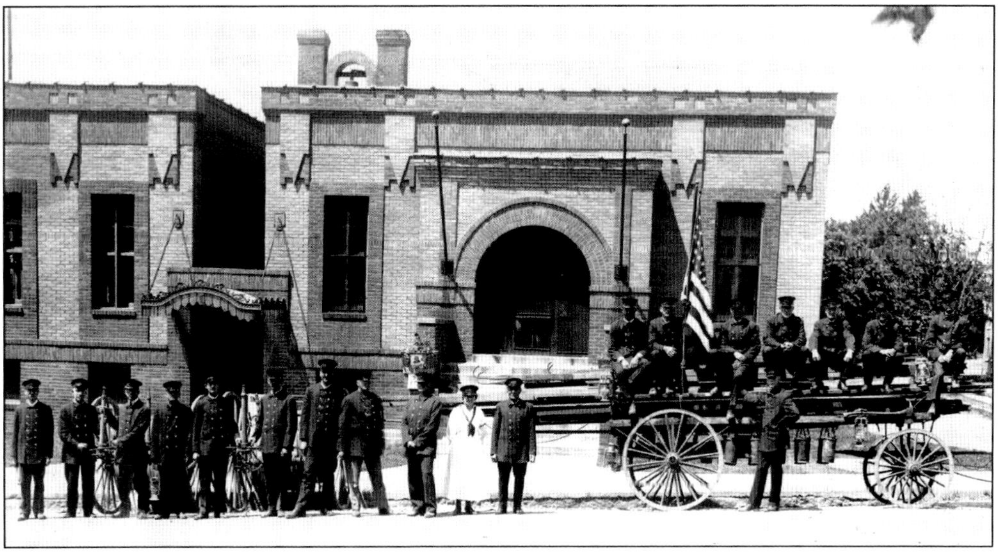

The Preston firemen posed for a photo on June 13, 1920 at their annual picnic. From left to right are Pete Wilson, George Pooler, Earl Turck, Homer Barnes, R.J. Rick, Harvey Winnega, John Brusse, Matt Strom, Dall Levey, Ladice Dovenberg, George Dovenberg, Herman Kuhl, Oscar Austin, Bert Fraser, Frank Schwartz, Andrew Nordahl, Frank Pickett, Bay Kerr, and Walt Volkman.

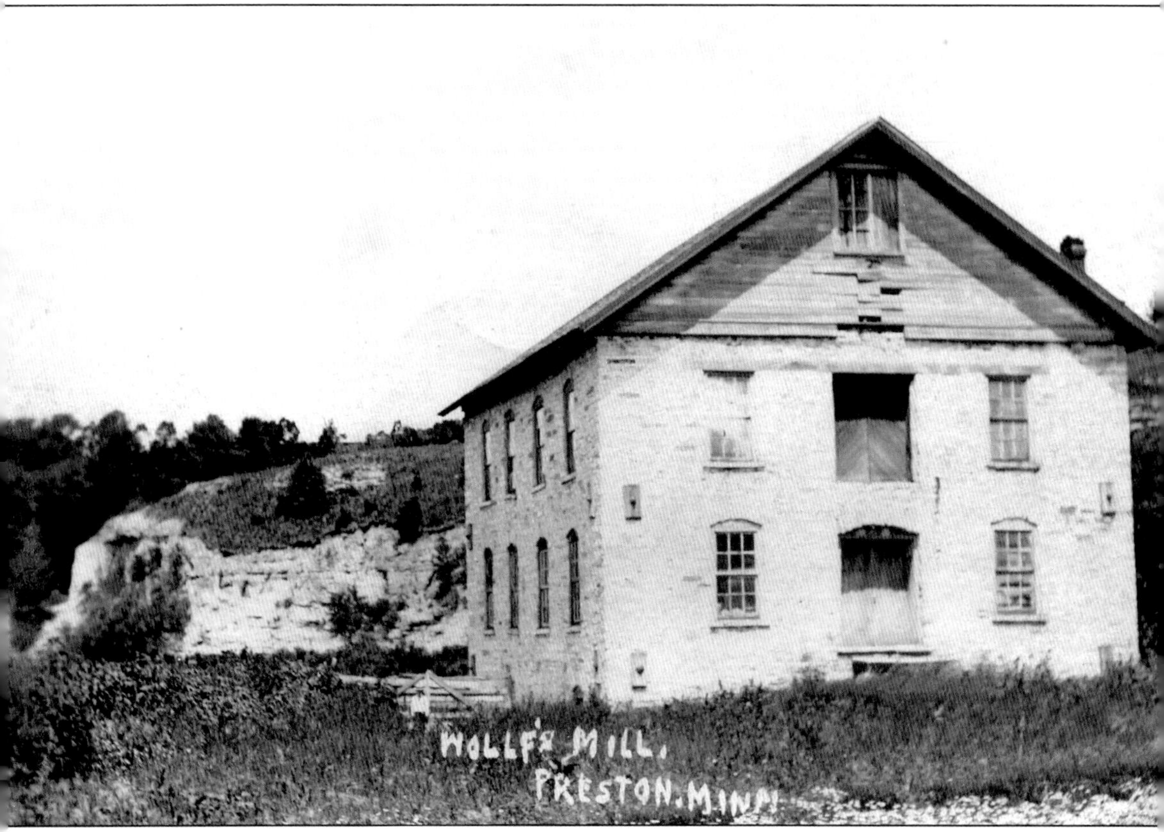


Before Frank Wolfe bought this mill near the fairgrounds in the early 1900s, it was the Conkey Bros. feed mill, and before that it was the Schweitzer & Weybright Woolen Mill. Wolfe ran it as a dairy and feed store. On Sunday morning, July 20, 1907, a fire was discovered inside the building. The individual who discovered it was able put the fire out by breaking in through the front door and dousing the flames with a few buckets of water. It was immediately suggested that the fire had been set deliberately and the fact that the grounds were littered with beer bottles and cigar stubs only added to the mystery. The area near the mill was locally known as the Jungles, a place of rowdiness and drinking parties. Frank Wolfe was a staunch supporter of the temperance movement and when the mill burned entirely the following week, the town buzzed with rumors and gossip that the drunks in the Jungle had burned the mill in revenge for Wolfe demanding that they leave his property. The monetary damage due to the fire was in excess of $3,000 and Wolfe's insurance policy only covered $1,300 of that, but nevertheless, by November of 1907, Wolfe advertised that he had completely rebuilt and repaired the mill. In April of 1915, the "fire fiend" was busy once again when another fire at the mill was discovered. This time, however, owner Frank Wolfe was arrested on suspicion of the arson, though he was later exonerated when a grand jury refused to indict him. The mill eventually burned down for good in the 1920s.

# *Three*
# Some People of Preston

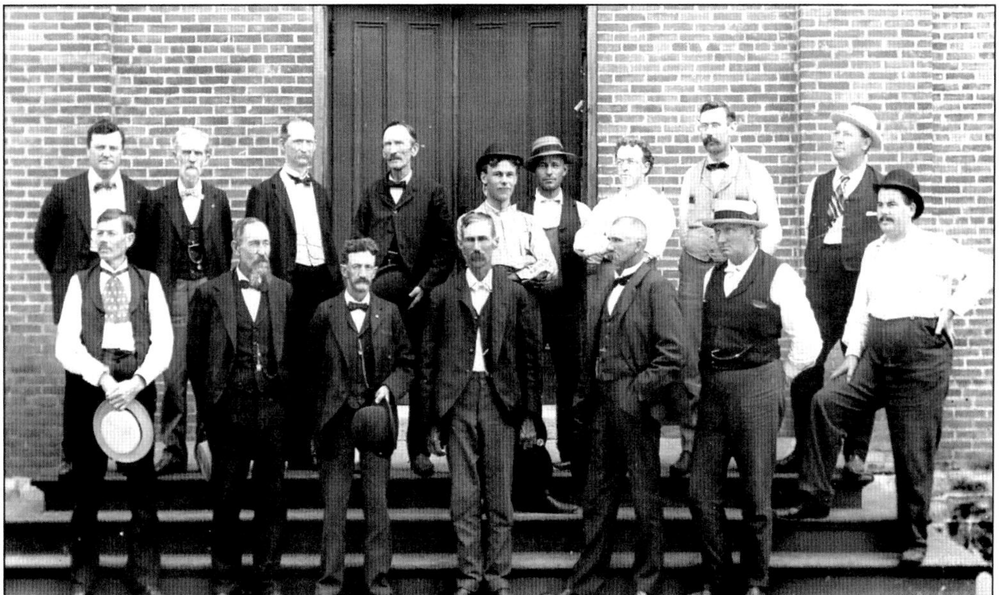

The Fillmore County courthouse employees posed for a picture around 1900. In the back row, from left are County Treasurer E.A. Highum, and Probate Judge E.V. Farrington. The only other positively identified man is Registrar of Deeds Tom Garratt (at far right, in a white shirt). During his off hours, Garratt was the manager of the Preston Tigers indoor baseball team. In 1910 he became a cashier at the National Bank of Preston, which later became the Farmers and Merchants State Bank. At the time of his death from pneumonia in 1934, Garratt was the bank's president.

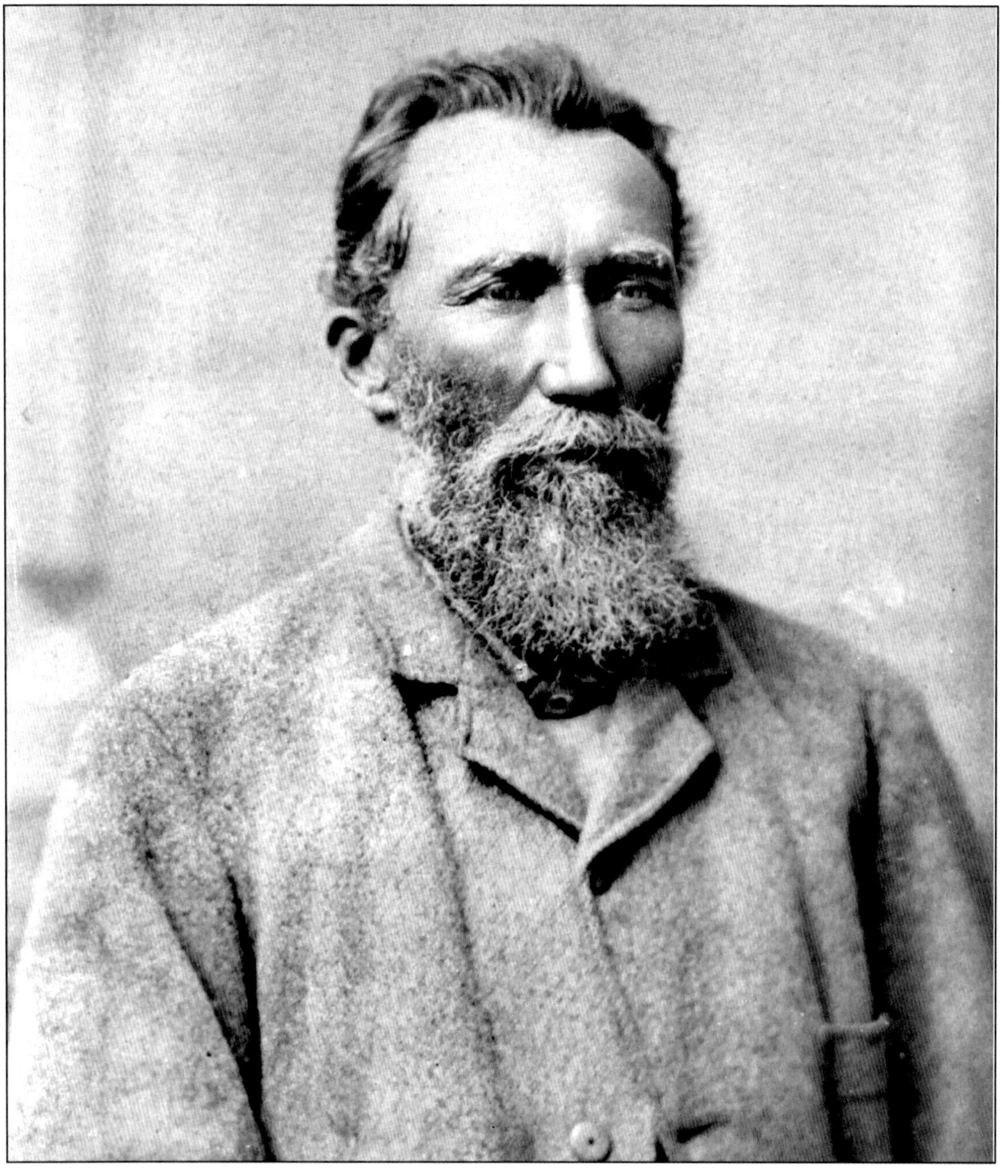

John Kaercher, the founder of Preston, was born in 1831 in the Alsace, then a province of France. He lived in Canada, Illinois, and Iowa before coming to Preston in 1855. He built Fillmore County's first gristmill along the north banks of the Root River. The building would remain standing for the next 110 years. After the financial panic of 1857, Kaercher lost the mill and later regained it, only to lose it again. He subsequently ran mills at Chatfield, Hampton, Fillmore, and Troy, only to have them succumb to fires, floods, and other various misfortunes. He landed back on the south branch of the Root River with a debt of $30,000 and no assets except "lost faith and confidence in every quarter." He swore that he would live to pay up every dollar of debt. He built a mill at Clear Grit a few miles north of Preston. Within ten years the mill was one of the largest in southern Minnesota, marketing over 100 barrels of high-grade flour daily, and selling to markets in Chicago and as far east as Albany, New York. In 1877 a well-known milling publication hailed, "Honest John" as "the maker of probably the best straight spring flour now manufactured in the United States, if not in the world."

James P. Tibbetts (1830–1904) owned "pretty near half of Preston" at one time, people were known to say. His tombstone at the Crown Hill Cemetery is today, still, the largest on the grounds. Born in Bangor, Maine, Tibbetts worked as a traveling photographer and jewelry salesman throughout New England and Canada (then the British Provinces) before heading west. He arrived in Fillmore County in 1856 and began establishing businesses. Not only was he the largest property owner in Preston, but he owned drugstores in Fountain and Lanesboro as well. His home, as shown below in the 1874 illustration, was a well-kept and impressive structure. J.P.'s son, Cushman, was for many years a local promoter of shows and entertainments. He even ran for Sheriff in the early 1920s but was arrested and thrown in jail by the incumbent sheriff Cy Christiansen and charged with libel. Cushman had been distributing leaflets in Mabel accusing Sheriff Christiansen of being lenient on bootleggers. Cushman disappeared shortly thereafter from Preston and when he died in 1937, penniless and ill with diabetes, he was a resident of the La Crosse Poor Farm.

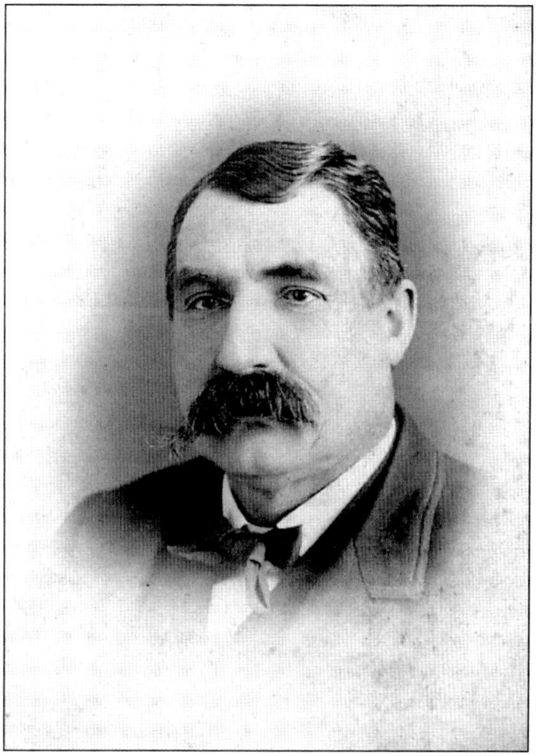

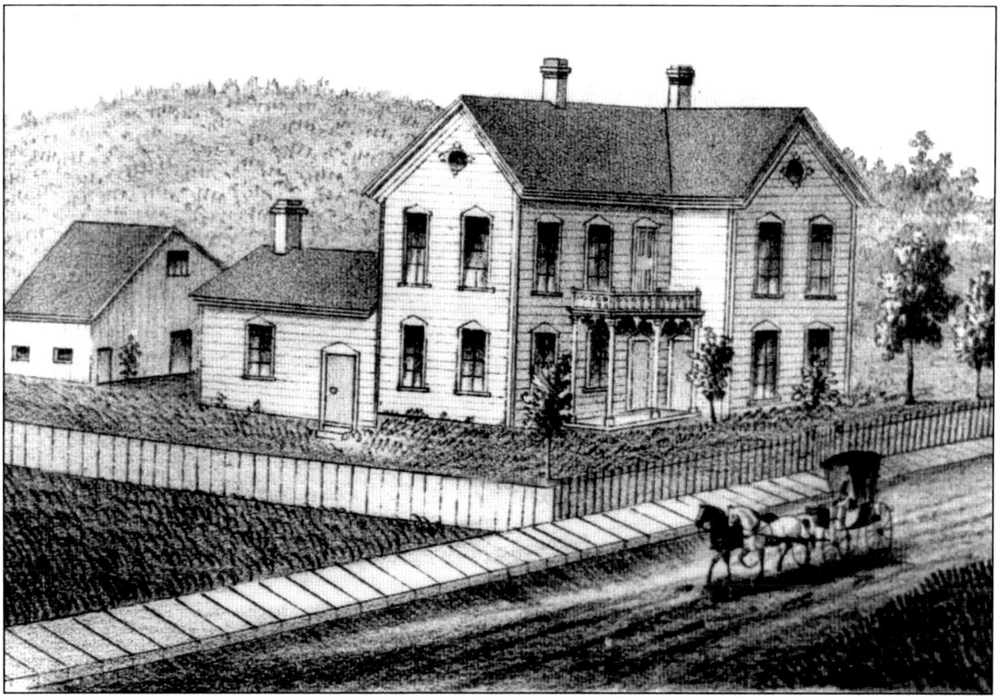

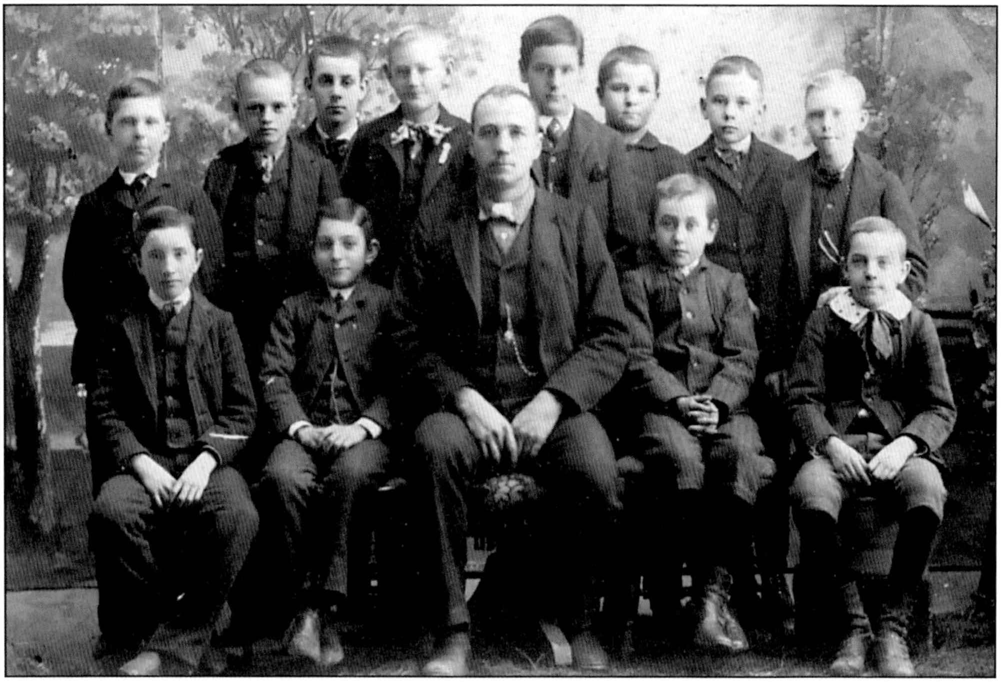

Aaron L. Sleyster (1856–1902) was a Preston teacher, artist, and poet, as well as the town's most popular photographer from 1883 until 1899. He published a book of poetry called *Hours of Pleasure* in 1893. In the top photograph he poses with his students. Pictured from left to right are the following: (front row) William Taylor, Charles Pettit, Sleyster, William Merril, and Paul Fife; (back row) George Pooler, Alton Gray, Lee Slatter, Albert Hamre, Roy Kramer, Ed Remer, Sam Nisen, and John Hague. The bottom photograph is a whimsical shot of his wife, Elizabeth Sleyster (1860–1946) posing with a cow and milk bucket. The Sleysters left Preston in 1899 for a new home in Roberts, Wisconsin. In November of 1902, the people of Preston were shocked to hear that Aaron Sleyster had suddenly died of "the black diphtheria." As his death notice in the *Wykoff Messenger* stated, "Mr. Sleyster was still in the prime of life and had reason to hope and expect that his years of usefulness would be many."

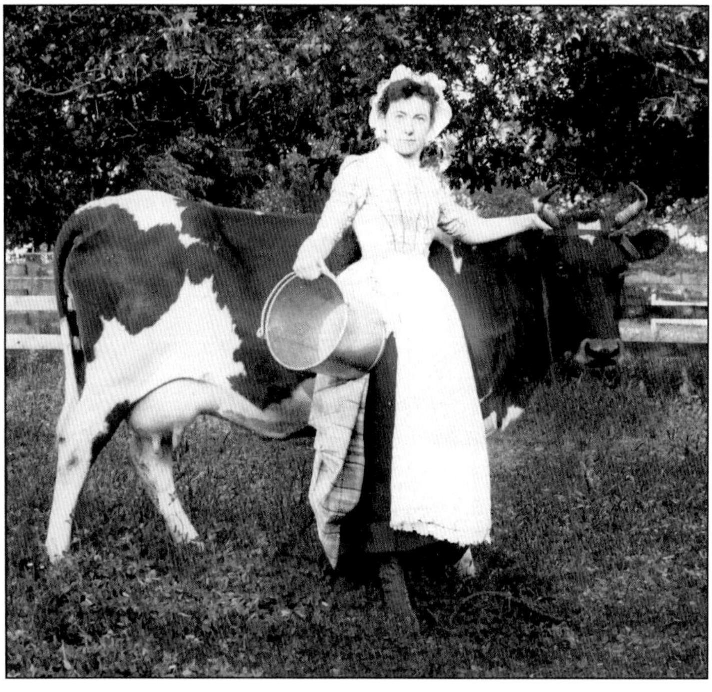

By the 1890s people were willing to travel great distances by horse and buggy to have their photographs taken. Here, Henry (1835–1916) and Ann (1843–1906) Terbeest (the author Al Mathison's great-grandparents), pose at A.L. Sleyster's studio in Preston. The Terbeests' farm was located about 14 miles from Preston, just west of Greenleafton. The *Preston Times* wrote in 1896 of Sleyster's photographic skills: "His pictures of old age are a study, representing the lives of each individual, some showing lines of hardship and care, others delicately portray that sweet sympathy we often read among the wrinkles of old age, where the heart has become tender with sorrow and the soul elevated and broadened so it soothes and blesses all it comes in contact with."

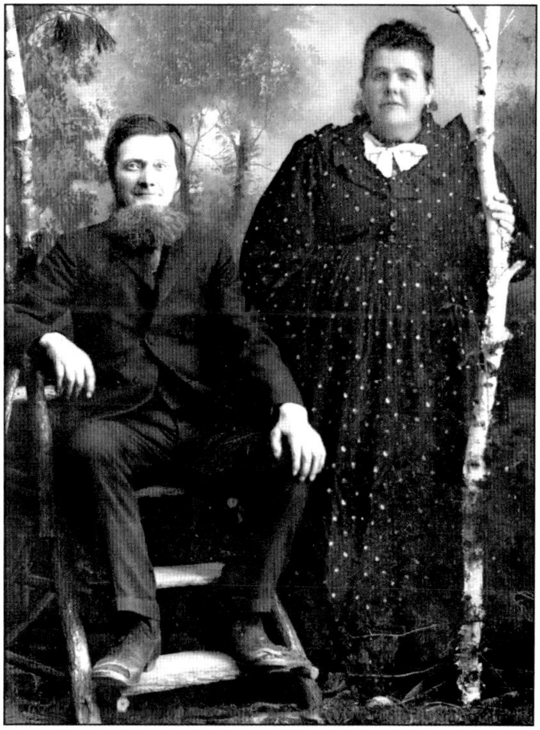

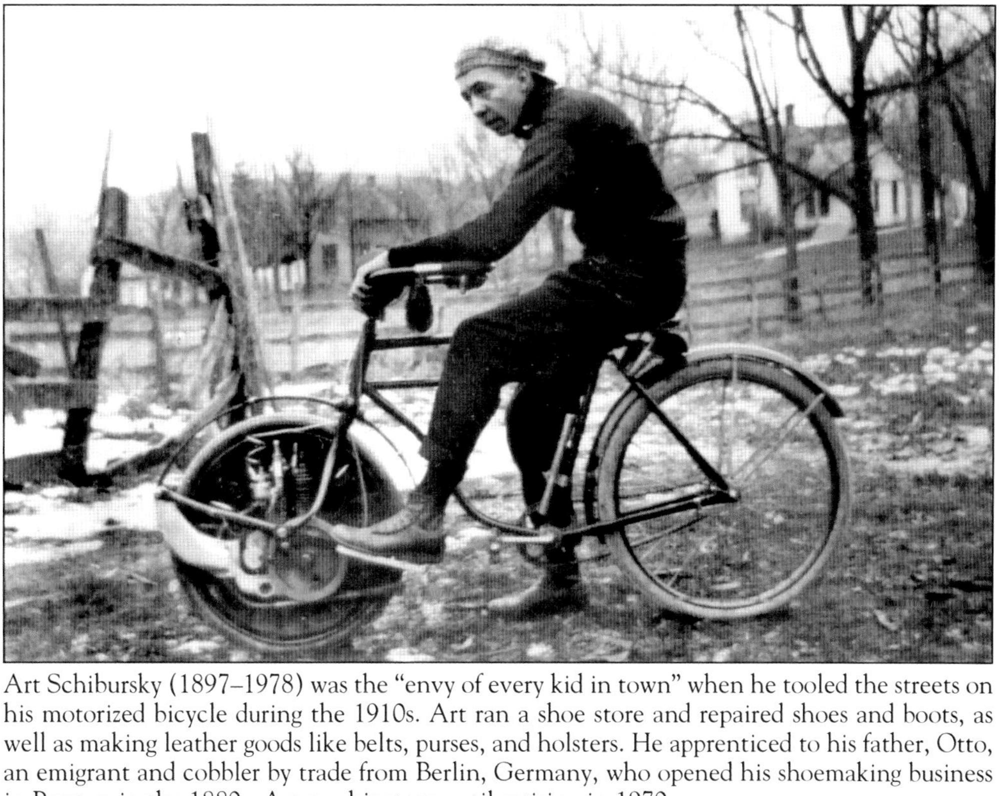

Art Schibursky (1897–1978) was the "envy of every kid in town" when he tooled the streets on his motorized bicycle during the 1910s. Art ran a shoe store and repaired shoes and boots, as well as making leather goods like belts, purses, and holsters. He apprenticed to his father, Otto, an emigrant and cobbler by trade from Berlin, Germany, who opened his shoemaking business in Preston in the 1880s. Art ran his store until retiring in 1970.

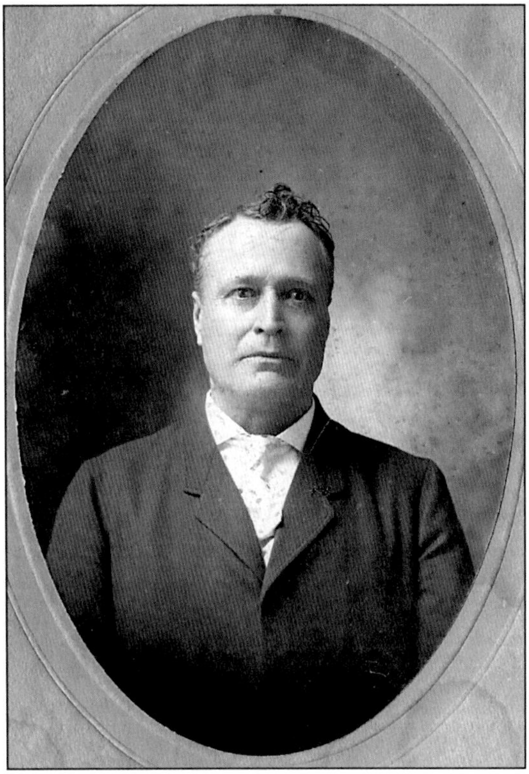

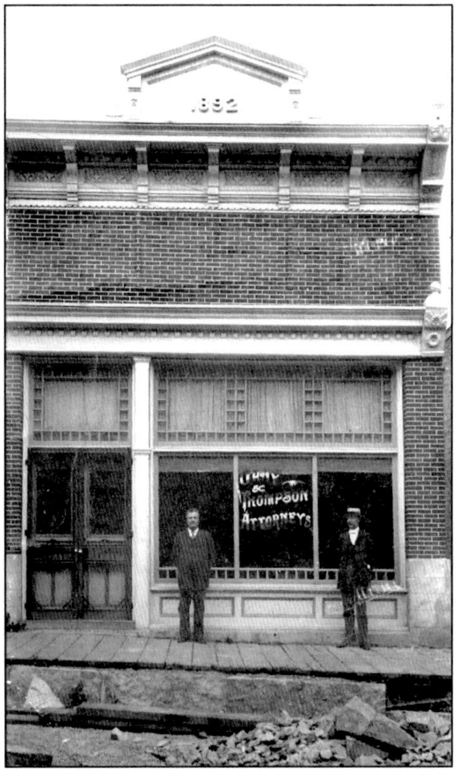


Archie Gray (1845–1932) was originally from New York, moving with his parents to Newburg in Fillmore County in 1854. He taught school for ten years and later served as County Commissioner and Clerk of Court. Pictured at right are Gray and his law partner, R.E. Thompson (1857–1925). The two bought this building on St. Anthony Street just east from the courthouse in 1898. Gray was a community leader and promoter of the Preston public school system, serving as school board president for 39 years. He was well-known as a defense lawyer and was very successful in defending men who had been charged with murder. These trials took him all across Minnesota and the neighboring states, as far west as Deadwood, South Dakota. He secured a verdict of "insane" in the case of a Professor Gifford of Decorah, Iowa, who was charged with murdering his wife. He used to lecture children on his way home to the Limerick neighborhood on the importance of clean living and the evils of using alcohol and tobacco. He was active in the Republican Party, serving as a delegate to the National Convention. More than one person remembered him for his pronouncement that: "I have voted the straight Republican ticket for fifty years and I am proud of it."

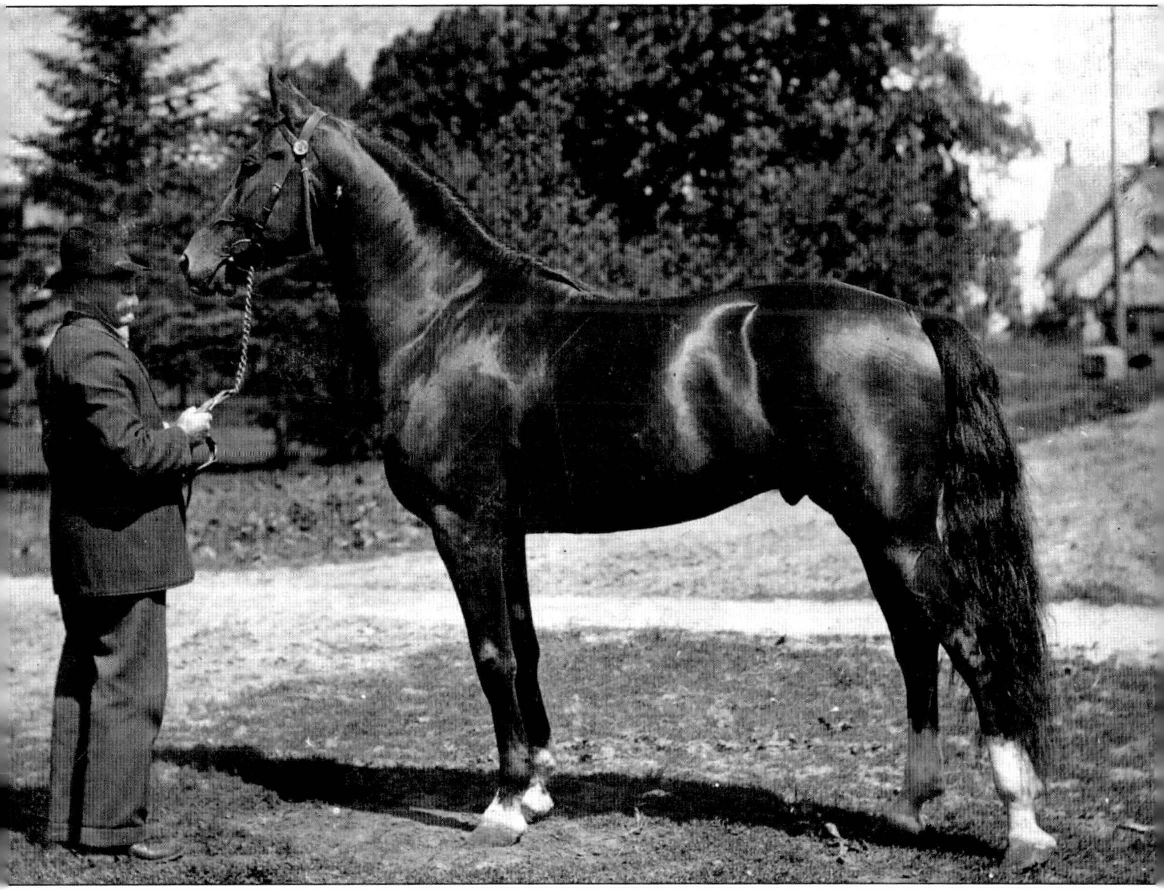

For many years Marvin T. Grattan (1848–1940) was Preston's most colorful and outspoken citizen. One of the most widely known horsemen in the Midwest, he was the owner of the Preston Stock Farm. He despised the automobile and here he poses with one of his purebred American Trotter horses. Grattan was a Civil War veteran and he served a term as Preston's mayor in 1884. In the 1920s Grattan moved to Decorah, Iowa. He returned to Preston for a Memorial Day program in 1933. Grattan was then 85 years old and was described as having a "spry and of wonderful mind." Just a month later Grattan shot and killed a man at the Winneshiek County Fair in Decorah over an argument about a horse race. Grattan was sentenced to life imprisonment at hard labor, though Iowa's governor later pardoned him. Grattan spent his final days at the Iowa Old Soldier's home in Marshalltown, Iowa.

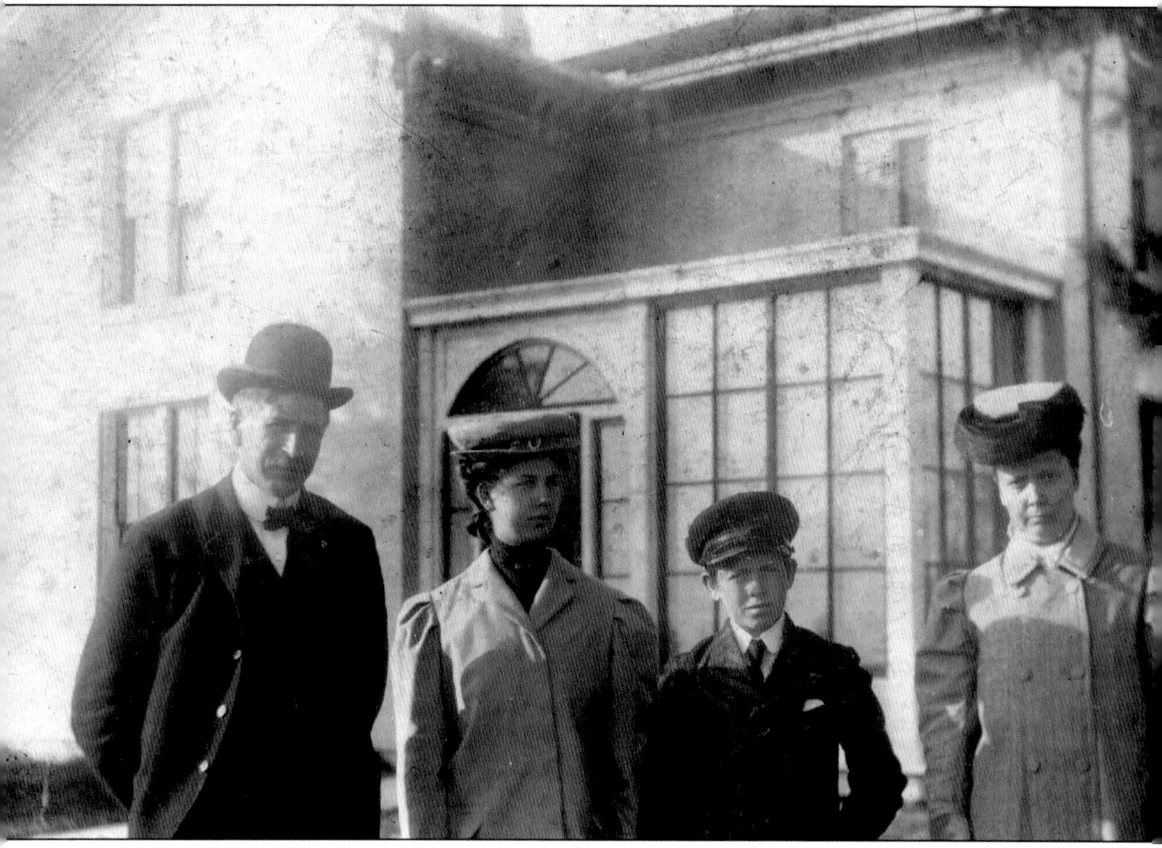

When John C. Mills died at the age of 81 in 1940, all Preston businesses closed their doors in his honor. Mills was born in Preston Township to a pioneer family and during his long life, held many prominent positions in agricultural, historical, and church organizations. His farm was located near Isinours, north of Preston. He was greatly interested in the introduction of pureblood stock of all kinds—sheep, cattle, hogs, horses, dogs, and chickens. He traveled to Europe and was the first farmer in the county to import Poland, China, and Yorkshire hogs as well as Oxford and Hampshire Down sheep. In 1909 he sold a pedigreed Shorthorn bull to oil tycoon John D. Rockefeller.

Before she married J.C. Mills in 1896, Emma Allen was for many years the superintendent of schools of Fillmore County. She also was appointed to the Board of Regents of the University of Minnesota. She stepped down from these positions when she married Mills. In a speech late in her life, Emma referred to her marriage as "40 years of rather humdrum life as housekeeper and homemaker in this village."

The entire county was shocked when John C. Mills was suddenly arrested in 1933, thrown in jail for the charges of tax evasion and perjury. The *Preston Republican* was outraged and wrote: "Think of it! A man whose reputation as a law abiding citizen has for 73 years been above reproach is herded like a murderer or an assassin to the 'stir'." Mills was a leader of the Taxpayers League. When his case went to trial, a jury deliberated for twelve hours before returning a verdict of guilty for filing a false tax return. Mills paid a fine of $400.

Shown in the picture from left to right are John C. Mills, Vivian Dowdell, William Dowdell, and Mrs. Emma Allen Mills. The Dowdells were the orphaned children of Mrs. Mills' sister and were raised by the Mills. As John C. and Emma had no children of their own, they bequeathed their house on Chatfield Street (built in 1864) to the Fillmore County Historical Society. The house still stands today as a private residence.

Henry Nupson (1852–1914) was a native of Norway who immigrated to America when he was five years old. He grew up on a farm near Harmony and in 1887 was elected sheriff of Fillmore County and moved to Preston. He served as sheriff for ten years and then became an auctioneer, traveling throughout the Dakotas, Iowa, and Minnesota practicing his trade. Known for his deep resonant voice, people said that when Henry Nupson opened his mouth, "the hills would ring." In 1912 he was elected mayor of Preston and served in that capacity at the time of his death from pneumonia. At his funereal march (shown below), 120 fellow Masons marched solemnly back up Fillmore Street from the Crown Hill cemetery where he was buried.

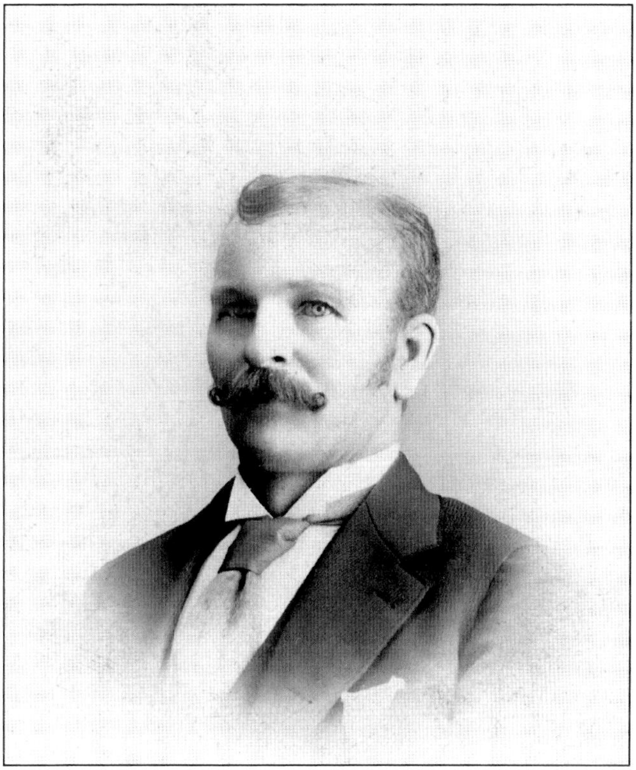

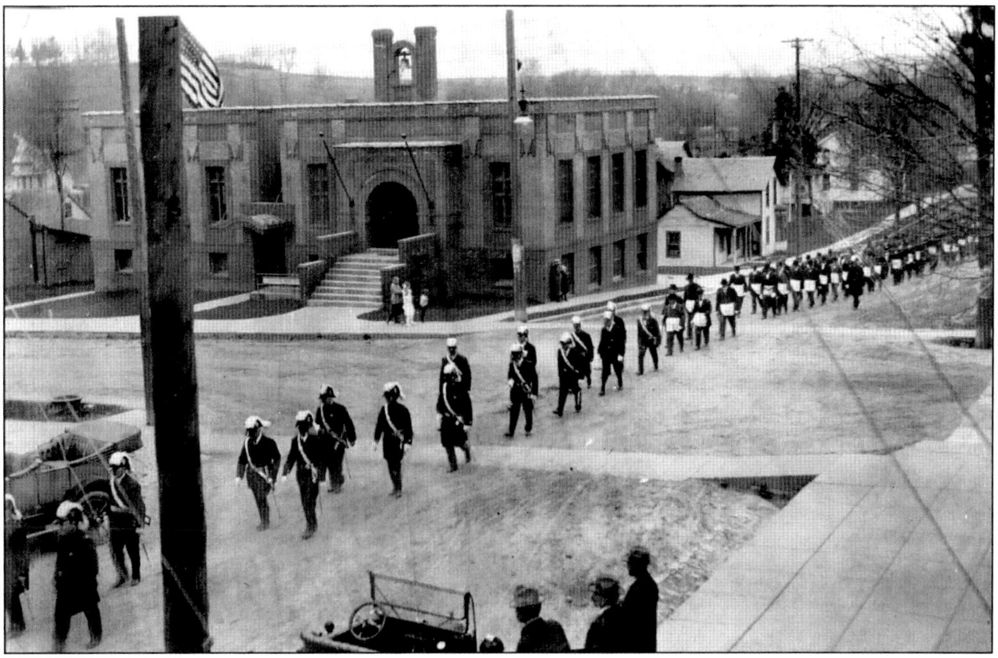

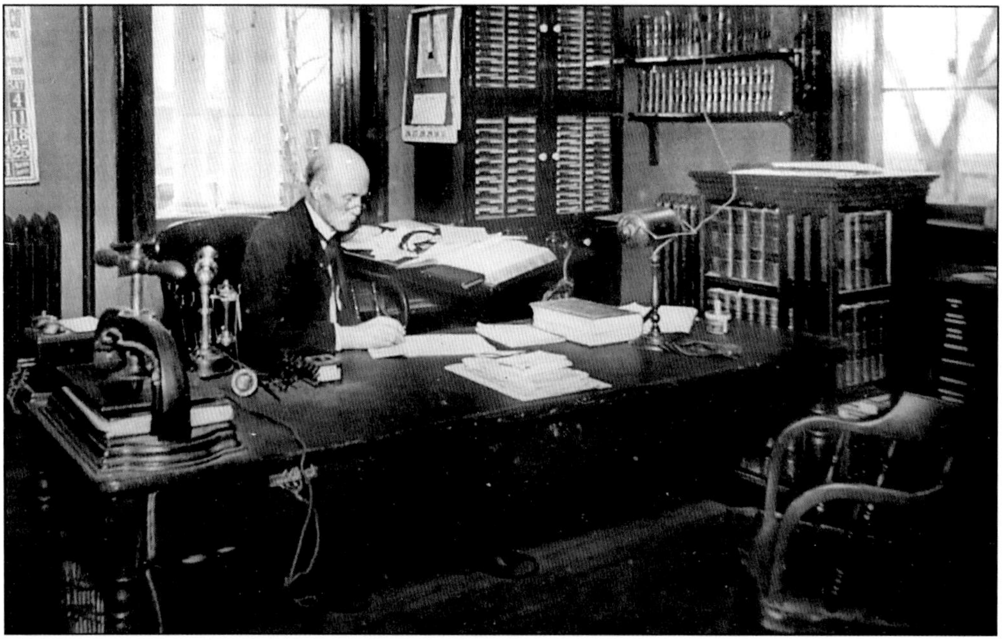

A rare view into the interior of the old courthouse shows Judge Eugene Varnum Farrington (1836–1907) at his desk in 1906. Farrington was born in New York and came to Fillmore County in 1858. He served as a soldier during the Civil War and then was a representative to the Minnesota House for two terms. In 1882 he became judge of probate of Fillmore County and held the position for 25 years.

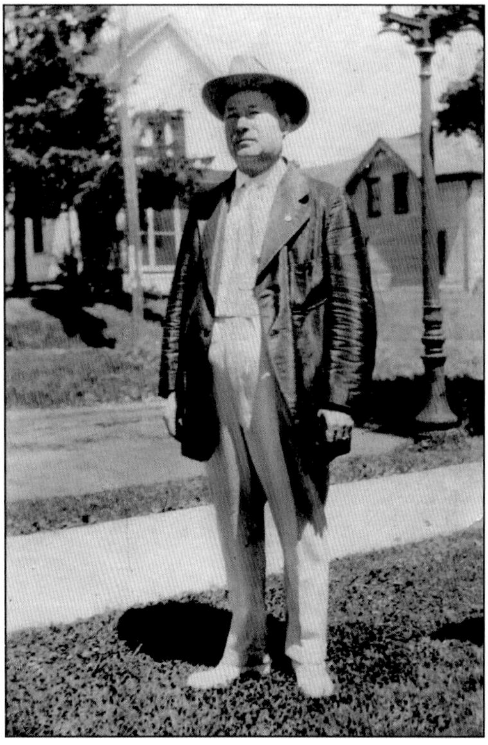

John W. Hopp (1868–1931) was a Preston attorney and served as mayor from 1914 to 1916. Hopp was born and raised in Preston and after attending law school in the Twin Cities, he began his practice back in his hometown. Over the years he served as county attorney, mayor and state senator. He was known as a great orator and "never failed to give a message worthy and appropriate for the occasion." In late May of 1931, John Hopp checked himself into a La Crosse hospital. "To recuperate for a strenuous term of court," he told friends. A day later, the 63-year-old lawyer was dead from apparent heart problems. The entire town of Preston was shocked and saddened.

When Doctor George A. Love died in 1930, at the age of 80, he had been practicing medicine in Preston for 56 years. A common saying around Preston was that the genial Dr. Love's presence in the sick room served as a wonderful restorative. All five of his sons became doctors and dentists, including Dr. George R. Love, who practiced medicine with his father in Preston from 1912 to 1930. Another son, Dr. William Love, was a victim of severe shell shock during World War I and was institutionalized for the rest of his life.

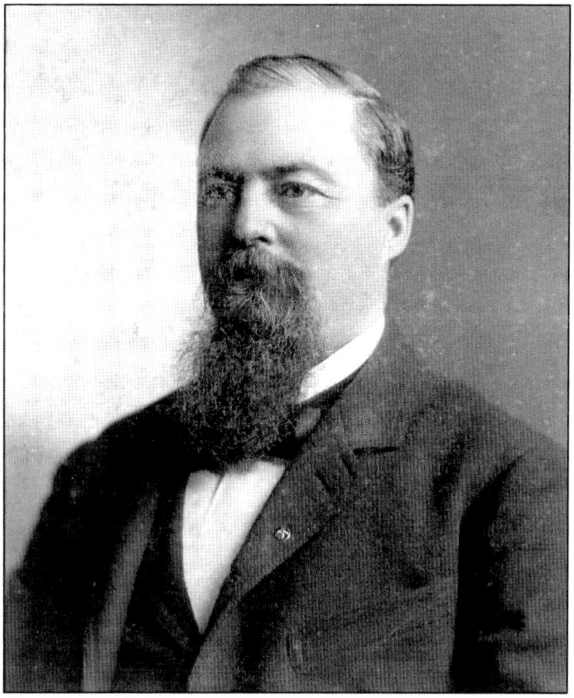

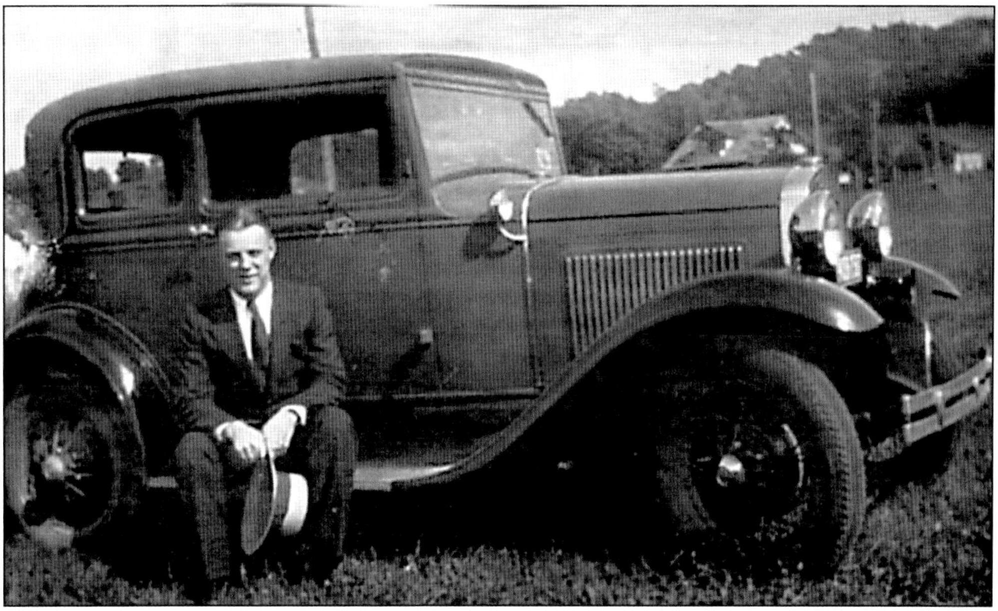

Doctor Jesse Potter Nehring (1904–1964) came to Preston to practice medicine in 1930 and for the next 34 years was the town doctor. It was reported that he assisted in the births of nearly 6,000 babies without the loss of a mother. Doc Nehring also served as county coroner from 1944 to 1967. He was a partner in the building of the Preston Nursing Home in 1963 and was well-known for his house calls as well as his "medical skill, hearty laugh and jovial nature." Commenting to the *Preston Republican* in the 1960s, Doc said, "the old country doctor is fast disappearing from the scene, just as did the horse, the harness maker, the blacksmith, the ice man and the old-fashioned butcher shop."

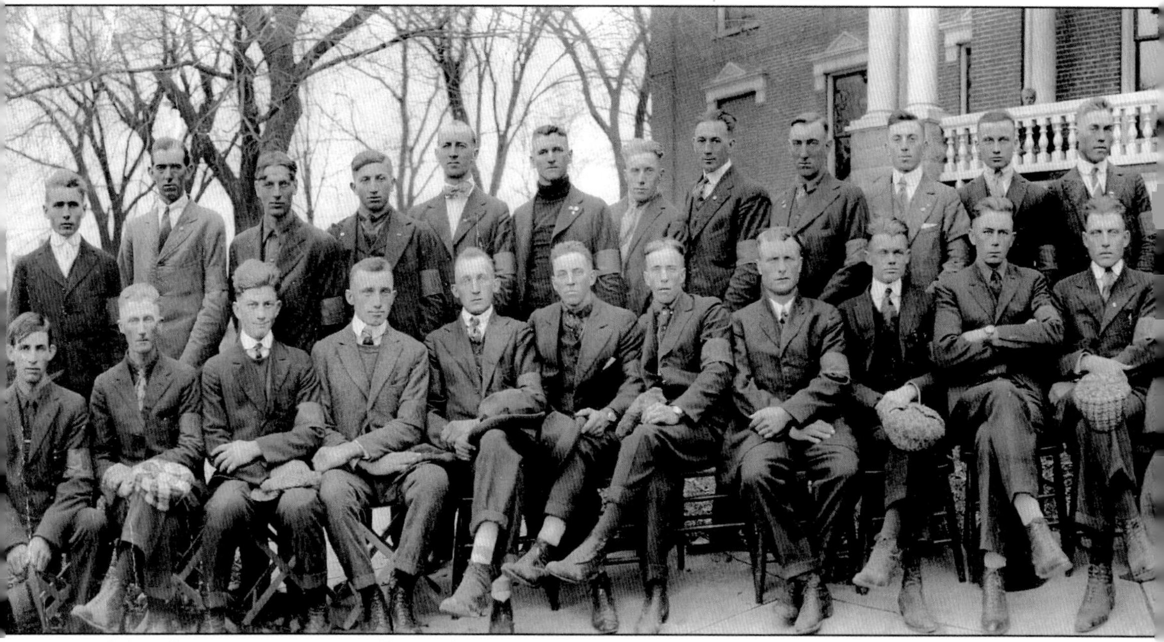

(*above*) Starting in 1917, all men between 18 and 45 were required to register for the draft. Each registrant was called before the draft board (made up of local officials) and his particular case decided upon.

Standing in the back row right in front of the American flag is Fillmore County Sheriff E.K. Blexrud, who was a member of the Fillmore County Draft Board during the war. Fillmore County sent over 800 men into service from a registration list of 7,000. During World War I, 48 Fillmore County men were to die over seas, including 11 Preston area men. Among them was Frank C. Viall of Preston. He was assigned to the 61st Infantry Supply Company and was killed in action while bringing up ammunition just eight days before the Armistice was signed. The American Legion Post in Preston was named in tribute to Viall, who was 25 years old at the time of his death.

(*right*) A group of American Legion members, who were also veterans of World War I, posed for a photograph on Memorial Day, 1929. Pictured from left to right are the following: (front row) William Pooler, Dr. Clarence Quanrud, Lynn Siniff, Harvey Winnega, Frank Bammart, J.F. Anderson, D.E. Broadwater, Moppy Anderson, Lee Krough, Clarence Seelye, William Boelter, and Mike Karp; (second row) Dr. E.K. Love, Floyd Frankson, Art Stegner, Carl Peterson, Oscar Gillund, unidentified speaker, Porter Remington, Tim Grebin, George Perry, and William Hare; (back row) D. A. McVeety, Major Flynn William Holton, George Potter, and Casper Tollefson.

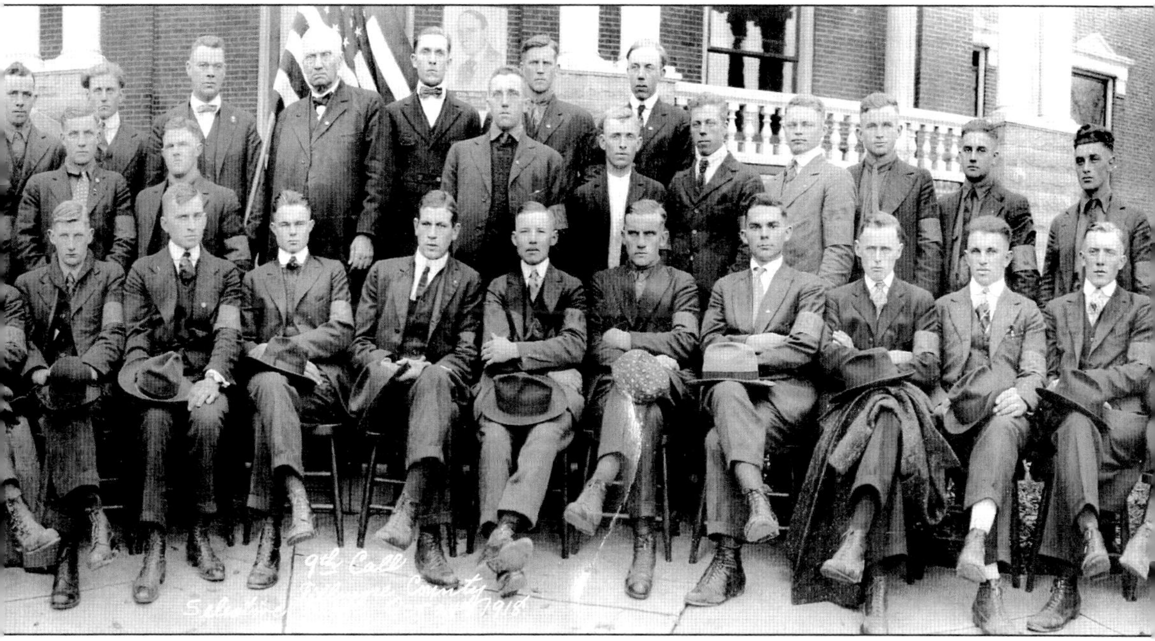
9th Call
County
1918

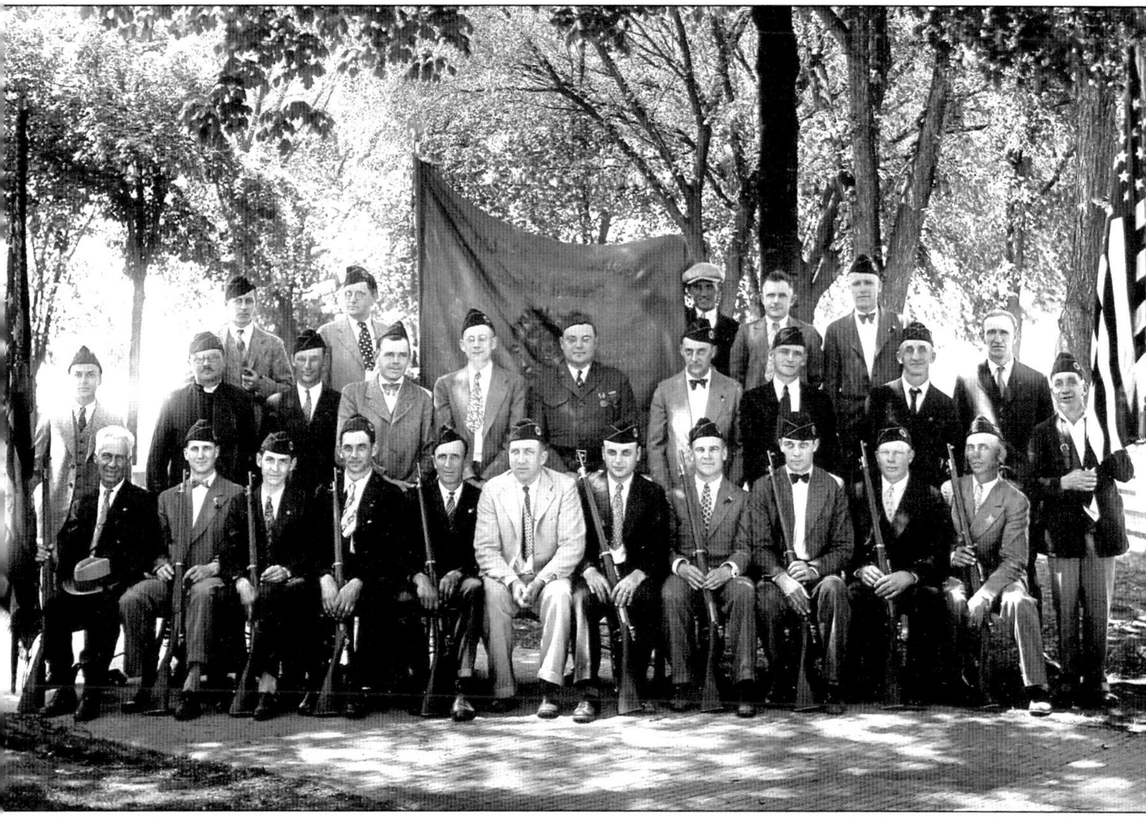

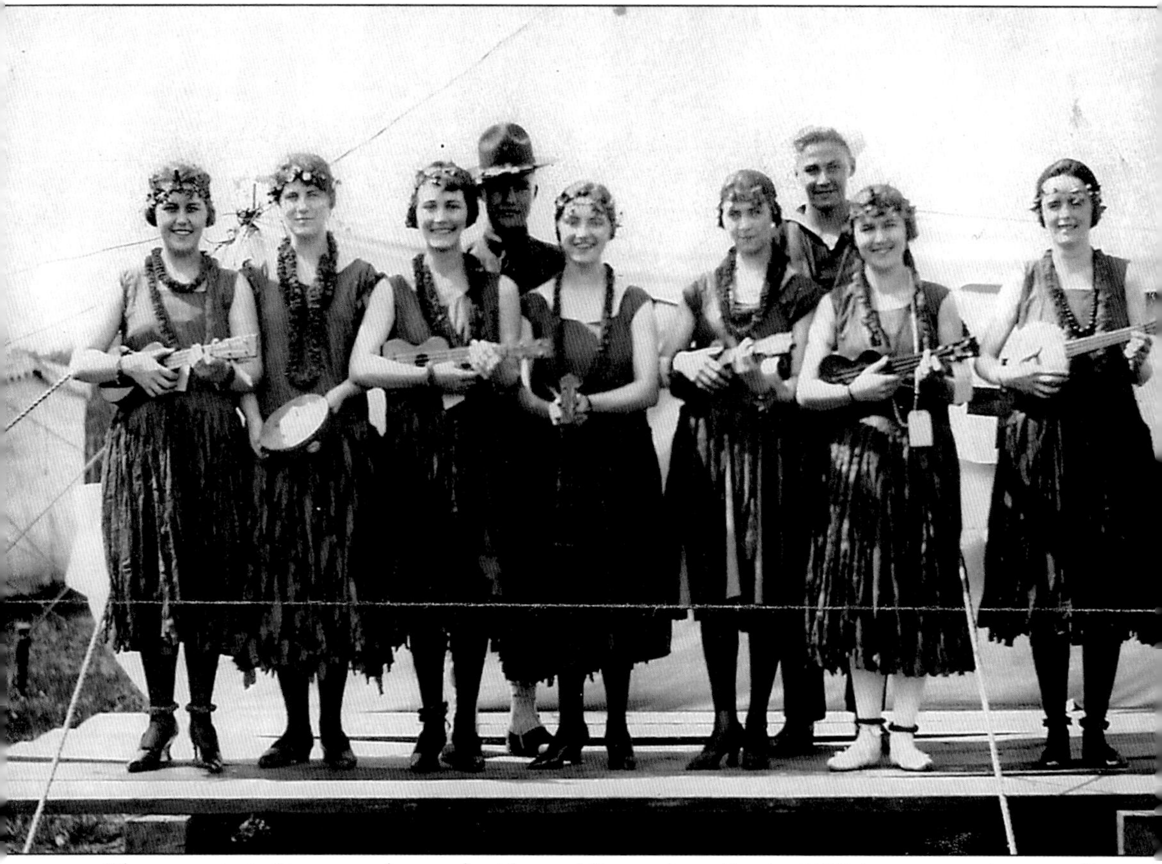

These patriotic Preston gals posed with a soldier and a sailor in 1918 in a promotion to sell Liberty bonds. Buying a $100 bond provided the U.S. enough money to feed a soldier in France for seven months. Another $35 would provide the soldier with a rifle with a bayonet on it. A second $100 bond would furnish him with "1,000 cartridges for it," with enough left over to "purchase a good sized bomb to throw in a dugout, or demolish a machine gun together with the Hun operating it." All in all, the Preston district—which included Carimona, Forestville, and Preston Townships—raised a total of $102,450 during the Liberty bond drives. Pictured from left to right are Allene Michener Anderson, Gladys Garratt Brokken, unidentified, unidentified, Kathleen Meighen McElroy, unidentified, Chris Anderson, Laura Michener Newell, and Lulu Hester Crotty.

Jake Kumm stands in front of his barbershop located on Main Street. When he retired from the barbering business, Kumm had spent $53^1/_2$ years cutting hair in Preston. Kumm was raised on a farm near La Crosse and came to Preston in 1903. In 1933, a newspaper ad for Jake's shop read: "Service, Cleanliness—Our Motto."

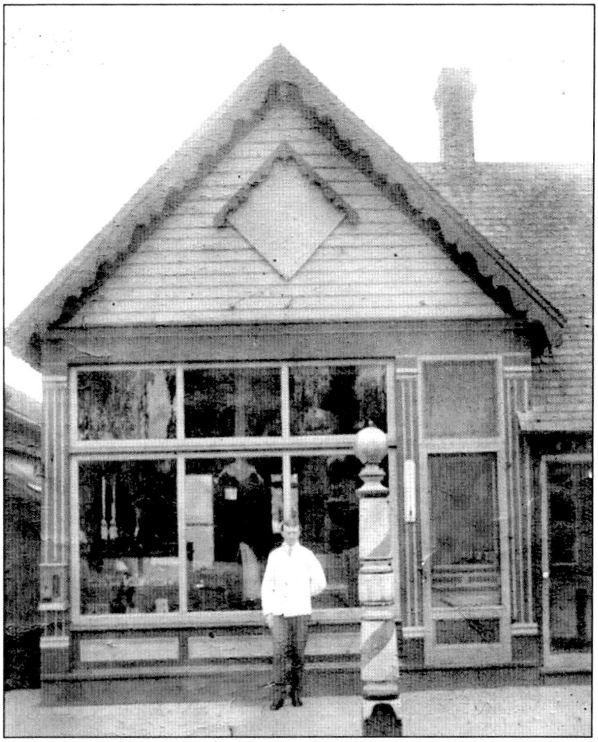

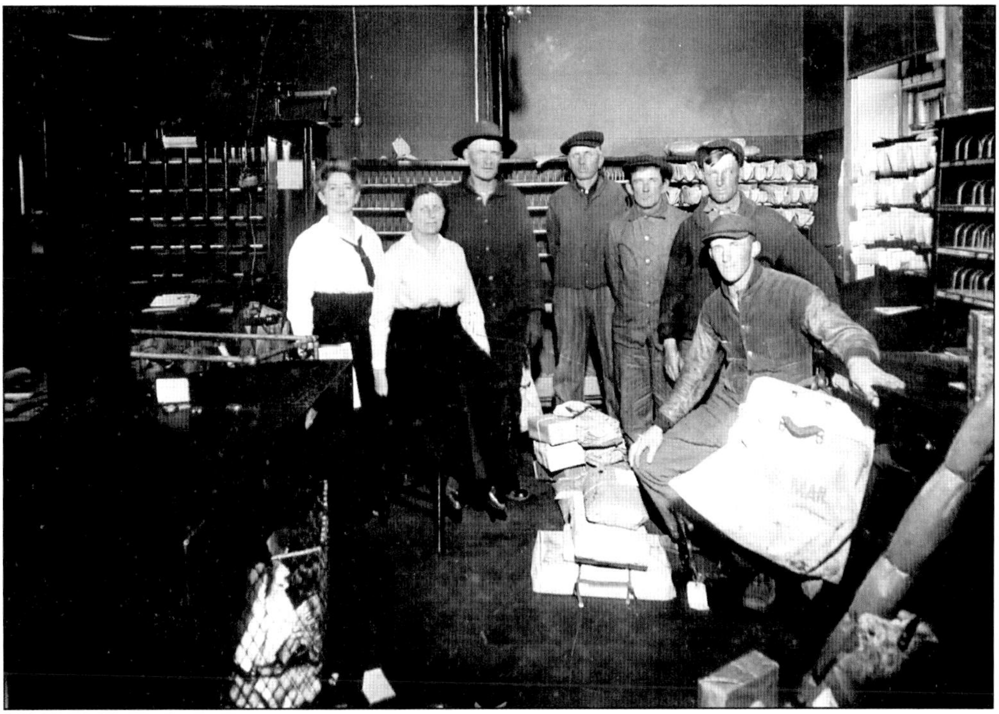

The Preston Post Office employees took a break for a photograph in 1921. From left to right are Hulda Hahn, Lily Winnega, Harvey Clark, Carl Hanning, George Kaump, George Chandler, and Paul Snyder.

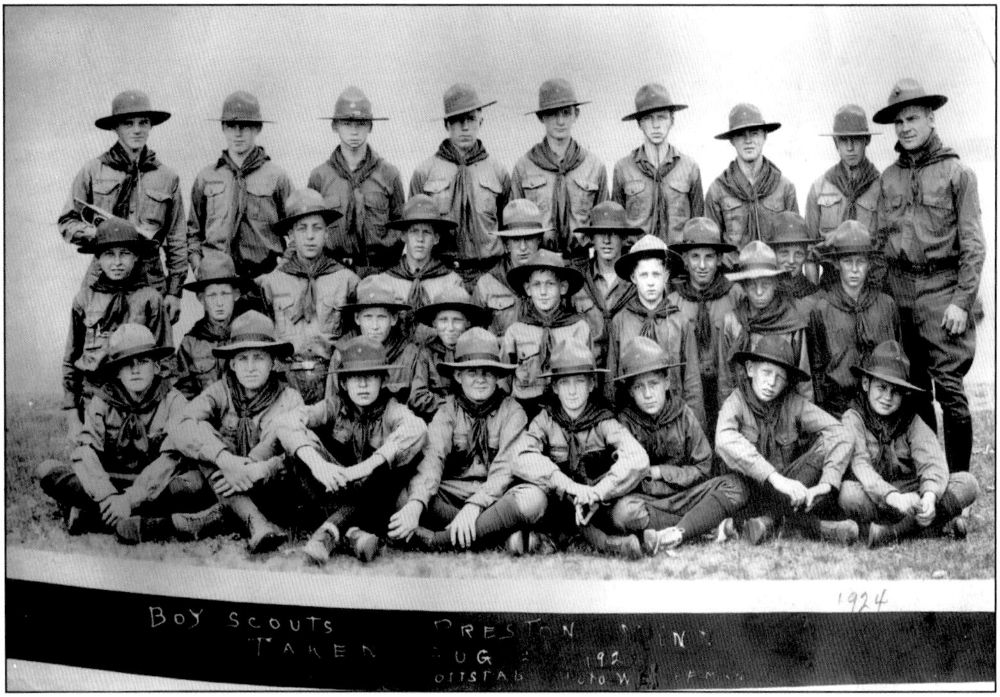


This photograph of the Preston Boy Scout Troop was taken at Roberts Lake near Fairbault on Aug. 2, 1924. Pictured from left are as follows: (front row) Carl Christenson, Eugene Hovelson, Thane Schoenbaum, Warren Ryan, Harold Christenson, Harold Ause, L. Grabau, and Fransis Barnes; (second row) Wesley Johnson, Carol Kaump, Paul Lange, Howard Gartner, Wilbur Utley, Alfred Austenson, and Donald Krause; (third row) Orval Ause, Marshall Ebert, Robert Rick, Kent Laugen, Paul Gartner, and Joe Rasmussen; (fourth row) Veron Wilder, Phil Gartner, Veral Wolfe, Anon Engle, Walter Wilder, Lloyd Levey, Fritz Olson, Lud Gartner, and Moppy Anderson (scout leader). The photo below shows the Troop of Boy Scouts at the Canadian border in the summer of 1925 as they went for a weeklong camping trip into the wilds of Canada.

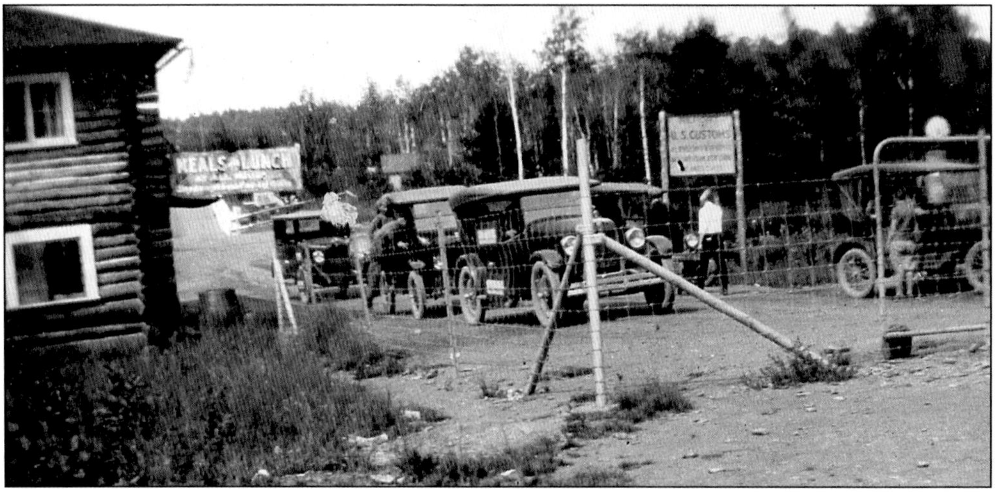

# *Four*
# Business and Commerce

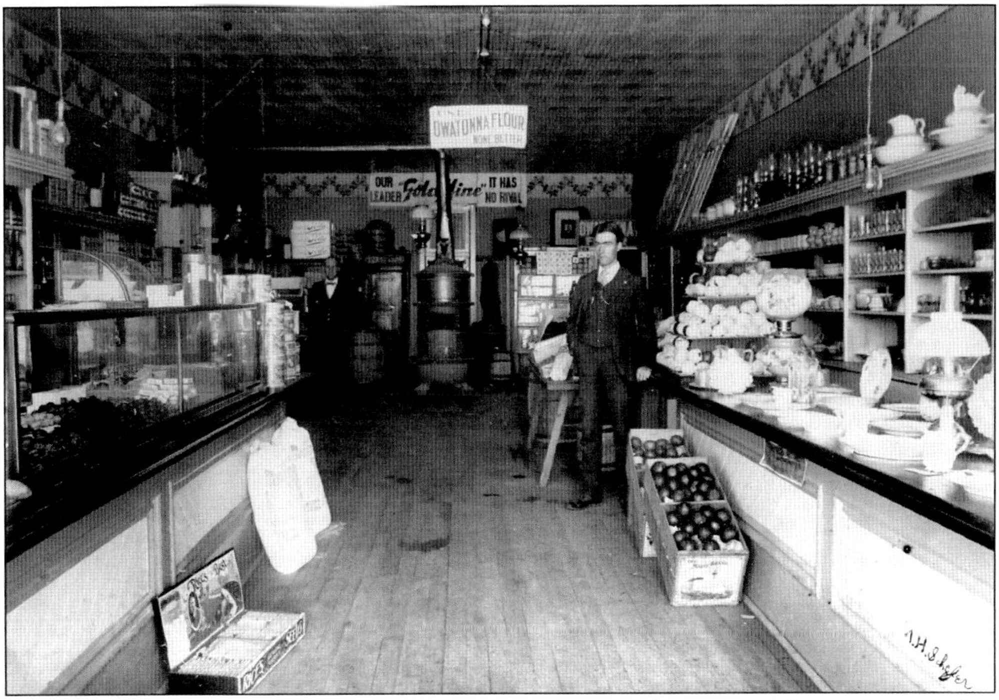


In the early 1900s, the Read Bros. Grocery and Crockery was located on Fillmore Street, below the Grand Opera House. They started their business in Preston in 1901, and a few years later the *Preston Times* was effusive in their praise, writing that the Read Bros. had "revolutionized the grocery business of Preston by introducing specialties and desirable features unheard of previous to their time." Pictured from left are Ed Read (1874–1950) and Will Read (1876–1941).

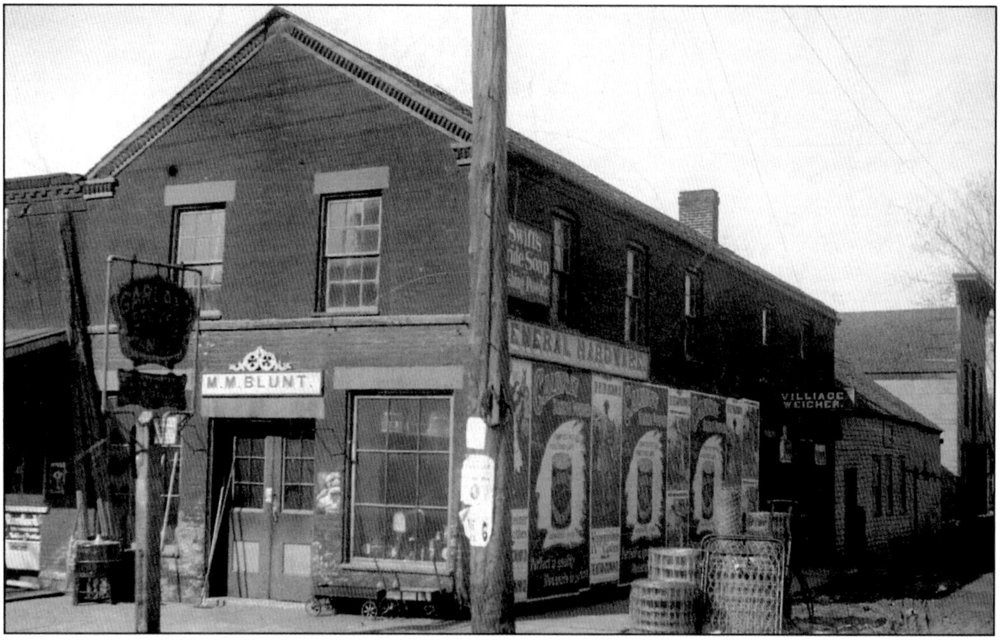


There was nothing more important than a hardware store for a growing community. M.M. Blunt operated his hardware business on the southwest corner of St. Paul and Main streets from 1897 to 1915. Pictured below is the interior of his original building, which was torn down in 1907. The interior shot shows a large stock of builders' supplies and hardware, as well as tin copper and sheet ironwares. Specialties of the store were Majestic steel ranges, cooking and heating stoves, as well as cream separators, buggies, cutters, sleighs, and farmers' tools.

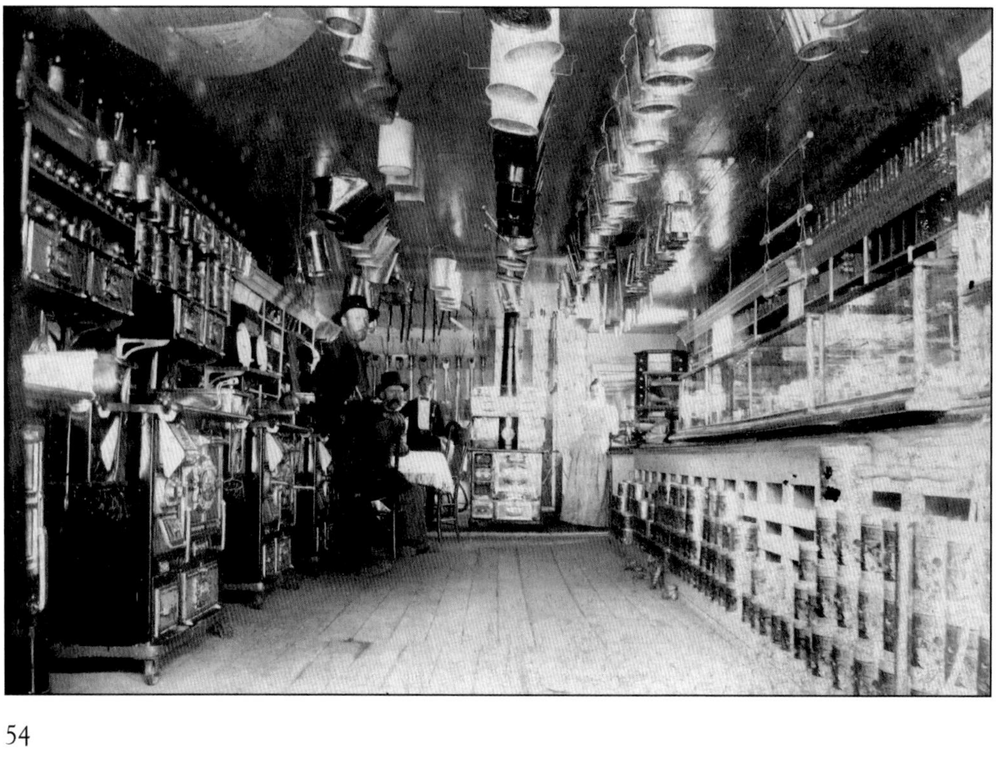

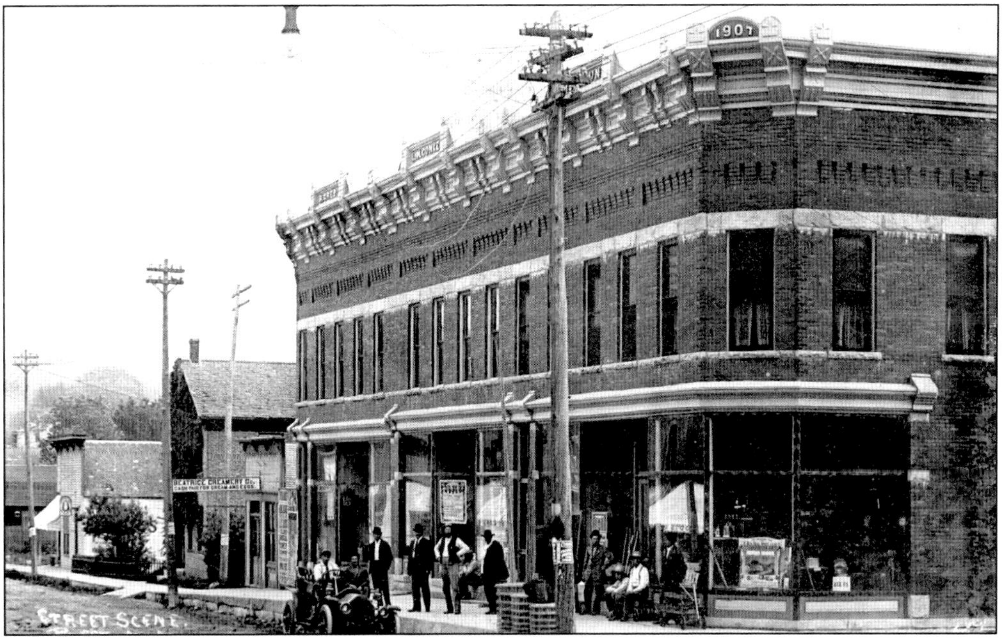


Called the "best brick block in the county," the buildings of Blunt, Conkey, and Grebin were built in 1907. While the construction was going on, M.M. Blunt moved a temporary building into the middle of St. Paul Street and conducted his hardware business from there.

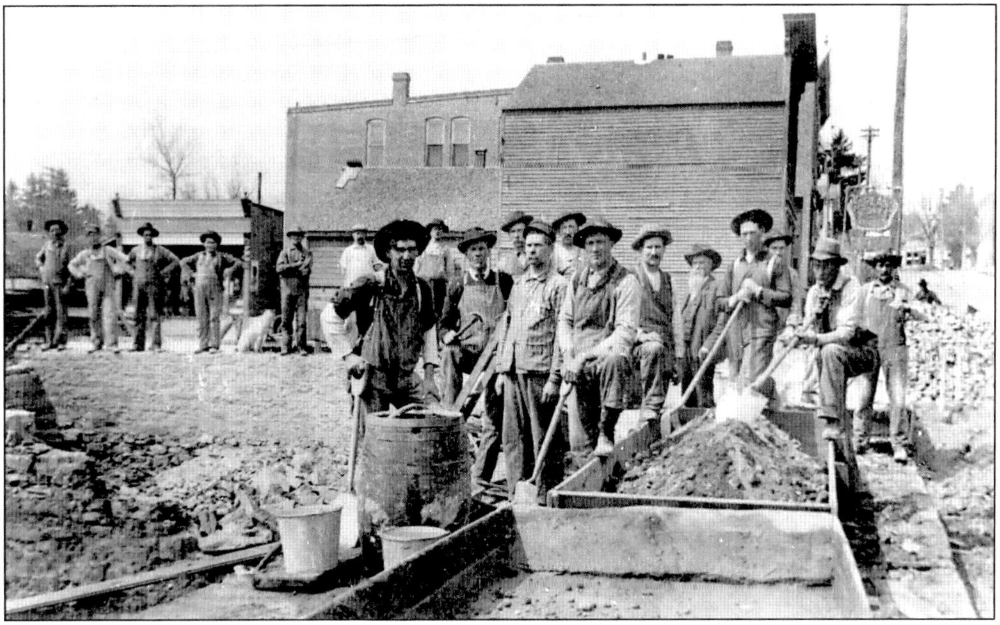

Construction began in April of 1907 and by September the new buildings were ready for occupancy. Pictured is the building crew at an early stage of the construction. From left to right are as follows: (front row) Bill Bakey, Herman Christianson, ? Viall, Romen Grebin, Ed Joseph, Jerry Vickerman, Charlie Morgan, Wadden Vought, unidentified, Dick Schultz, and Herman Schroeder; (back row) unidentified, Frank Camber, unidentified, Major Flynn, Jim Johnson, unidentified, Herman Kuhl, and Gage Viall.

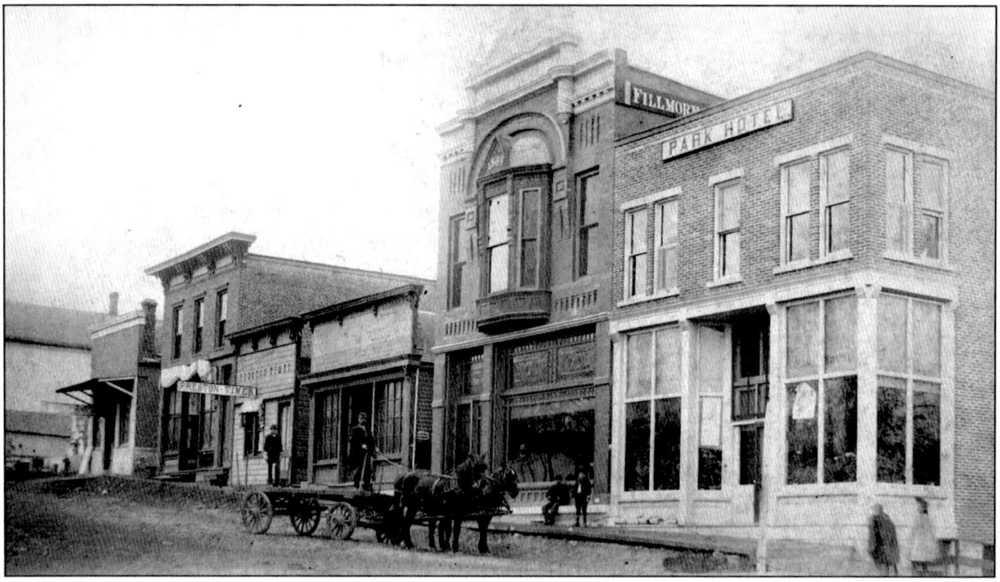


In 1896 the *Preston Times* called for more hotel space in Preston. "Time and again people have come to this office seeking information as to rooms, the latest being the manager of the troupe now playing at the Opera House. On being questioned why (he) did not go to the hotels, he said that the Park was full and (there were) only three rooms left at the Tibbetts, which was entirely inadequate for his company." Even though it was thought the Park had no room for expansion, the owners added a third floor, which was completed a few years later

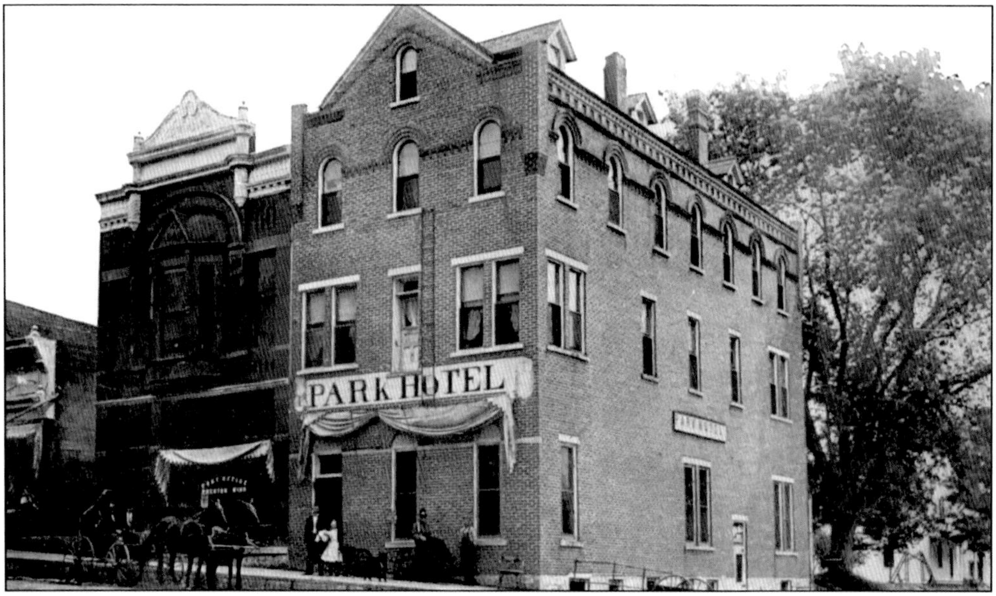


Henry Winnega and his wife, Lydia (Pfister) Kerr, took over the Park Hotel from William Smith in 1936. Winnega died the following year at the age of 44, and Lydia ran the hotel for the next 20 years. She consistently charged $2.50 a night for her best rooms and 50¢ a night for the top floor rooms, which were usually rented out to working men from the Spies Mill. Kerr did the laundry and cooking in the basement. Her normal charge for a meal was 50¢ or as she later recalled, "whatever somebody was able to pay."

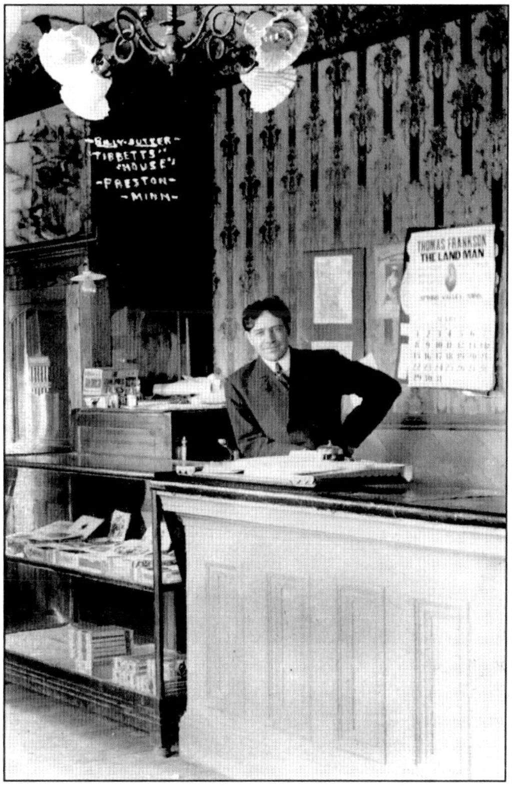


In 1905 the *Preston Times* said that the Tibbetts House was a "well ordered and excellent hotel, finely appointed, neatly kept and completely equipped in every particular, while the table and service is unrivaled. The Tibbetts is popular with the boys on the road and the house is modern throughout heated by steam, lighted by electricity, etc." Shown below is an advertising card that was handed out to travelers at the railroad depot.

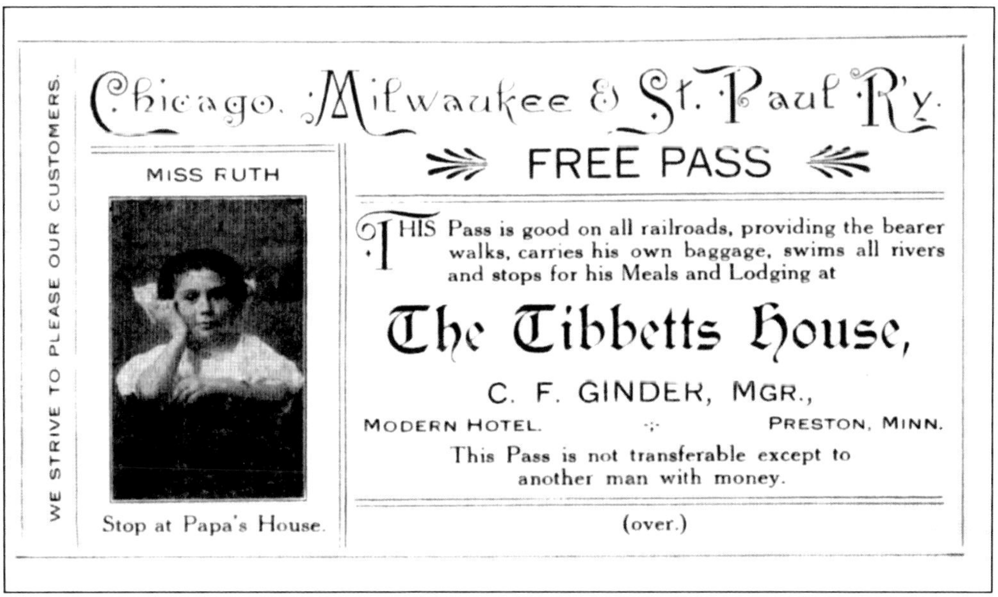

WE STRIVE TO PLEASE OUR CUSTOMERS.

Chicago, Milwaukee & St. Paul R'y.

FREE PASS

MISS RUTH

Stop at Papa's House.

THIS Pass is good on all railroads, providing the bearer walks, carries his own baggage, swims all rivers and stops for his Meals and Lodging at

The Tibbetts House,

C. F. GINDER, MGR.,

MODERN HOTEL. PRESTON, MINN.

This Pass is not transferable except to another man with money.

(over.)

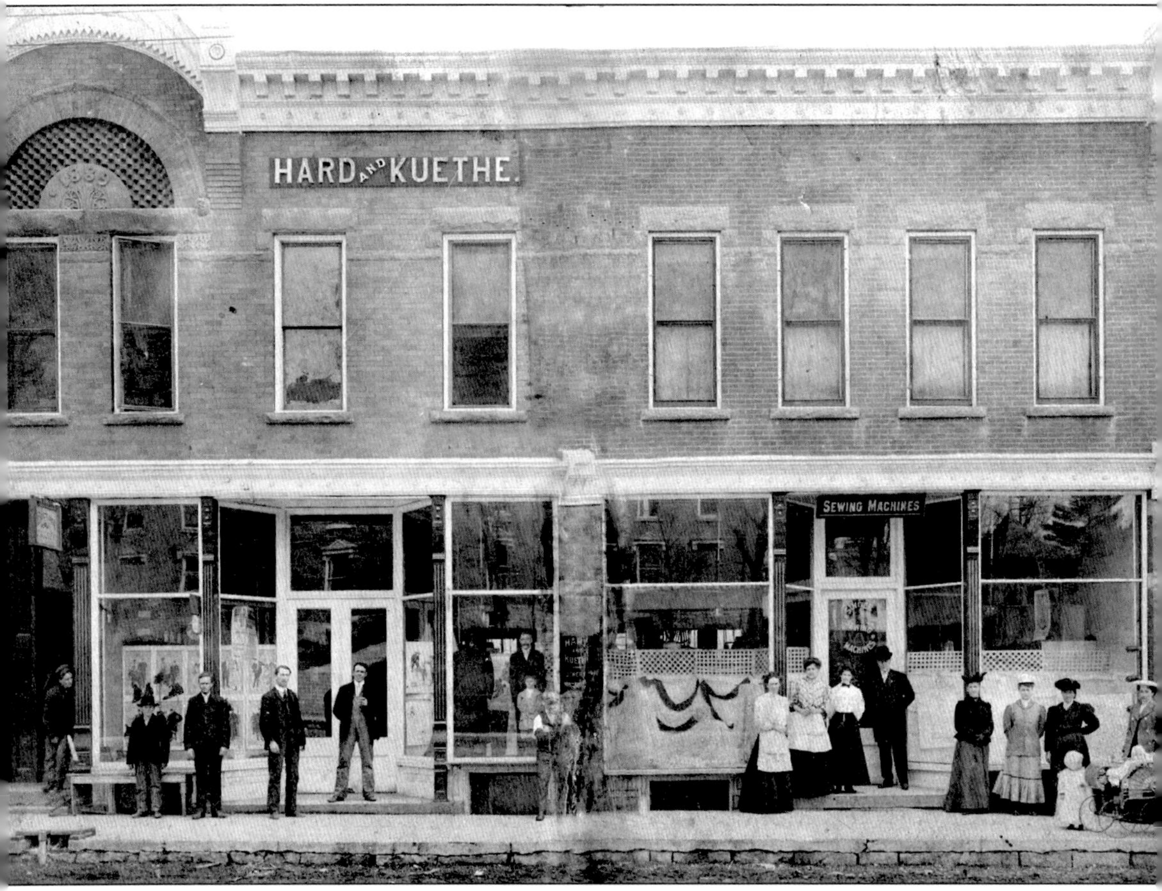


Called by many the "Old Reliable," the mercantile store of Hard and Kuethe was located on Main Street. It carried a full line of clothing as well as having a grocery department. George Hard (1843–1920) was a Civil War veteran who hailed from New York. Originally a photographer, Hard started a general merchandise store in Preston in 1881. He took Carl Kuethe (1855–1916) on as his partner in 1889. At one time the company employed eight sewing machine operators on the second floor of their building. A reporter from the *Spring Valley Sun* wrote in 1903, "in one hour we saw more goods on sale than we have seen under one roof outside the Twin Cities. The building is 120 by 75 feet, high ceiling, lighted by 100 incandescent lights and half a dozen arcs, and heated by steam. Every few feet we found a clerk and each clerk was busy. The pen fails to do justice to the enterprise. It must be seen to be appreciated."

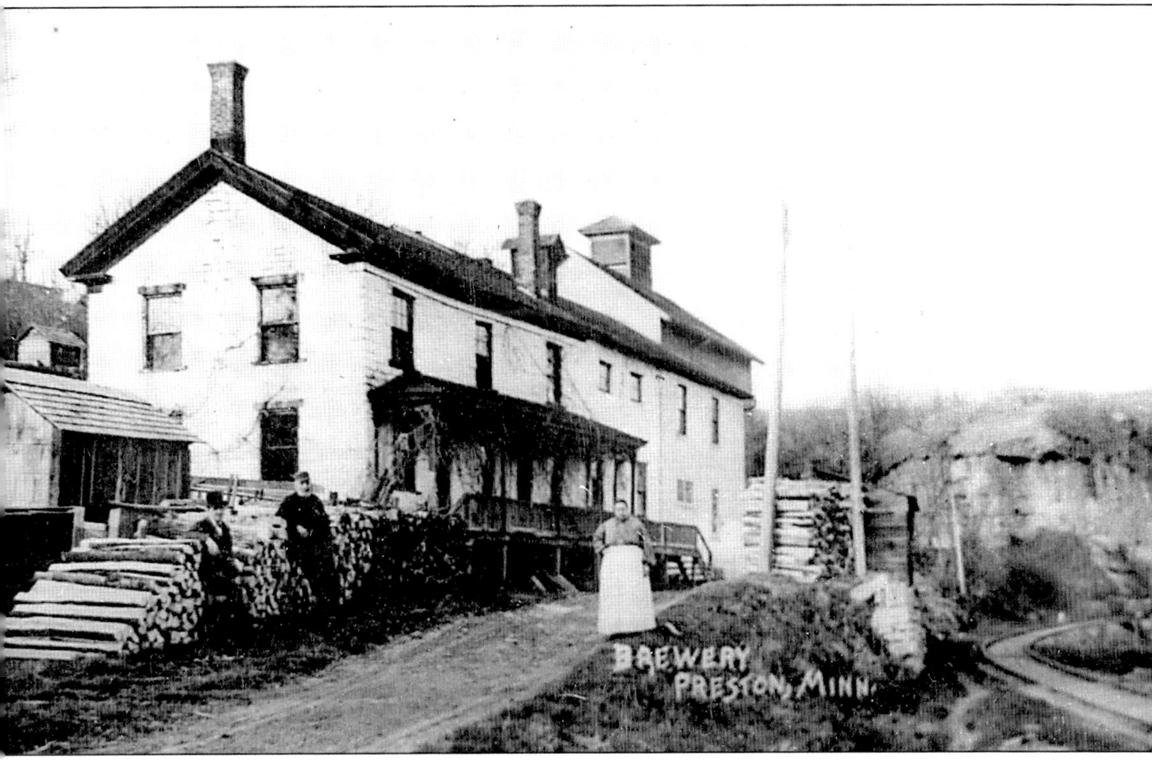


The Preston Brewery started beer production in 1859 and closed in 1878 before being reopened in the late 1880s by Yager and Luhman. Their newspaper ad of the era stated: "Our beer is made from hops and malt—no rice, no glucose. It is the VERY BEST on the market and stands the medical test. Send in your orders. Families supplied at reasonable rates." Two of the beers produced over the years at the brewery were called "Peerless" and "Forget Me Not." During Prohibition, the brewery's owner, August Knapp, produced soft drinks for a couple years before closing down the brewery for good.

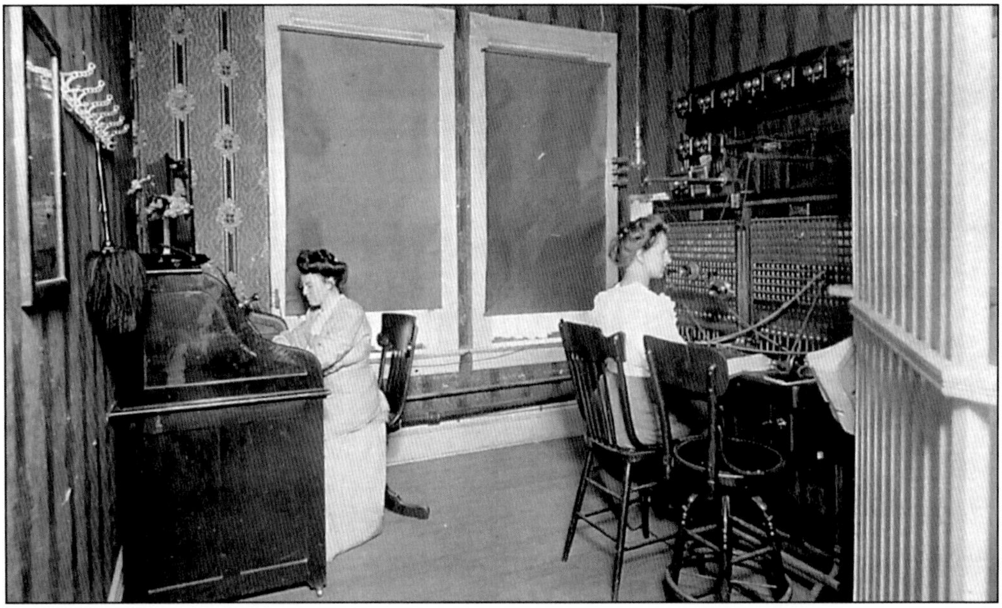

The first telephone call from Preston took place in 1895, when Mayor M.R. Todd of Preston called the mayor of Spring Valley. "The two exchanged greetings as solemnly and ceremoniously as though it had been the Atlantic cable which connected the two continents," the *Preston Times* said. By 1909, when this photograph was taken, there were six different long distance companies vying for business in Preston. Pictured are Anna Samp Convoy (left) and Bess Samp.

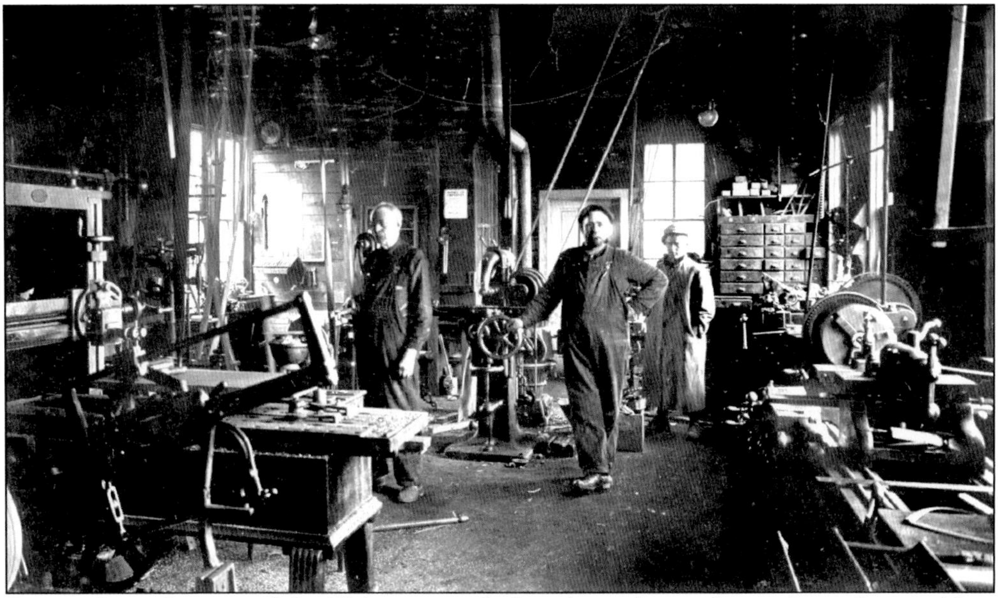

During the early years of the 20th century, before the widespread use of acetylene welding (around 1913), there were five blacksmith shops in Preston, including Preston Iron Works, owned by H.S. Popple and E.H. Cummings. With their lathes, saws, drills, planers, and other devices, they did repair work on all sorts of farm machinery and industrial equipment. They were also the builders of the Preston Gasoline Engine, which was built entirely in their shop. The engine was guaranteed for two years.

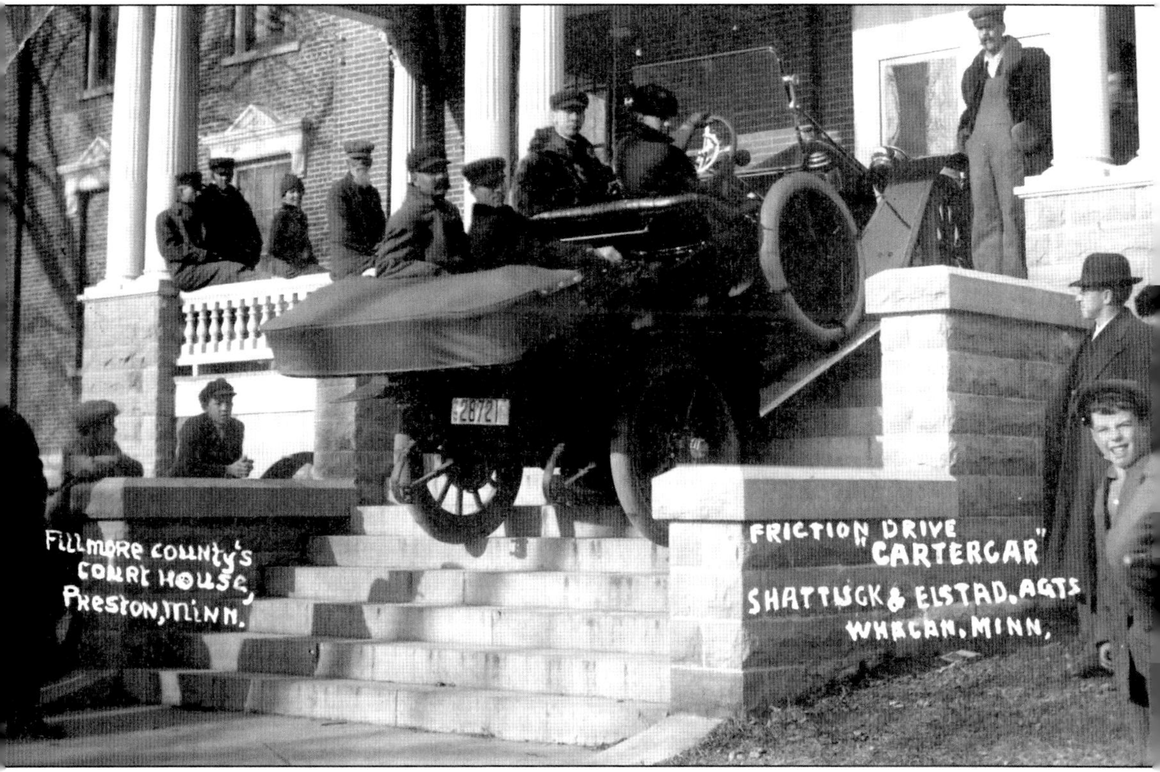


"The friction drive 'Cartercar' can climb anywhere." And to prove it, salesman Bert Shattuck from Highland (left rear seat) had one of his new 40 horsepower Cartercars driven up the courthouse steps. At the wheel was his business partner Torger Elstad. After going up and down the steps a few times, they loaded fifteen people into the $1,250 car and drove around the square. The Cartercar was in production from 1905 to 1915 and was known for its gearless friction drive transmission. The Cartercar company was absorbed by General Motors in 1909. This photograph was taken in December of 1912 and was later used as a local newspaper ad. The only other identified individual in the photograph is Louis Opperud (at top right), who was a pioneer blacksmith at Highland.

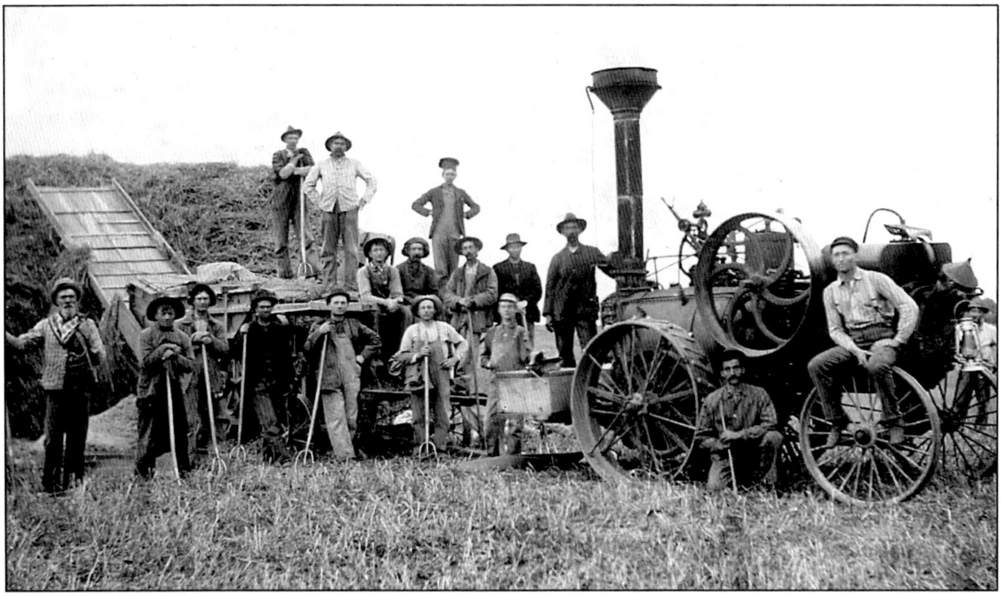

Threshing crews traveled the area during the harvest season. This photo was taken near Carimona. In July of 1922, Minnesota Farm Bureau Federation reported that the average wage for general farm work per day was $1.90. A one-day wage for haying was $2.20, while harvesting or shocking brought $2.40 per day. For those working by the month during the harvest season the average wage was $46.

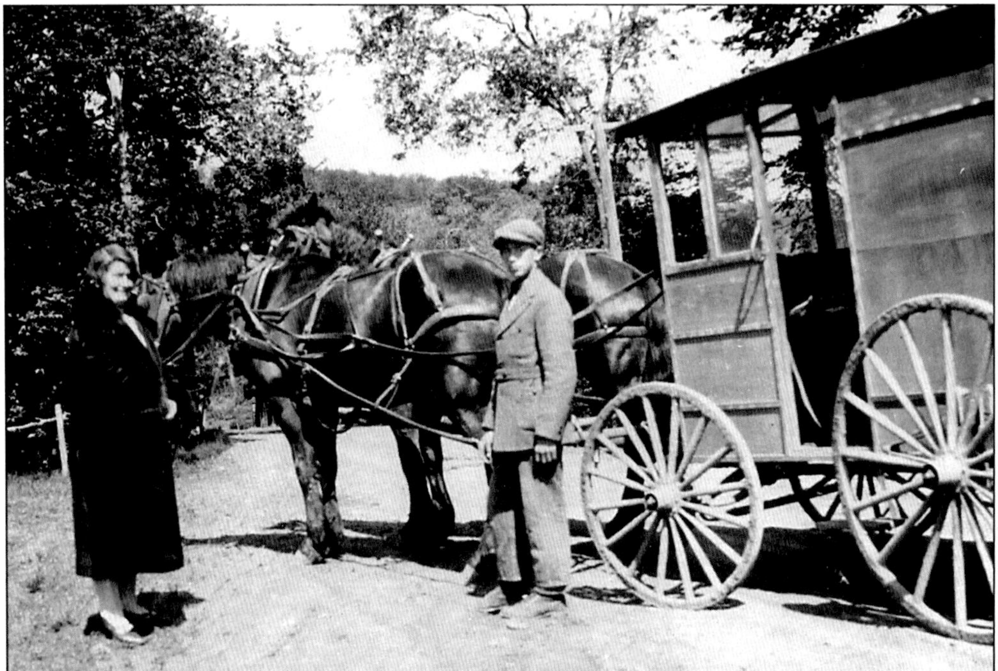

This 1926 photograph shows Burdette Maust and his mother, Grace Maust. The Mausts ran the Sunny Hill Dairy just outside of town and sold milk to individual families, restaurants, and grocery stores.

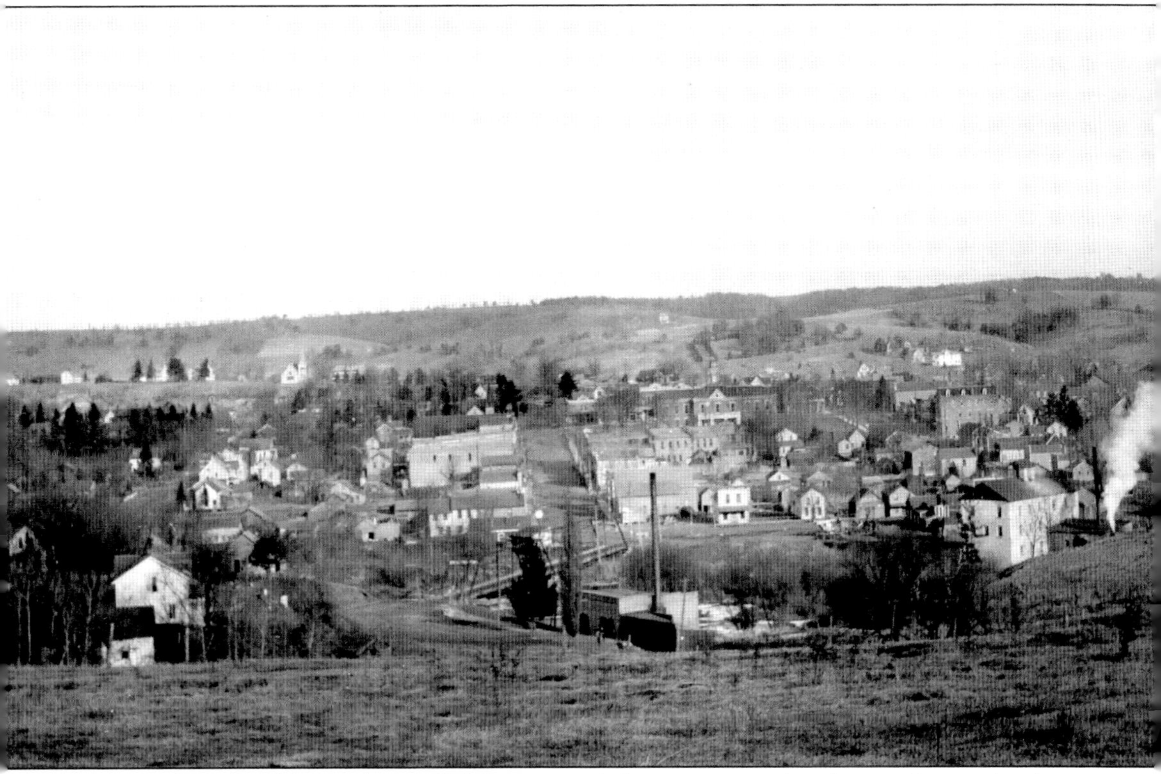

In 1912 when the old Kaercher Mill (shown at right) was renovated and opened up under the new management of Charles Spies and Sons, the *Preston Times* wrote: "The smoke is dense and black that comes out of the big smoke stack at the mill this week but there is no talk of enacting an ordinance declaring it a nuisance, on the contrary it is a welcome indication of the revival of the Preston milling business."

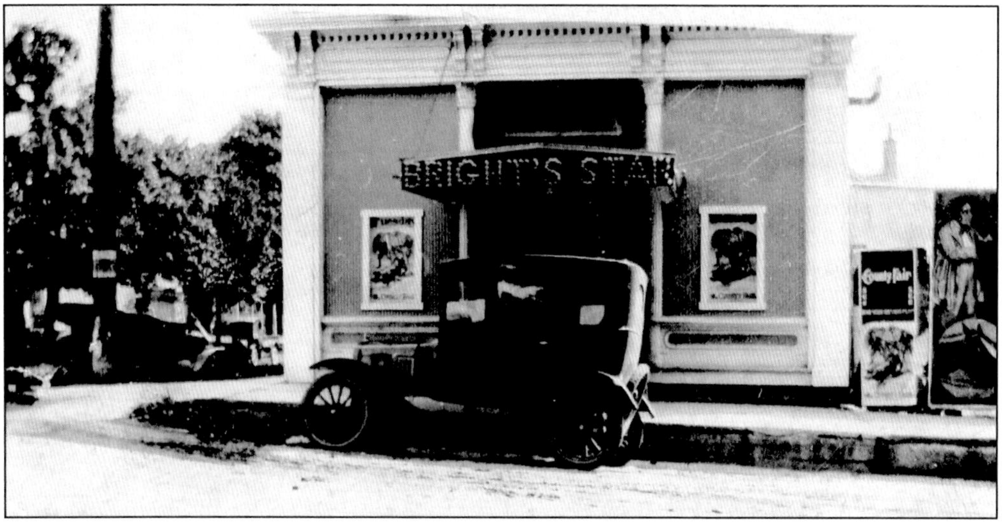


Preston's first moving picture theatre was called the Gem and was located at the southeast corner of Fillmore and St. Anthony Streets (the present location of Preston Eye Clinic). A former dentist named Dr. George Harrington opened it in 1911. Harrington had a good voice and sang songs to piano accompaniment as the silent movies played. When he died in 1920, the theatre was sold to Ross Bright of Iowa, who renamed the theatre Bright's Star. Bright installed intake and exhaust fans to assure his audiences "an abundance of fresh, cool air, even at the second performance when the atmosphere always becomes stuffy." Bright died tragically in August of 1921 in an airplane crash just south of Preston

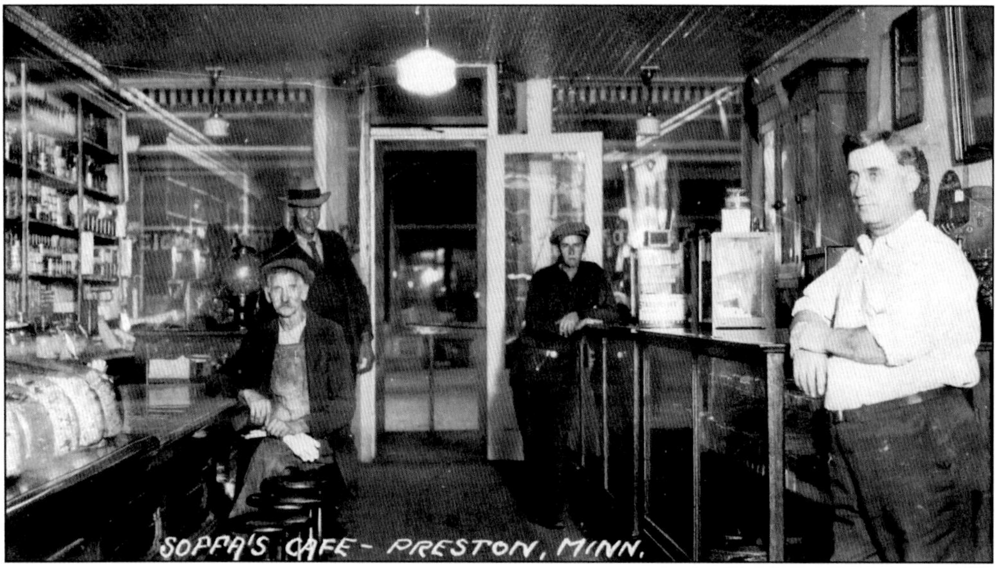


A 1927 ad for Soffa's Café, which was actually a grocery store in the old Tibbetts Drug Store building, advertises that it is: "The Place for FRUITS, CIGARS, TOBACCO. Largest assortment of candy in town." In another ad the following year, Soffa advertised a pool room and bowling alley on the premises. Born in Duma, Syria, John Soffa, pictured at front right, was in the restaurant and grocery business in Preston for 12 years. Before that he had been a barber in Granger, Minnesota. He died suddenly of a strangulated hernia in La Crosse on New Years Eve in 1929.

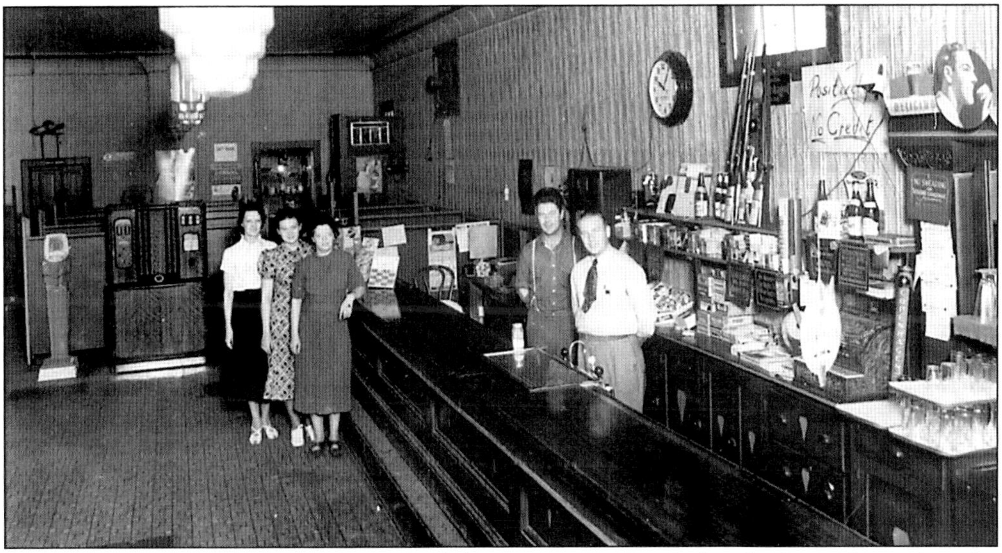

This is a c. 1934 photo of the interior of the Green Lantern Café, which was located at the southwest corner of Main and St. Anthony Streets. Pictured from left to right are Carrie Brink, unidentified, Isabelle Langum, Herman Brink, and Mervin Langum (owner). The Langum family's living quarters were in the rear area of the building. A newspaper ad that year heralded the end of Prohibition and boasted of the Café's "Quality Beer Service as well as a Quality Food Service." The owners bragged that the beer was always cold and came served in sterilized glasses. "Enjoy it at the tables, in the booths, the lunch counter, the bar or in the open air Terrace Garden. 101 Comfortable Seats!"

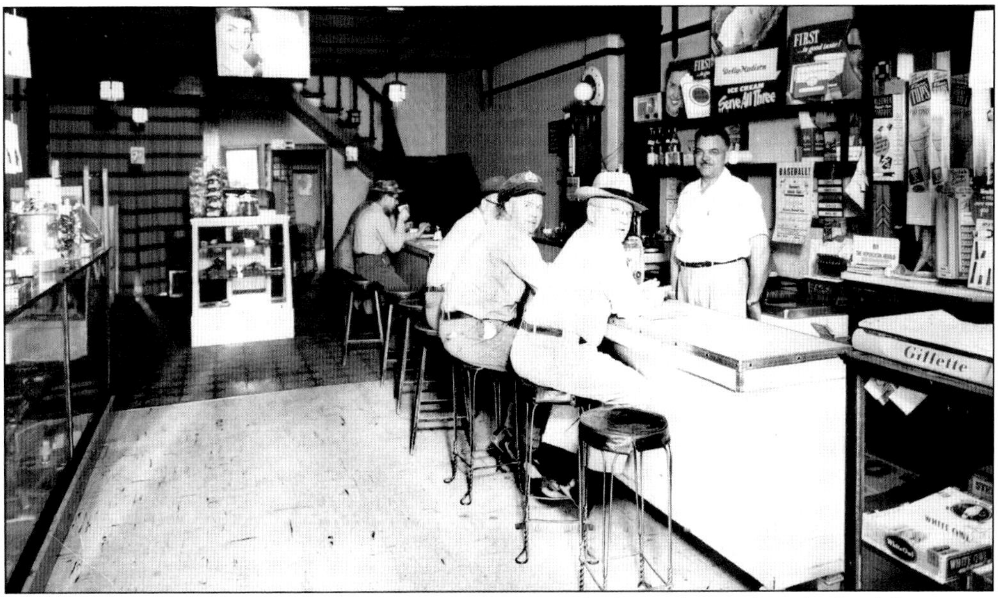


Here is an inside view of the Preston Confectionery, which was located on St. Paul Street just west of the courthouse (now Tom Byrne's office). The restaurant had previously been called Kerr's. Sitting on the stools from left to right are Lud Gartner, unidentified, Chris Evenrud, and Al Ellinger. Standing behind the counter is owner Alton Olson, who had farmed south of town on the Ridge Road before opening the restaurant.

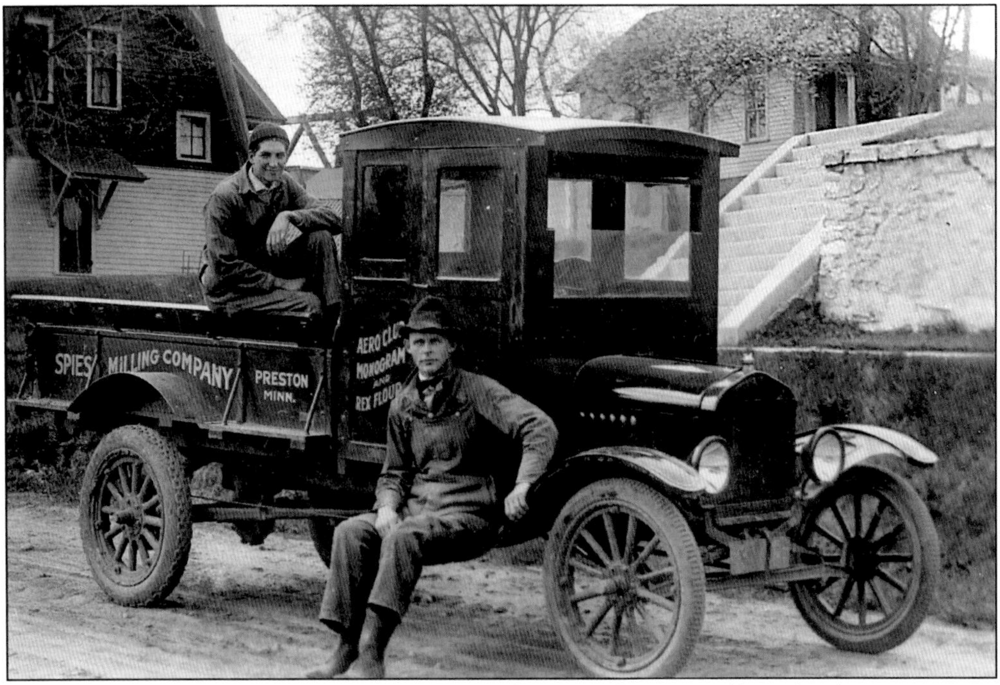


Herb Spies, sitting on the fender of his truck, came from a milling family. In previous generations, his grandfather, Henry Spies, ran the Carimona Mill and his father, Charles Spies, ran a mill in Wykoff. Spies served as Preston's mayor from 1930 to 1945 and then again from 1948 to 1951. He died in 1959.

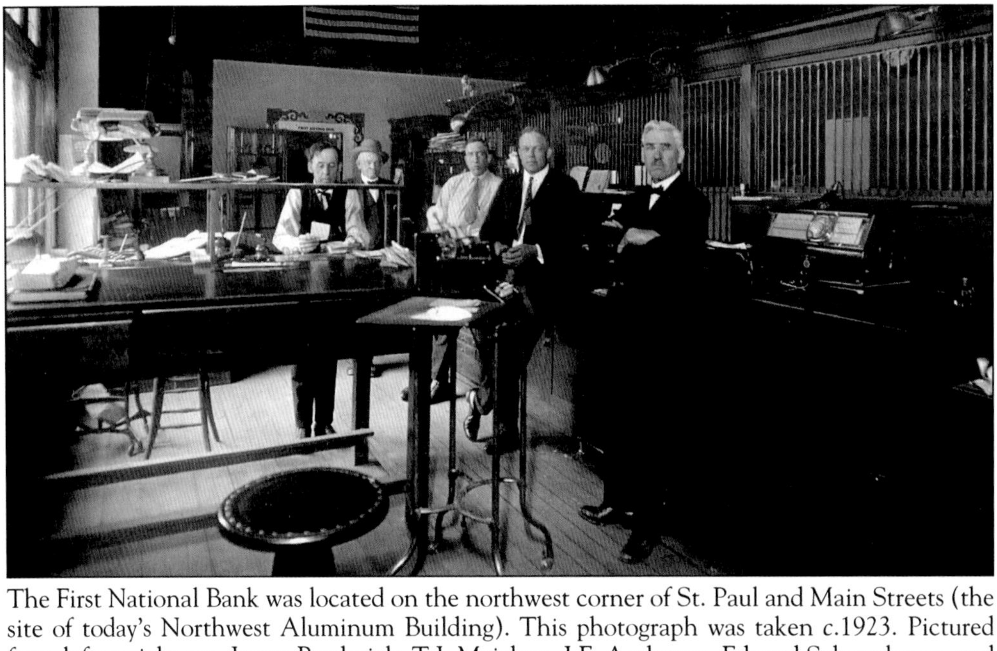

The First National Bank was located on the northwest corner of St. Paul and Main Streets (the site of today's Northwest Aluminum Building). This photograph was taken c.1923. Pictured from left to right are, James Broderick, T.J. Meighen, J.F. Anderson, Edward Schoenbaum, and Christopher M. Anderson. In 1939, the citizens of Preston were shocked when the bank was suddenly closed when examiners "discovered the misappropriation of funds by its employees."

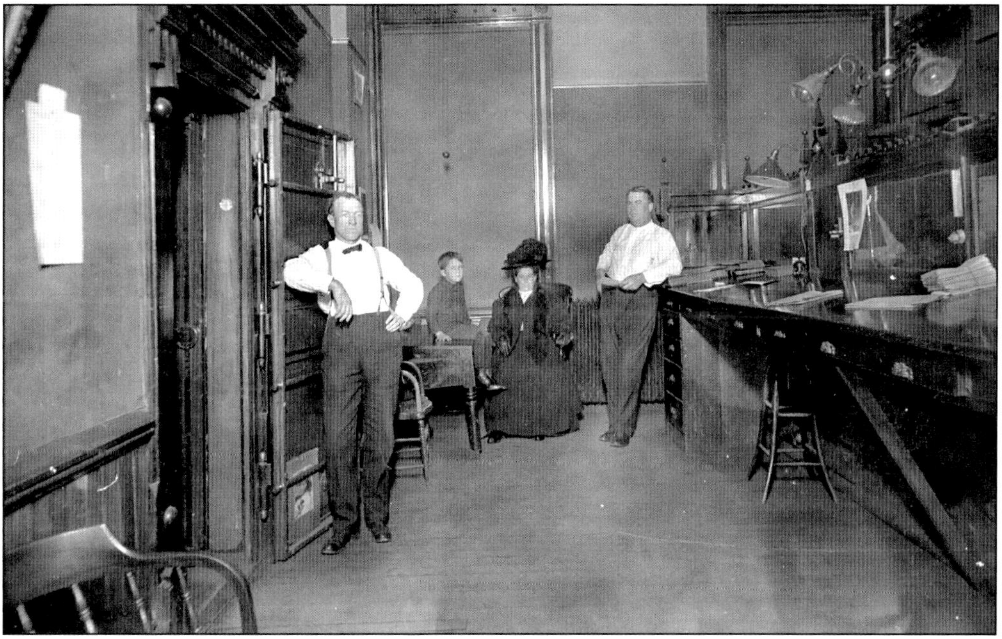

The Farmers and Merchants Bank was located on Main Street. The bank was organized by 46 stockholders in March of 1911 with a capital of $25,000. Two months later, the new bank took over the business of the National Bank of Preston. Pictured from left are unidentified, Wils Garratt, Effa (Terwilliger) Garratt, and Tom I. Garratt.

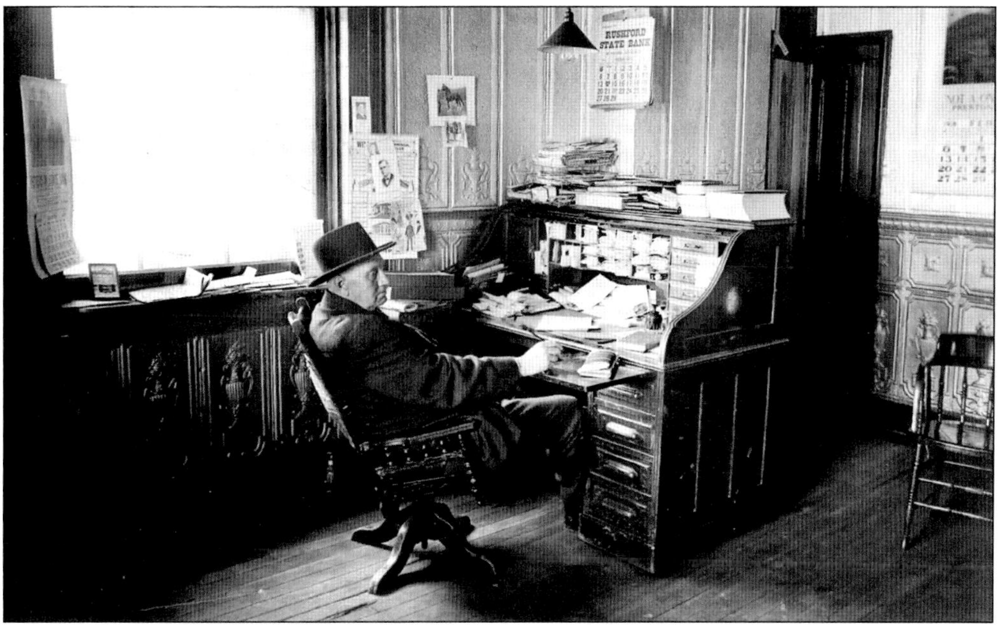


This picture was taken in 1916 of *Preston Times* owner/editor Samuel Langum (1857–1921). Langum was elected Fillmore County Sheriff in 1880 when he was just 23 years old. It was said that he was the first native-born son to hold an elective position in the county. He bought the weekly newspaper, *Preston Democrat* in 1887 and changed its name to the *Preston Times*. Besides running the newspaper, he served several terms in the Minnesota House.

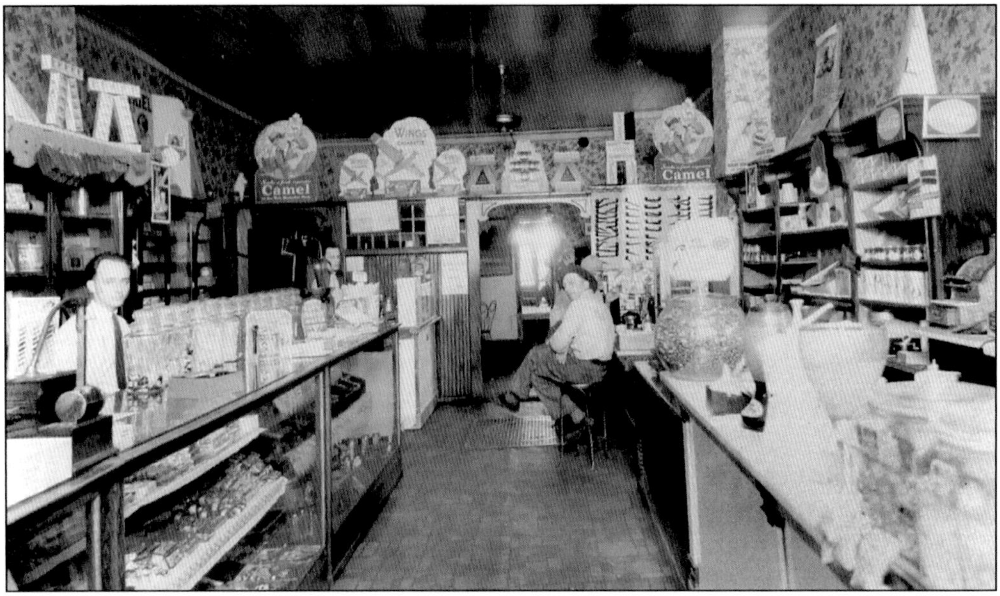

Andy Chilson started his restaurant, called Andy's Candy Store, in 1926, in the building that originally housed the J P. Tibbetts Drug Store. On the day he opened for business, Andy put 38¢ into the till for change, all the money that he had. The business had its up and downs, selling mostly confections, ice cream, candy, popcorn, peanuts, and tobacco products. It was a struggle to make it through the Depression, though it helped when Prohibition ended making it possible to sell beer to his customers. This picture was taken around 1933. Pictured from left to right are Andy Chilson, Foster Chilson, and Herman Aug. Chilson sold the business in 1945.

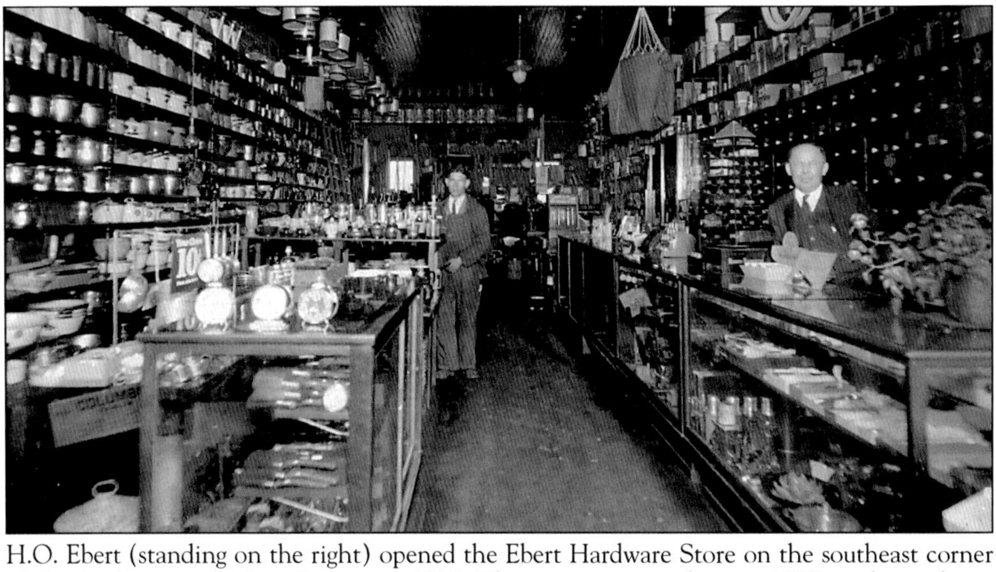
H.O. Ebert (standing on the right) opened the Ebert Hardware Store on the southeast corner of St. Anthony and Main Streets in 1911. This picture was taken in 1927, with employee Walter Dreier in the background. One of the store's specialties was making tin cupolas for farm buildings. The store would remain the Ebert family up through the 1980s. "H.O."—as everybody called him—was born in Heron Lake, Minnesota, in 1875. He was a Spanish-American war veteran, and died suddenly in 1932. H.O.'s sons, Herman and Marshall, ran the hardware store for the next several decades up through the 1980s.

# *Five*

# DIVERSIONS

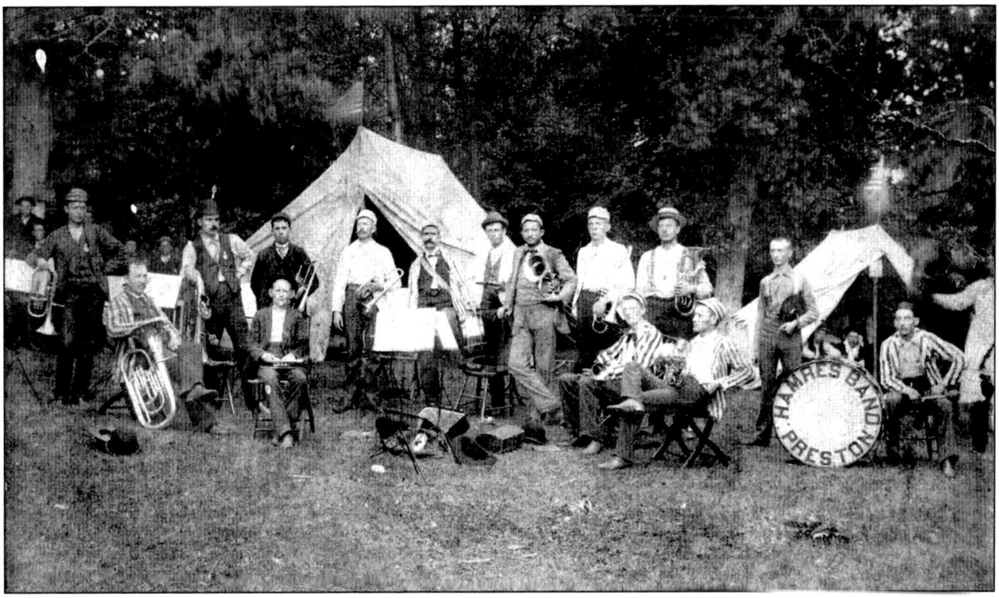


Hamre's Brass Band is seen here in a photo taken at Well's Grove near Preston in July of 1890. The band was about to embark on a weeklong camping trip. The Hamre Band had a statewide reputation and played locally for skaters at the Tibbetts Roller Skating Rink, at special events in the courthouse park, and at the county fair. John Hamre, originally from Ohio, was the leader of the band. He left Preston in 1895 and died in Bemidji in 1903 of tuberculosis at the age of 33. He was buried in Preston and his old bandmates led the procession to the cemetery playing a mournful funeral march.

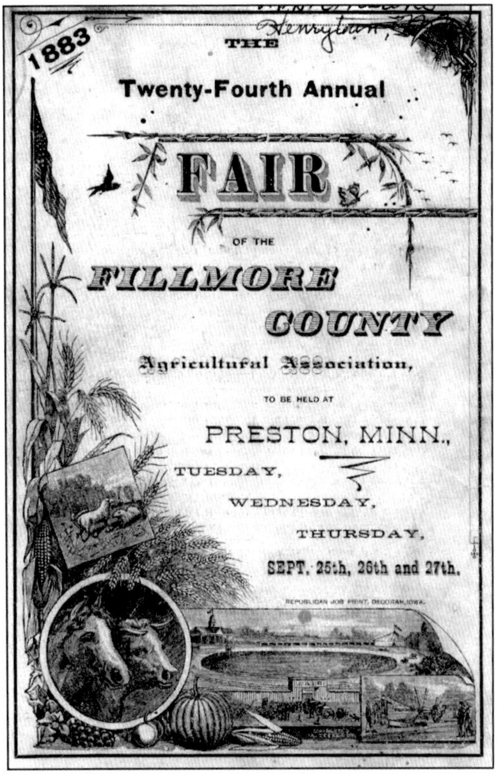


This is a fair bill from 1883. The Fillmore County Fair was originally called the County Agricultural Fair, with the first event held in 1861. In 1874, the fair was moved to Lanesboro for that year only. The following year the Village of Preston bought land at the current site of the fairgrounds and leased it to the Fillmore County Agricultural Society. Throughout the 1800s, the fair was held during the latter part of September, because farmers were too busy with field work during the summer.

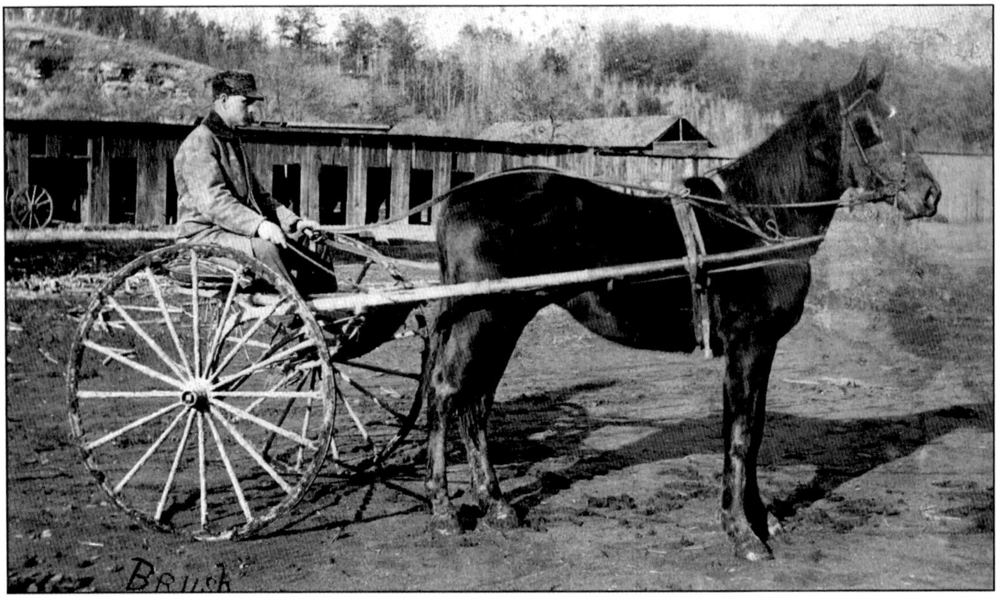


Horse and harness racing was a big event for many years at the Fillmore County Fair. In 1897, around the time this photograph was taken at the fairgrounds, the *Preston Times* commented on the popularity of horse racing. "Nine out of ten people will go further and stay longer to see an exciting horse race than they would to see the best agricultural exhibit. This is not only true of the town people but of the farmers themselves." The purses that year for the horse races were $100 prizes plus one "Special, free-for-all, purse at $125."

Known as "the team that made our city famous," the Preston Tigers Indoor Ball Club played their games at the Grand Opera House during the winter months. Pictured from left to right are team members: (front row) Clinton Kerr and B. Johnson; (second row) Fred Love, David Ploff, and Walter Foote; (third row) Herb Vickerman, Ed Schoenbaum, Manager Tom Garratt, E. Joseph, and A. Kerr. Considered the second best indoor baseball team in the country, they played the Chicago Spaldings in 1905 at Preston. The Spaldings won the series two games to one. Up to 1,000 spectators crowded into the Grand Opera House for each of the games. Special trains like the one pictured below took the Tigers and their enthusiastic fans to games on the road. In 1904 when the Tigers were still unbeaten, the *Preston Times* proclaimed: "The Tigers stand ready to play any team between oceans and, until they are defeated, we consider them invincible."

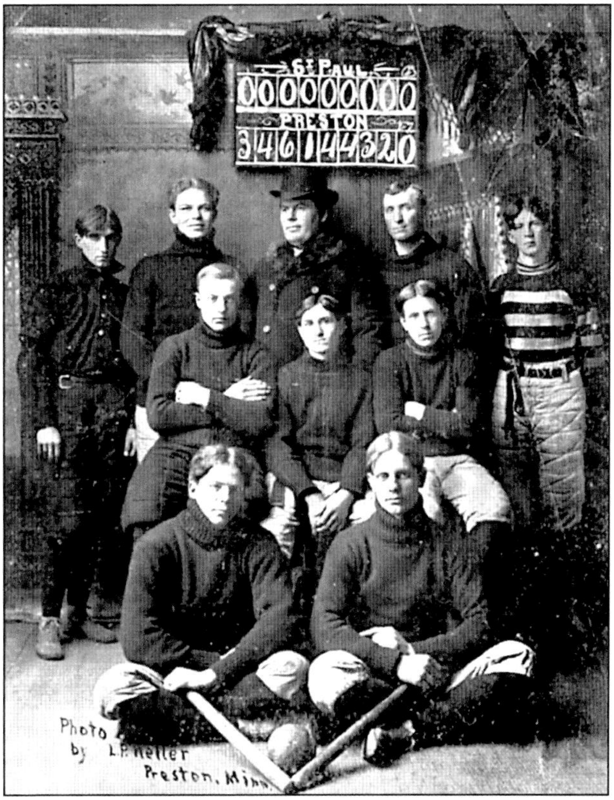


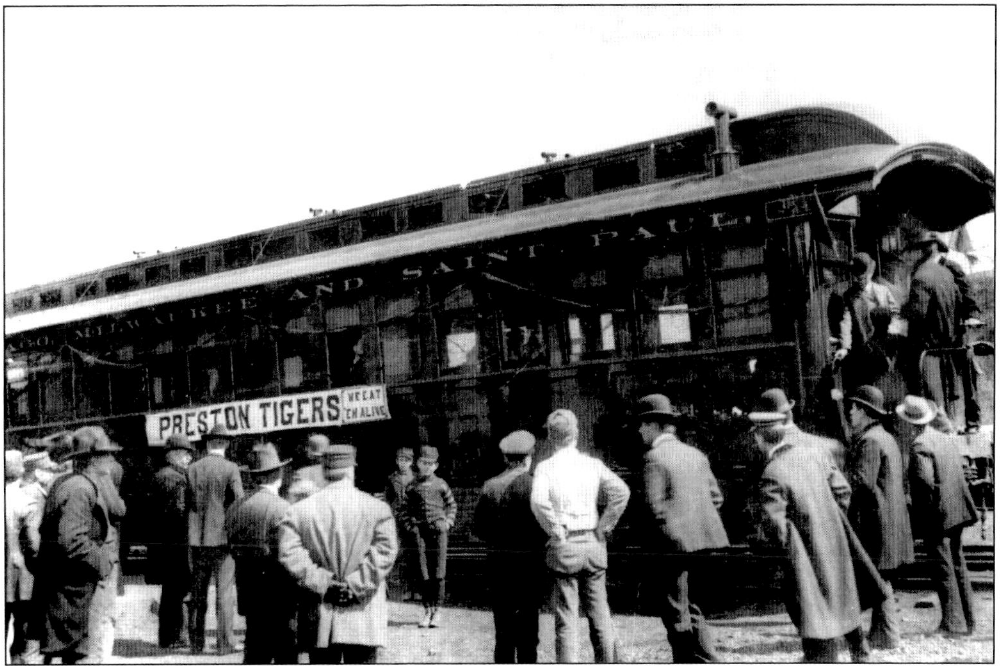

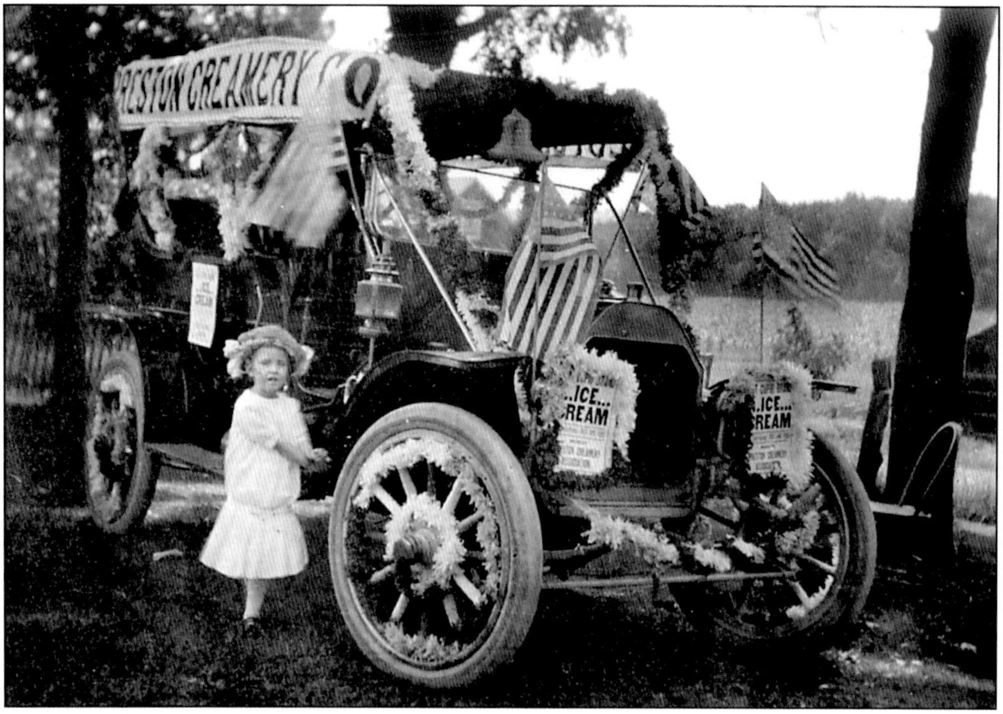


This was the Preston Creamery Association's entry into the Fourth of July parade in Preston in 1911 or 1912. Pictured is four-year-old Esther Utley (Mrs. Alden Pickett). Charles Utley (Esther's father) was the secretary-treasurer of the association when this picture was taken.

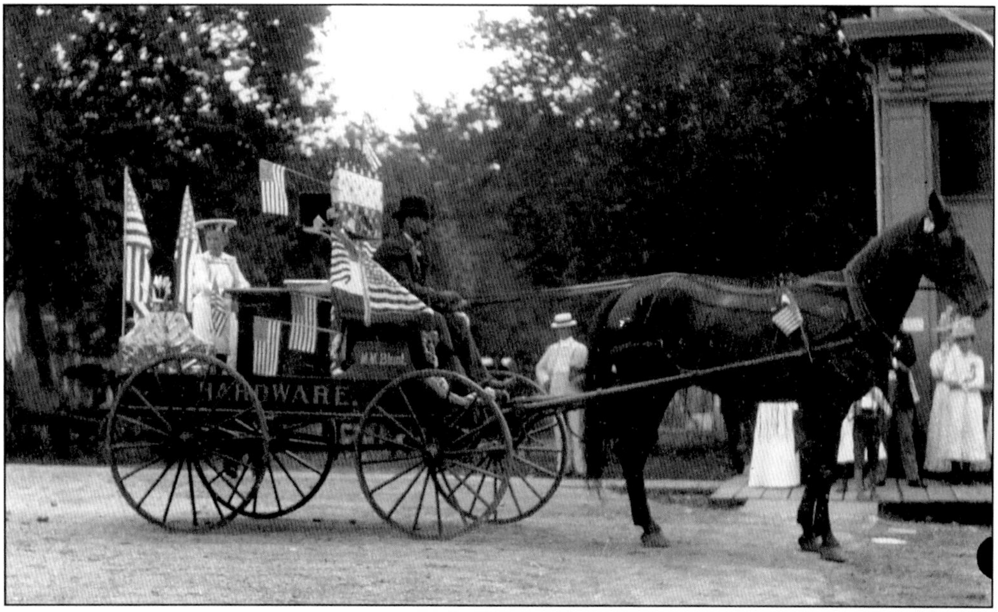


Hardware store owner M.M. Blunt sits in the driver's seat of his entry in the annual Fourth of July parade. In 1915, Blunt traded his store along with its complete inventory for a 347-acre farm in Glenwood, Minnesota. Blunt also owned five lots as well as his residence and barns two blocks north of the courthouse. Blunt died of an apparent heart attack in Glenwood in 1918.

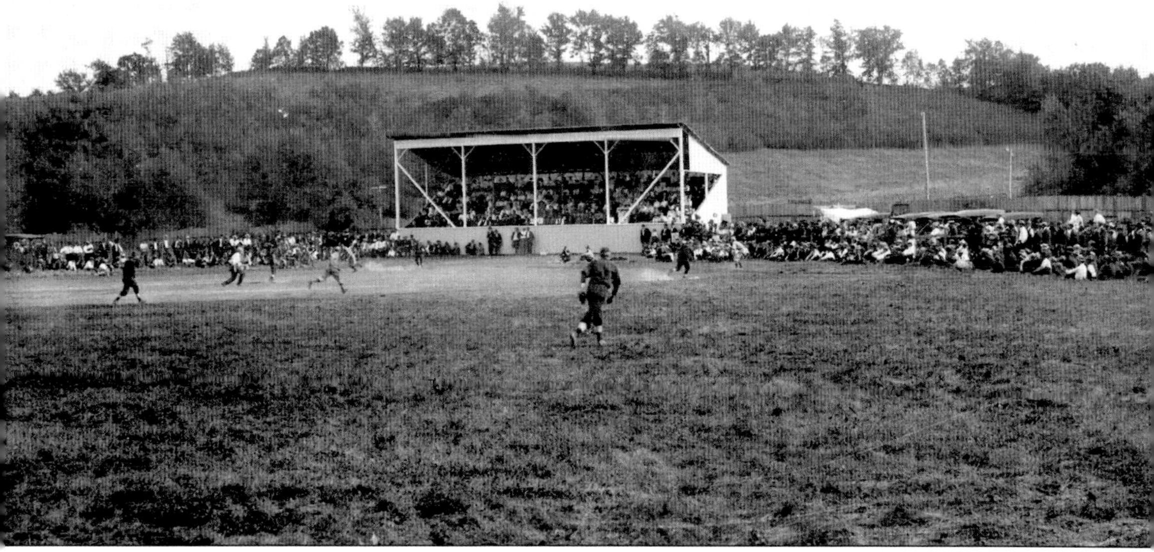

Outdoor baseball replaced the indoor version as the town's favorite sport. In 1910 a world championship series was held at the fairgrounds between two "Negro teams." The Leland Giants of Chicago and the Colored Gophers of St. Paul were widely acknowledged to be the greatest "colored teams in the world." The Giants won three games over the Gophers, claiming the title, as well as an $800 purse.

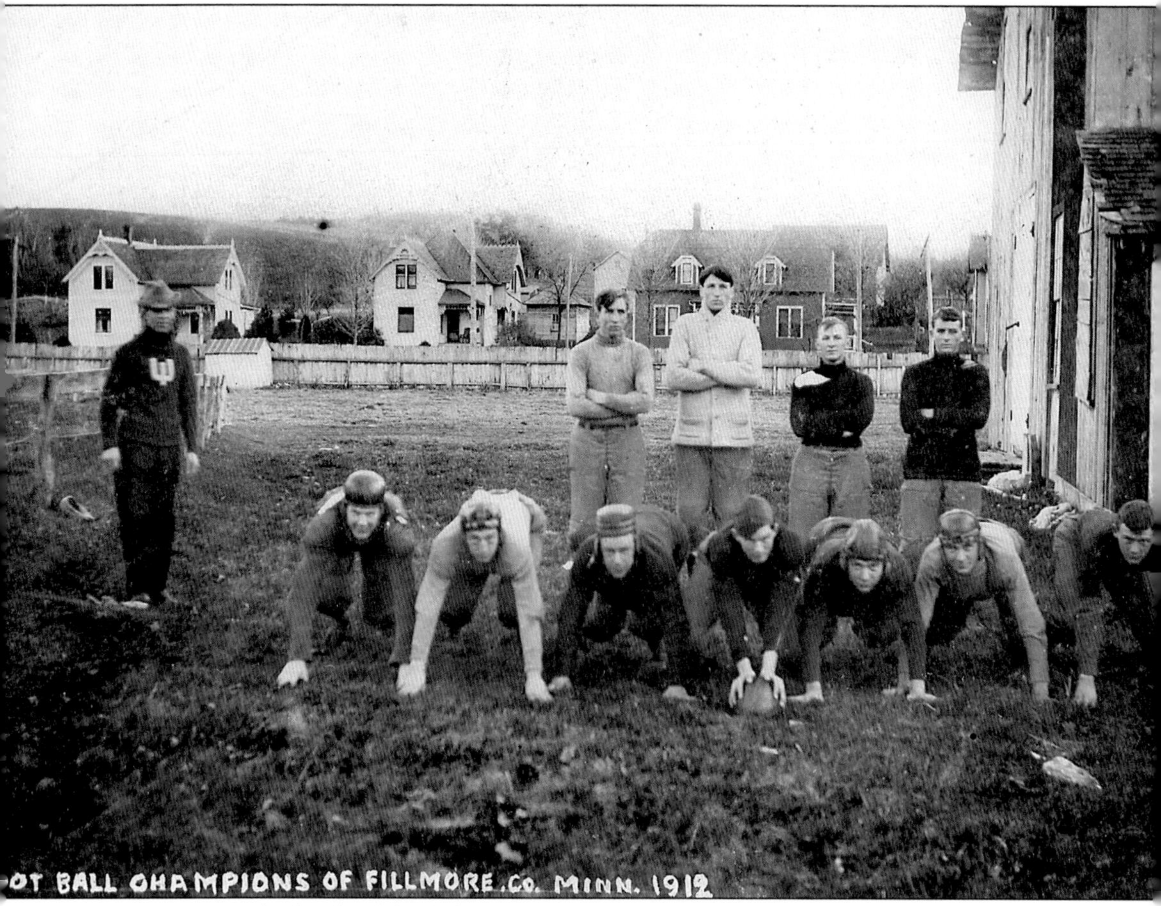


Preston's 1912 high school football team was crowned the Champions of Southern Minnesota after they beat Grand Meadow in November of that year. From left to right are as follows: (front row) Scotty Love, Ray Kuhl, Francis Snyder, Milo Vandale, Leonard Snyder, William Nelson, and Tim Grebin; (back row) Coach Shipton, Chris Anderson, Knute Inglebret, Leslie "Slip" Kruppenbacher, and Claude Shook.

Tim Grebin was Preston's city clerk from 1933 through 1957, and for many years was the town's unofficial historian. Knute Inglebret would go on to become Fillmore County sheriff, serving from 1926 to 1941, when he was forced from office after he shot up the Spring Valley Sales Barn with a tommy gun. "Slip" Kruppenbacher went on to serve as the president of the Mars Candy Company in Chicago from 1935 to 1959. Upon retiring, Kruppenbacher sold his Mars stock back to the company in 1962 for $5.4 million. He died the following year.

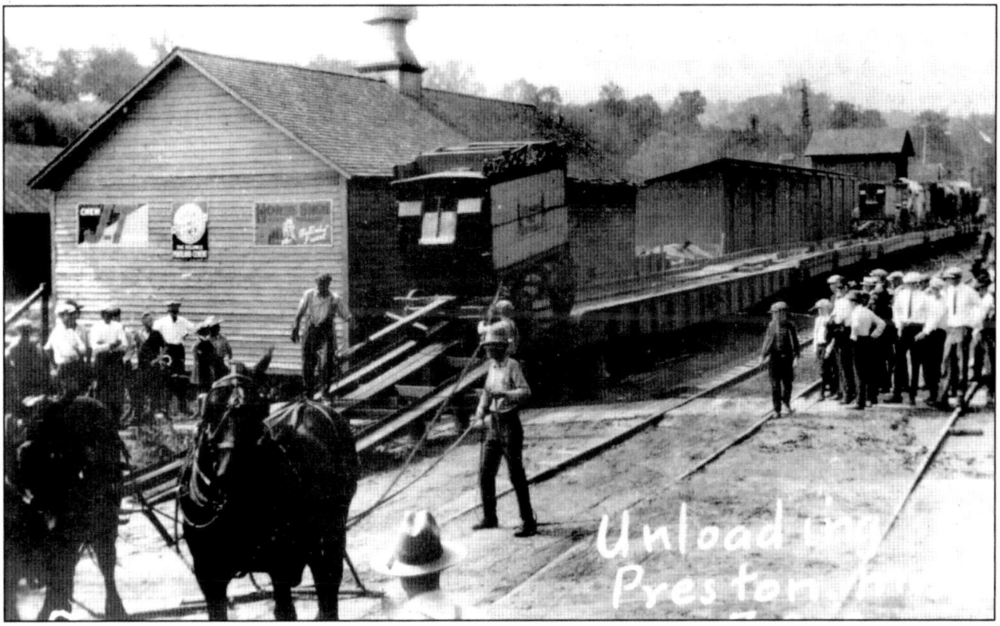

The World Brothers Circus unloads equipment and animals at the train depot in preparation for a big show in this July 4, 1927 photo. The circus boasted four rings of entertainment including performing polar bears, a horseback-riding leopard, golf-playing elephants, a lion that loops the loop as well as 50 "funny" clowns. It was called the "Biggest Wild Animal Circus in the World."

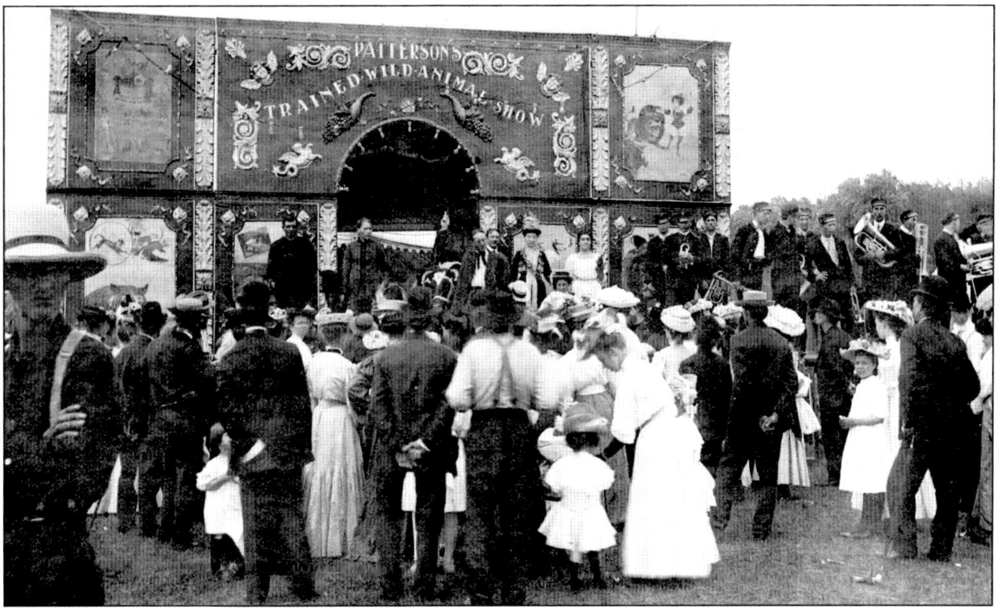


The *Preston Times* reported: "The man or woman with a grouch has no business at the Fillmore County Fair this year. You must go prepared to enjoy the blare of band and the million noises that aren't music. You must be keyed up to revel in the sight of thousands of chatting holiday makers, of bright decorations, of pretty girls, of sideshows and ballyhoos. Yes, it's going to be so much bigger and better than ever before that you will have to come at least two days and nights if you want to see it all."

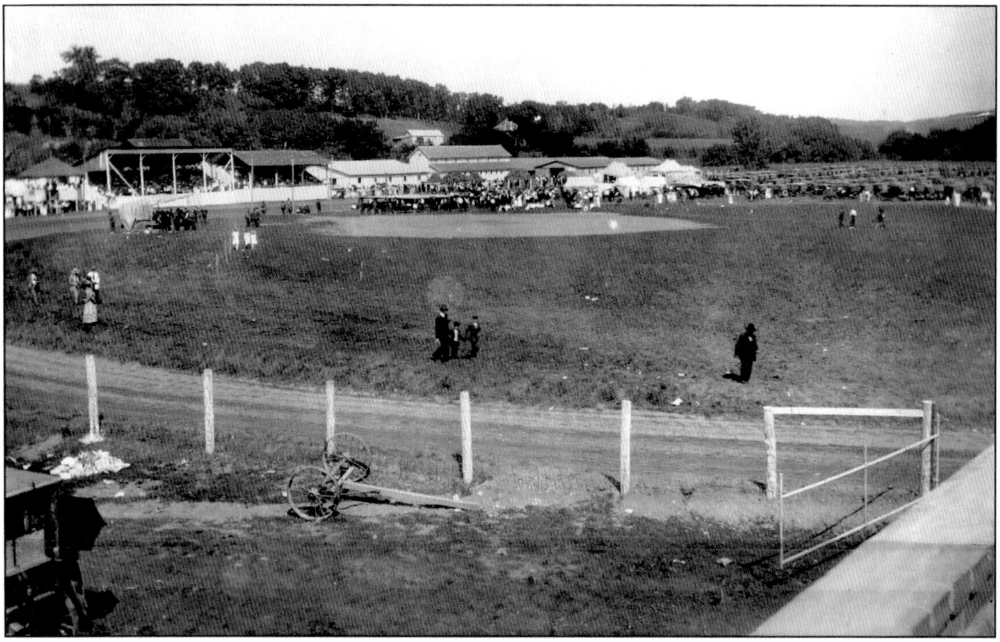

At the 1920 County Fair, the year that this picture was taken, 18-year-old Ethel Dare performed acrobatics in the air. Her performances included hanging by her toes and teeth on a ladder dangling from a plane after jumping from one plane to the other while they were flying in the air. The owners of the airplanes also gave rides to people willing to pay $15 for a 15-minute ride. "Everyone agreed that they got their money's worth."

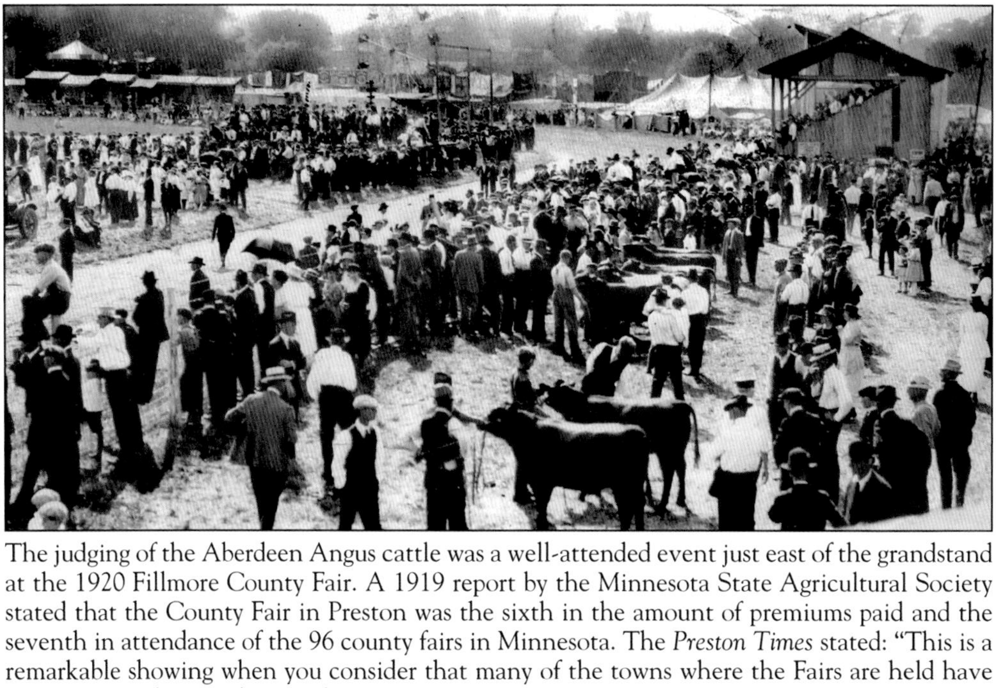

The judging of the Aberdeen Angus cattle was a well-attended event just east of the grandstand at the 1920 Fillmore County Fair. A 1919 report by the Minnesota State Agricultural Society stated that the County Fair in Preston was the sixth in the amount of premiums paid and the seventh in attendance of the 96 county fairs in Minnesota. The *Preston Times* stated: "This is a remarkable showing when you consider that many of the towns where the Fairs are held have several times the population of Preston."

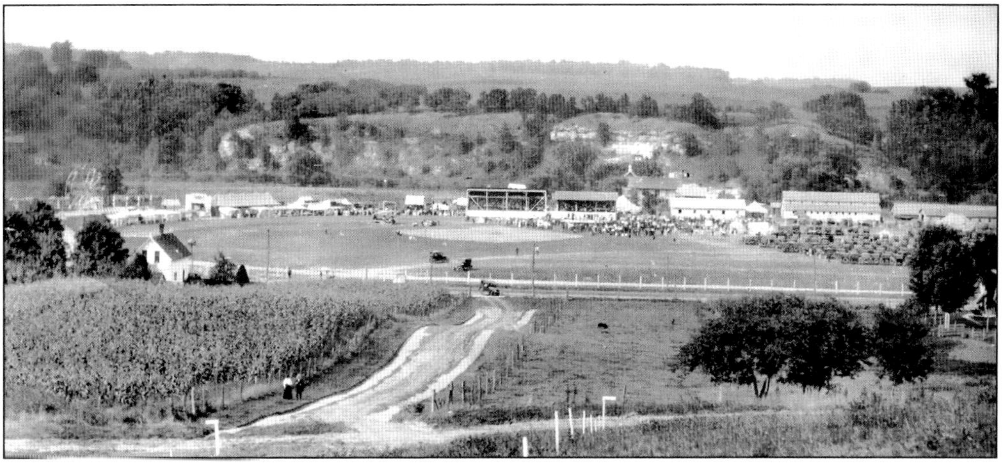

The County Fair was always hyped for weeks in advance in the local papers and the 1925 County Fair was no exception. It would undoubtedly be the "biggest and best yet!" The Fair did get off to a good start due to fine weather and 10,000 people in attendance the first night. But, the next day, vicious rumors swept the county that a young girl had died from infantile paralysis while attending the fair and that there were six other cases in the village of Preston. Another rumor that circulated throughout the county was that the price of admission to the fair had been raised to $1. Neither rumor was true but in the end the County Fair went over $3,000 in the hole.

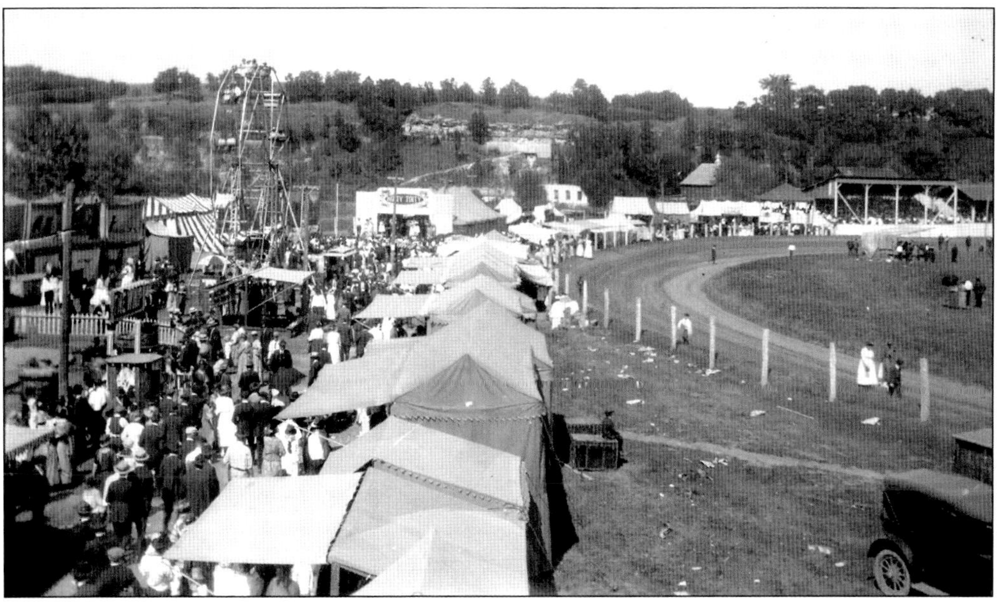

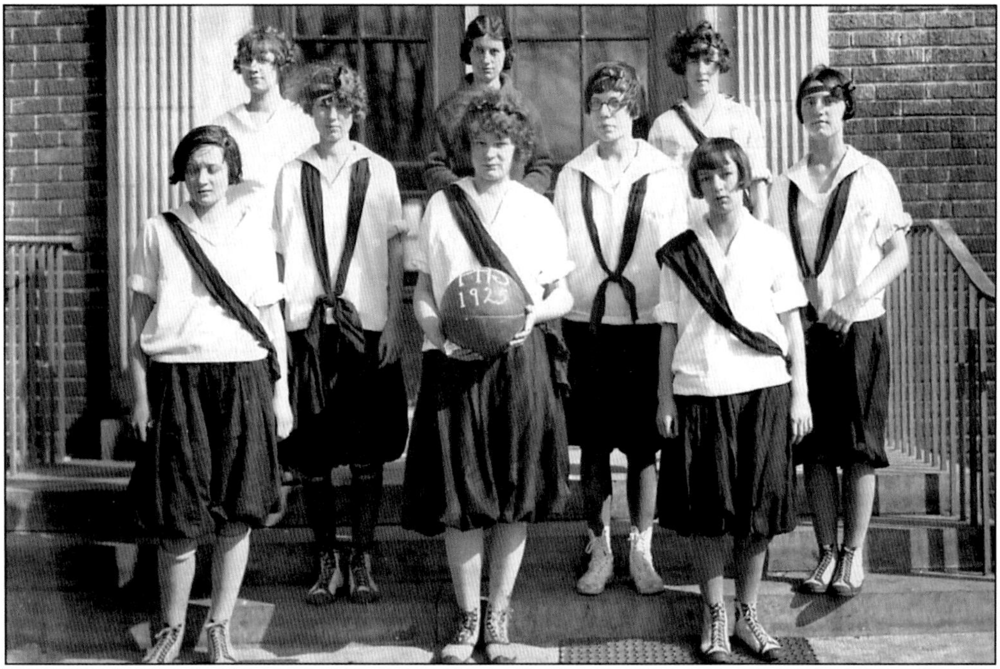

Preston High School put a girls' basketball team together for the first time in 1925. Pictured from left to right are team members: (front row) Tressa Barnes, Florence Keehn, and Bernice Grebin; (second row) Luella Peterson, Marion Bacon, and Marion Dent; (back row) Erma Peterson, Ann Carmody (coach), and Marian Krause. After losing a game to Mabel by the lopsided score of 33 to 11, one of the Preston boy basketball players consoled the team by saying, "Hard luck, girls, but remember this is only your first year at the game."

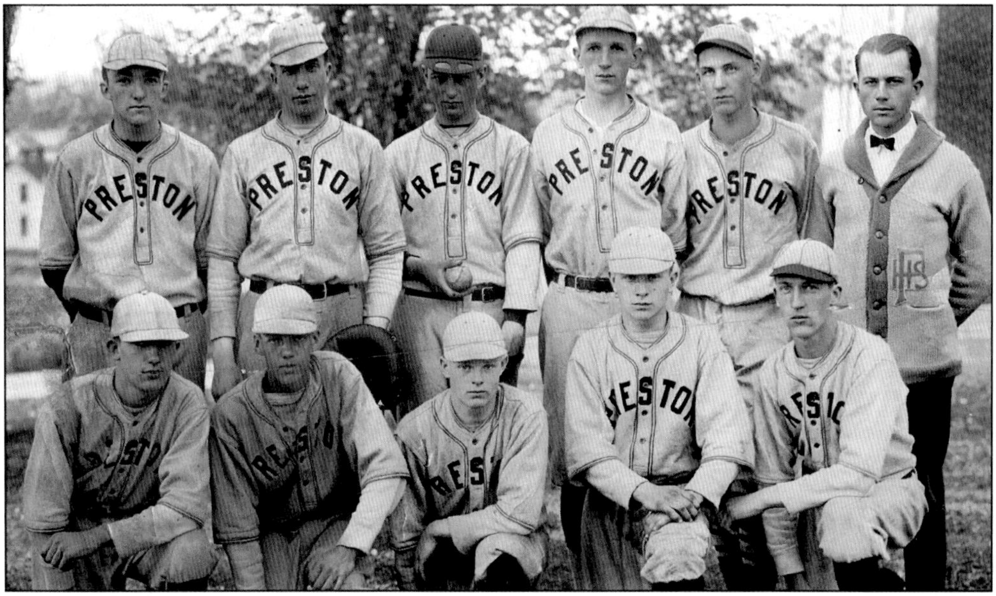


The high school's 1925 Baseball team is pictured here. From left to right are as follows: (front row) Robert Rick, Marshall Ebert, William Shanahan, Raymond Snyder, and Clarence Rick; (back row) Thomas Healy, Vic Bacon, Howard Garletz, Francis Grebin, James Clark, and Coach E. Hoff.

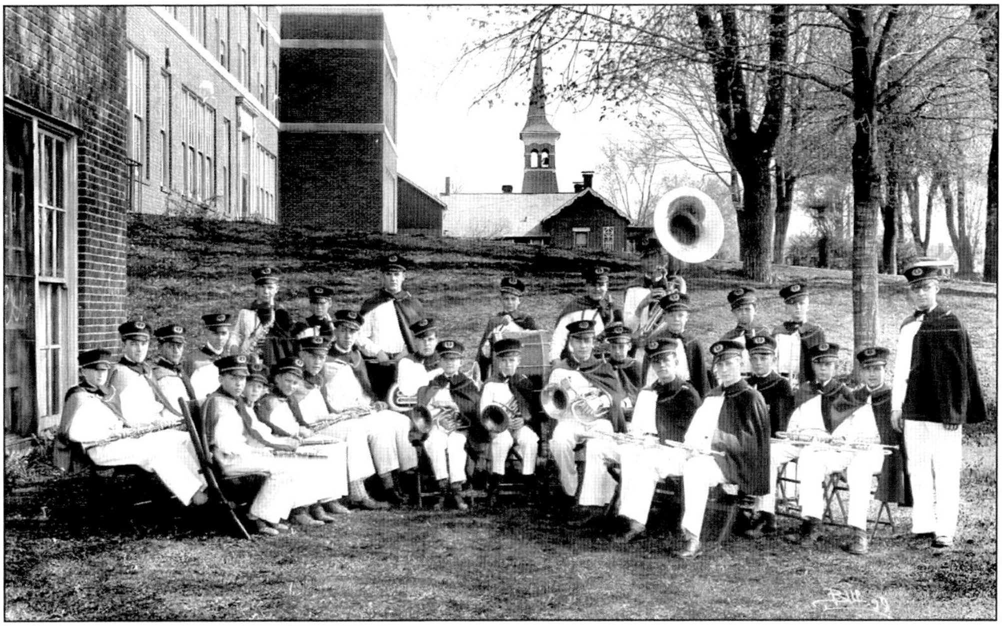

From the mid-1920s until the mid-1940s, the renowned Lanesboro photographer Matt Bue took Preston school pictures. Here is a photograph of the Preston School band, in 1928, with the spire of St. Paul's German Lutheran Church in the background.

Howard Karp was 11 years old in 1927 when this photograph was taken. He was the drum major for the Preston Junior Band and also for the Boy Scout Drum and Bugle Corps. He told a reporter at the time that his ambition was to "become a movie star or a violin player," and added, "I'm not so good as a drum major but they like me." In May of 1927, Howard led 60 members of the Drug and Bugle Corps in three parades in Rochester, as Preston was chosen to be the official corps at the National Court of Honor. The event was attended by the head of the National Organization of Boy Scouts, James West, of New York City, who personally congratulated Howard on a job well done.

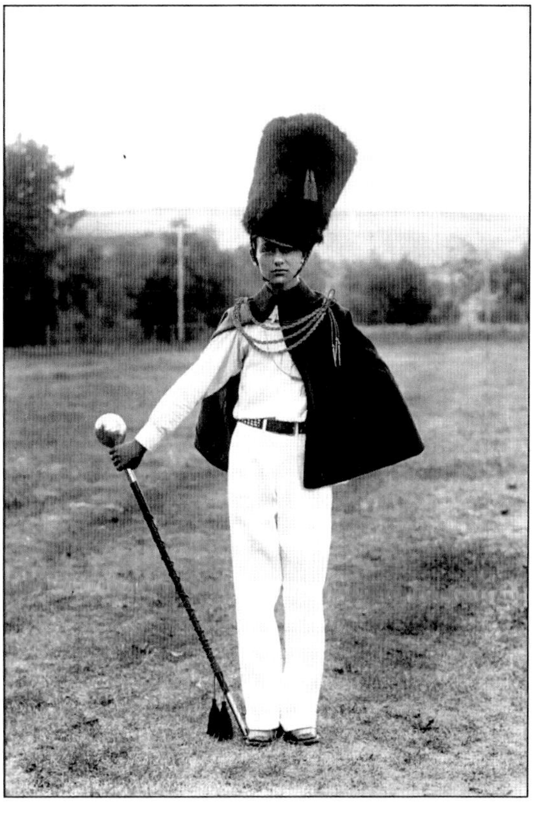

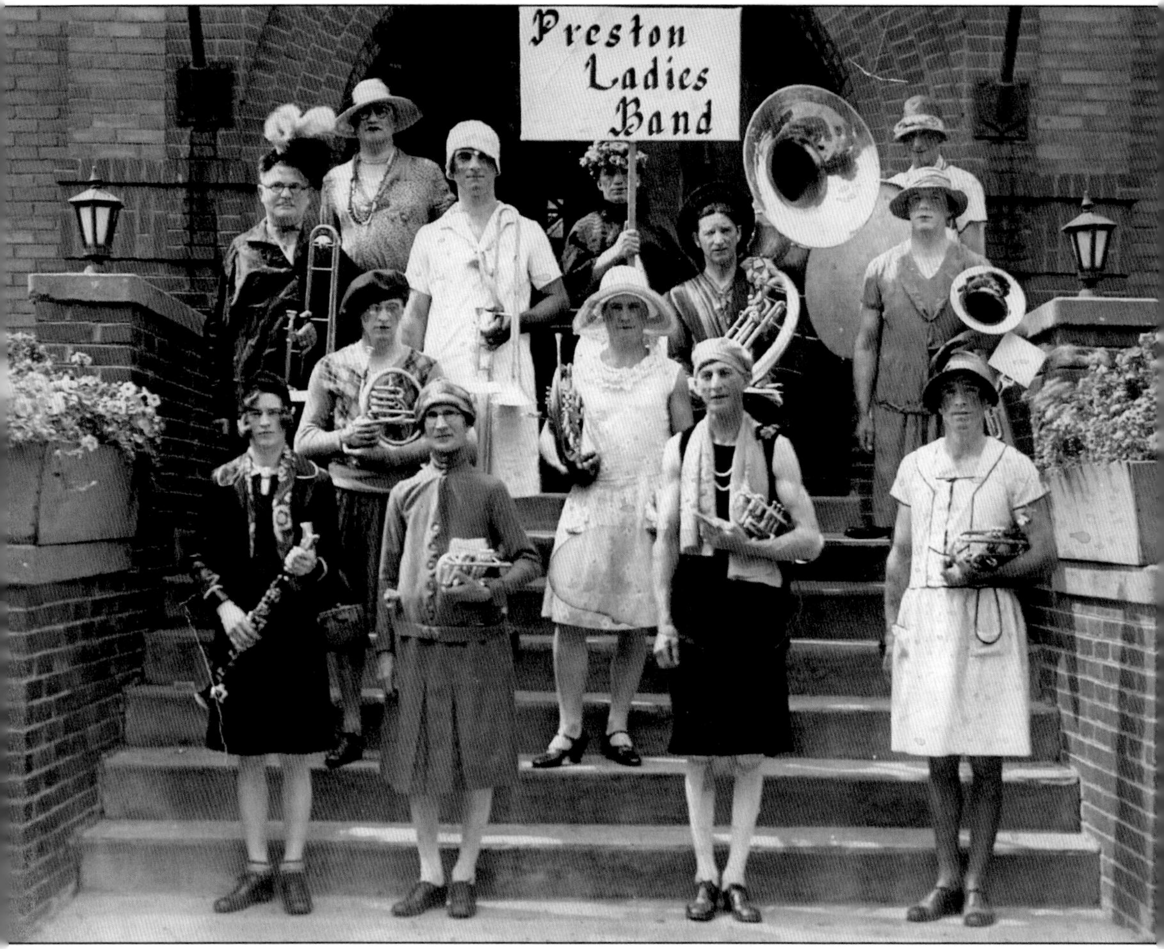


During the late 1920s, the local men who comprised the Preston Ladies Band created a sensation wherever they appeared. Besides being known for their stylish appearances, they were also recognized as outstanding musicians. Among their many appearances were the American Legion conventions at Austin, Winona, Rochester, and Plainview. They performed at the Fillmore County Fair and led the car caravan from Austin when the Preston basketball team beat Austin for the regional championship in 1929. They were photographed here by Matt Bue and their "lady nicknames" were printed in the paper. Pictured from left to right are band members: (front row) Alvin "Ethel" Hoines, Ed "Edwina" Norris, Lester "Minnie" Barnes, and Alvin "Evelyn" Cumming; (second row) Joe "Johana" Barnes, and Roy "Royola" Flatten; (third row) Floyd "Flora" Frankson, Wils "Wilsonia" Garratt, Jim "Jimima" Christianson, Pete "Petra" Gilbertson; (back row) Harold "Haroldine" Hopp, Mike "Miss" Karp, and Virgil "Virginia" Vickerman.

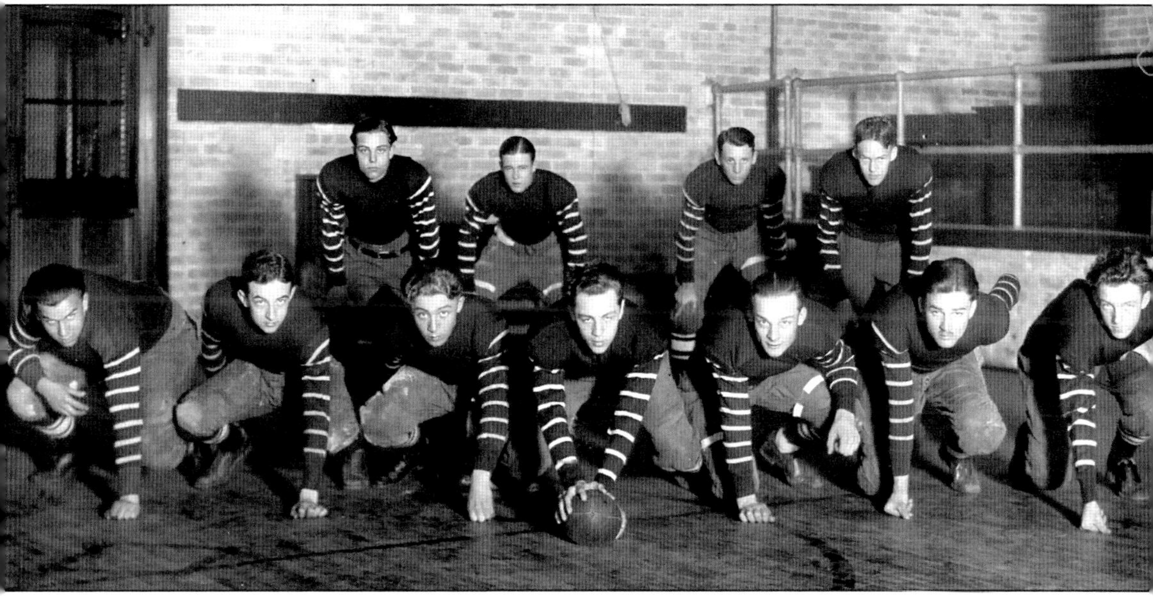

The 1927 Preston High School football team poses inside the gymnasium. Pictured from left to right are the following: (front row) Kermit Wiegand, Thane Schoenbaum, Faye Sikkink, Orval Ause, Leonard Stoskopf, Moody Kiefer, and Raymond O'Connor; (back row) Kenneth Pickett, Frederick Olson, Lloyd Jeffers, and Marshall Ebert. After an 18-0 victory over Lanesboro in early October, the *Preston Republican* wrote: "It can be truthfully said that Preston's team has never played a faster game of good clean football than they did Friday." In a rematch a few weeks later, Lanesboro beat Preston, 13-12. Preston was poised to score with the ball on the one-yard line when the final whistle blew.

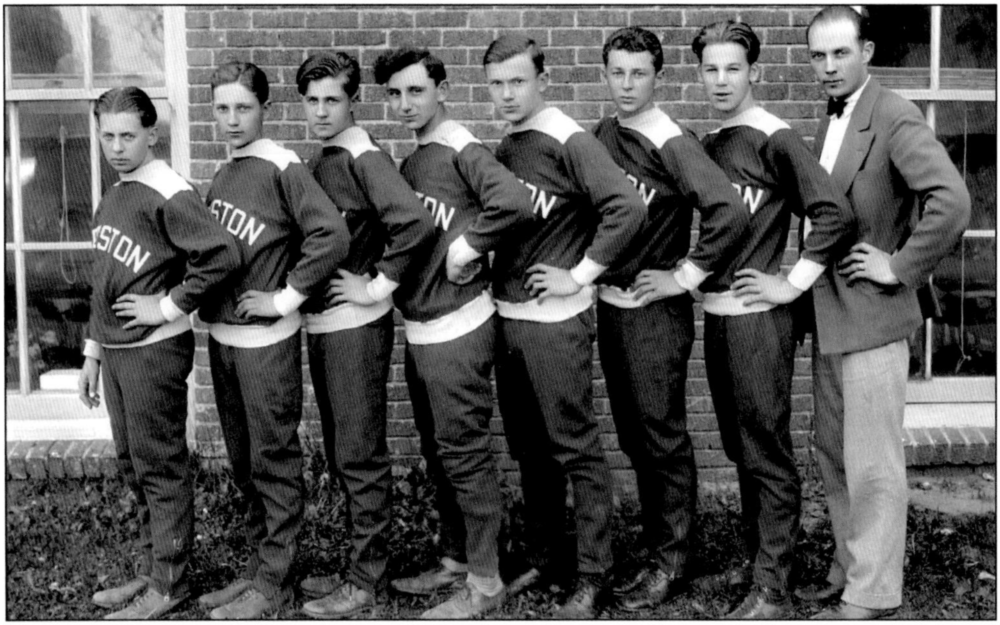

Here is the Preston High School track team of 1927. Pictured from left to right are Howard Bakken, Roy Riehl, Wilbur Utley, Hank Hartig, Howard Magdlin, Don Krause, Bud Wolfe, and Coach Lewis Krough. Don Krause broke a conference record that year in Caledonia when he ran the 100 yard dash in 11 seconds on an uphill track. He also broke the record for the broad jump, when he jumped 18 feet 6 1/2 inches.

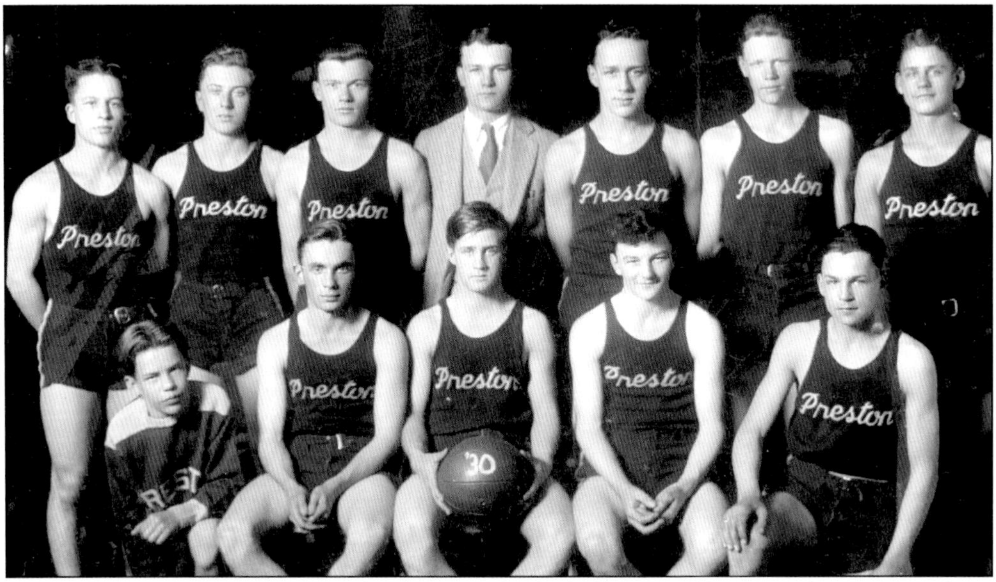

Shown here is Preston High School's 1930 basketball team: (front row) Herman Ebert, James Ryan, Wilbur Utley, Forest Sadler, and Robert Cleveland; (back row) Roy Schnaufer, Francis Roberts, Howard Magdlin, Coach Levi Krough, Harold Ause, Kenneth Hutton, and Arthur Ashton. The 1930 team did not achieve the success of the preceding 1929 team, which went to the state tournament in St. Paul. Unfortunately no picture of the 1929 team can currently be found.

## The Womanless Wedding

*Sympson-Levie Co., Bardstown, Kentucky*

*Directed by Miss Esther Dee Ladwig*

*Sponsored by Reuben Wells Chapter No. 69, O. E. S.*

*GRAND OPERA HOUSE, PRESTON, MINN.*

**Thursday & Friday, April 7th & 8th** 1927

*Cast of Characters*

Butler—Bert Fraser.
Punch Girls—Ray O'Connor, Thane Schoenbaum.
Present Takers—Leonard Grebin, Orval Anse.
Bride's Weeping Mother—Perlum Nelson.
Comforting Father—Moppy Anderson.
Bad Little Brothers—Alton Gray & Earl Broadwater.
Mr. Ikey Rosenstein—Ray Eischen.
Old Maid Aunt—Reuben Rappe.
Bride's Grandmother—Jim Broderick
Bride's Grandfather—Odd Langum.
Mr Charles Chaplin—Roy Flattum.
Uncle from Hutton—Charlie Lewis.
Aunt from Hutton—Harry Taylor.
Madame Schumann-Heink—William Thompson.
Twin Sisters—Vernie Smith, Casper Tollefson.
Fritz Kreisler—Glenn Snyder.
Mary Pickford—Joe Barnes.
Groom's Haughty Father—Dr. Towner.
Groom's Haughty Mother—Oscar Gillund.
Fashion Plate—Tim Grebin.
Country Cousins—Joe Christenson, Pete Gilbertson.
Mr. Patrick O'Grady—Chas. Durst
Rosie O'Grady—Ben Kostold.
Sis Hopkins—Loyal Ferdinandt.
Annie Laurie—Moody Kiefer.
Hen-Pecked Husband—Patsy Devine.
His Devoted Wife—C. A. DuMond.
Willie Schuls-en-Heim—E. W. Pflugradt.
Pres. Coolidge—Arthur Stegner.
Mrs. Coolidge—Dr. Quanrud.
Negro Mammy—Porter Remington.
Baby Sister—Major Flynn.
Sambo—Buddy Pflugradt.
Jumbo—Russell Sutton.
Mr. Thos. A. Edison—Joe Simonson.
Mrs. Edison—R. W. Pfister.
Flapper of 1927—Bill Shannahan.
Village School Ma'am—Irvin Harm.
Gen. Pershing—Lynn Siniff.
Marshall Haig—L. H. Krough.
Theda Bara, the vamp—Wils Garratt
Mr. John D. Rockefeller—Geo. Utley.
Mrs. Rockefeller—H. D. Gleason.
Madame Galli Curci—Jim Hall.
Mr. Henry Ford—Dean McKnight
Mrs. Ford—Art Noel.
Mr. Irving Berlin—John Hester.
Mrs. Berlin—Geo. Soffa.
Groomsmen—Everett Joseph, Eldon Kline.
Best Man—Leo Gartner.
Bishop—Otto Watts.
Paderewski—Frank Ibach.
Bridesmaids—Geo. Gartner, Orville Wolf, Sam Moe, V. I. Bergstrom.
Maid of Honor—Art Ehrman.
Ring Bearer—Paul Kabus.
Flower Girl—Cecil Snyder.
Pages—Lawrence Ristey, Roderick Pugh.
Trainbearer—Francis Grebin.
Bride—Herb Spies.
Groom—Guess Who? ? ?

**WARNING:** This particular play was composed, owned and produced by Simpson Levie Company, protected by copyright No. 70971, U. S. Copyright Office, Washington, D. C. Any person or organization attempting infringement, will be prosecuted to fullest extent, & damages collected

In another example of gentlemen dressing up as ladies, the Preston men put on the well-known burlesque "The Womanless Wedding" in 1927. The play was a benefit for the local chapter of the Order of the Eastern Star and was described in the *Preston Republican* as "continuous comedy . . . every minute was entertaining. One felt like a small boy at a five ring circus, 'You just couldn't see it all.'

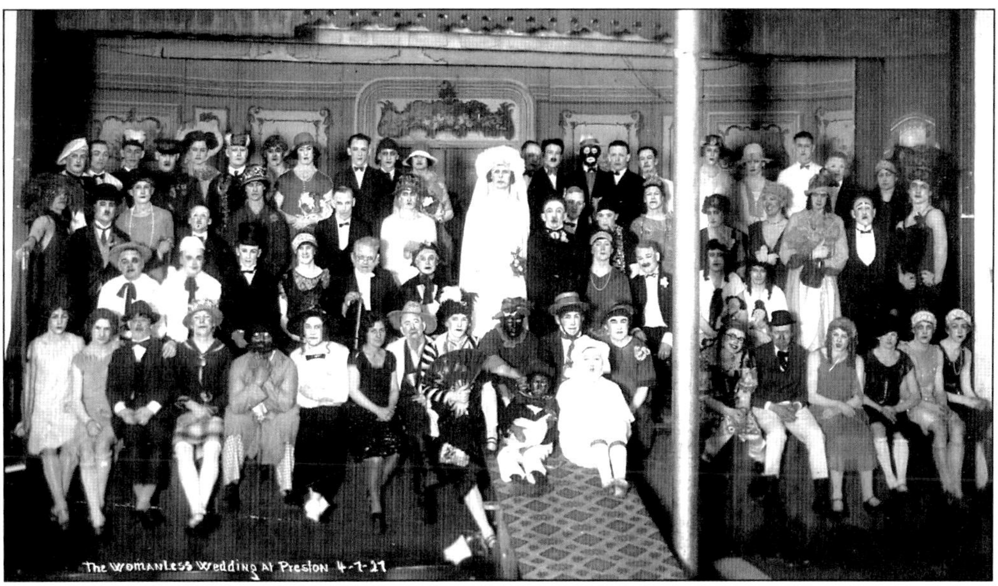

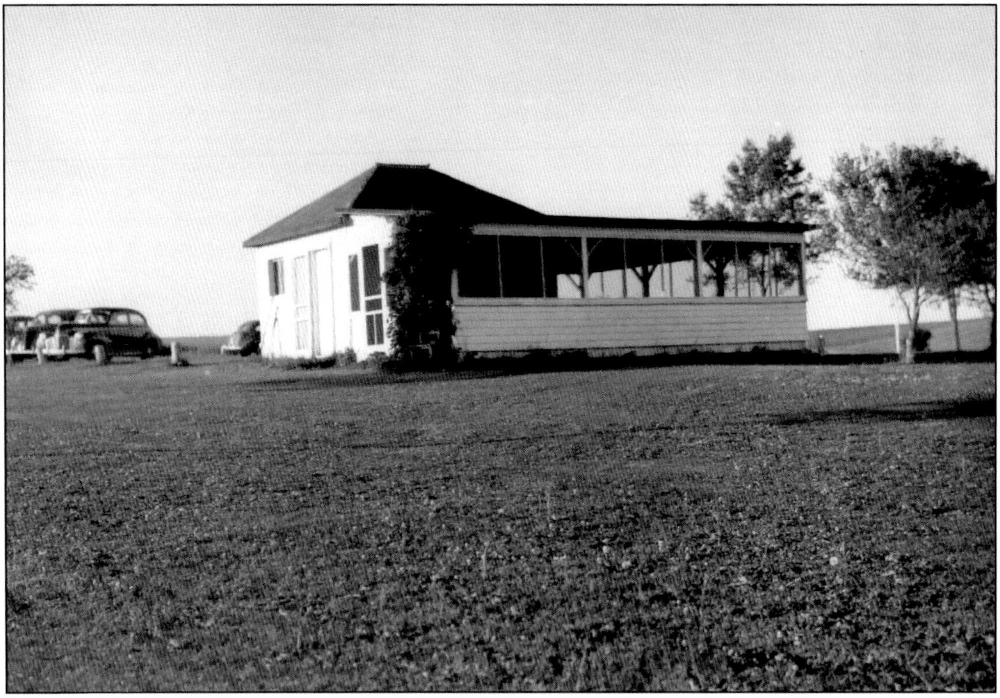

In its early days, golf was called Cow Pasture Pool. The first Preston Golf Club was built and ready for golfing by the spring of 1933. A short time later a tornado destroyed the clubhouse and a newer larger one was built. The original golf course was north of the site of the present golf course. There was no Highway 16 at the time. In 1938 a newer, larger golf course opened at its current site. A 1938 report says that the builders and club members took "forty acres of ditches, washes, ridges and bare ground and made a golf course." In 1946 Highway 16 was relocated past the golf course, with paving completed in 1949.

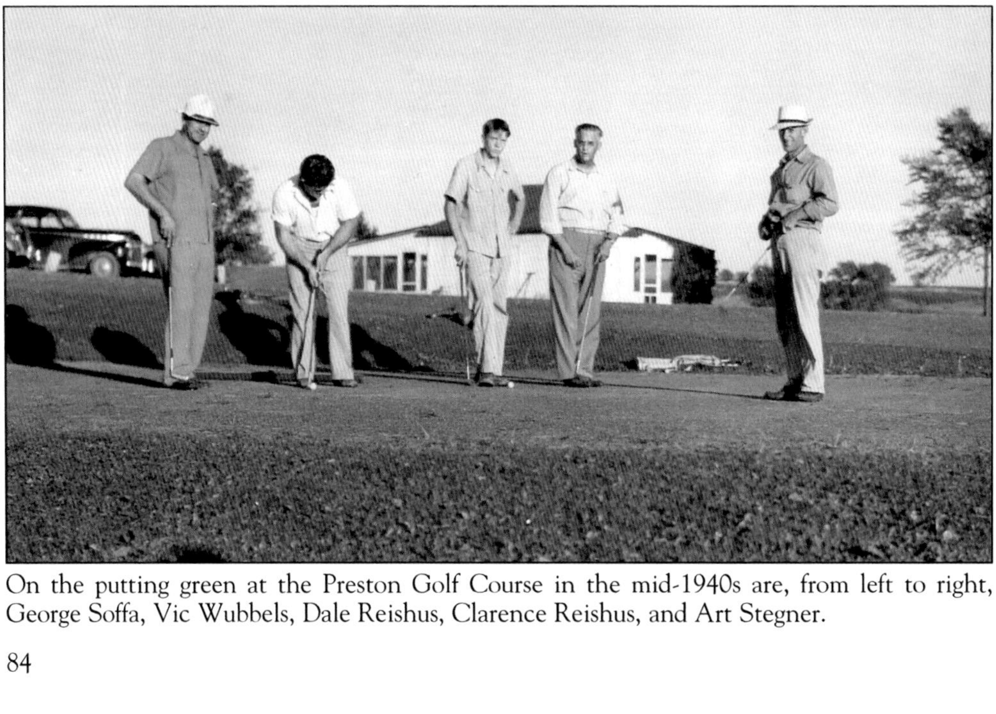

On the putting green at the Preston Golf Course in the mid-1940s are, from left to right, George Soffa, Vic Wubbels, Dale Reishus, Clarence Reishus, and Art Stegner.

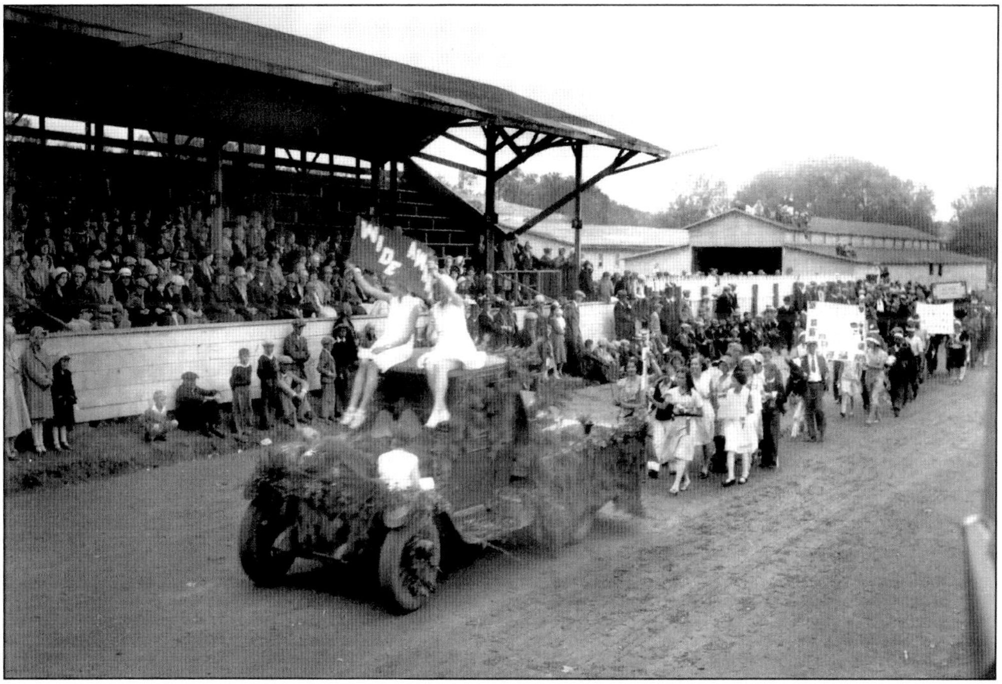

An annual event at the County Fair was the 4H parade, which took place in front of the grandstand. These two photos from 1938 show a couple of typical floats presented by the 4Hers. The Ostrander Orioles won the prize for best float. The other top four floats were: The North Canton Clippers, Fountain Friends, Highland Helpers, and the Empire Builders.

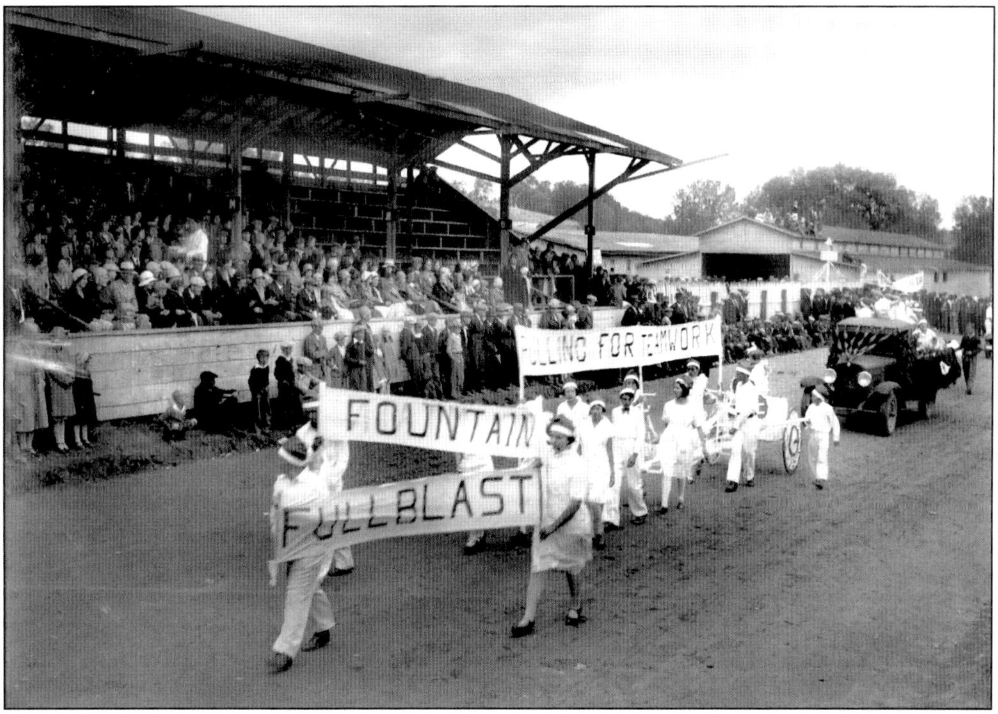

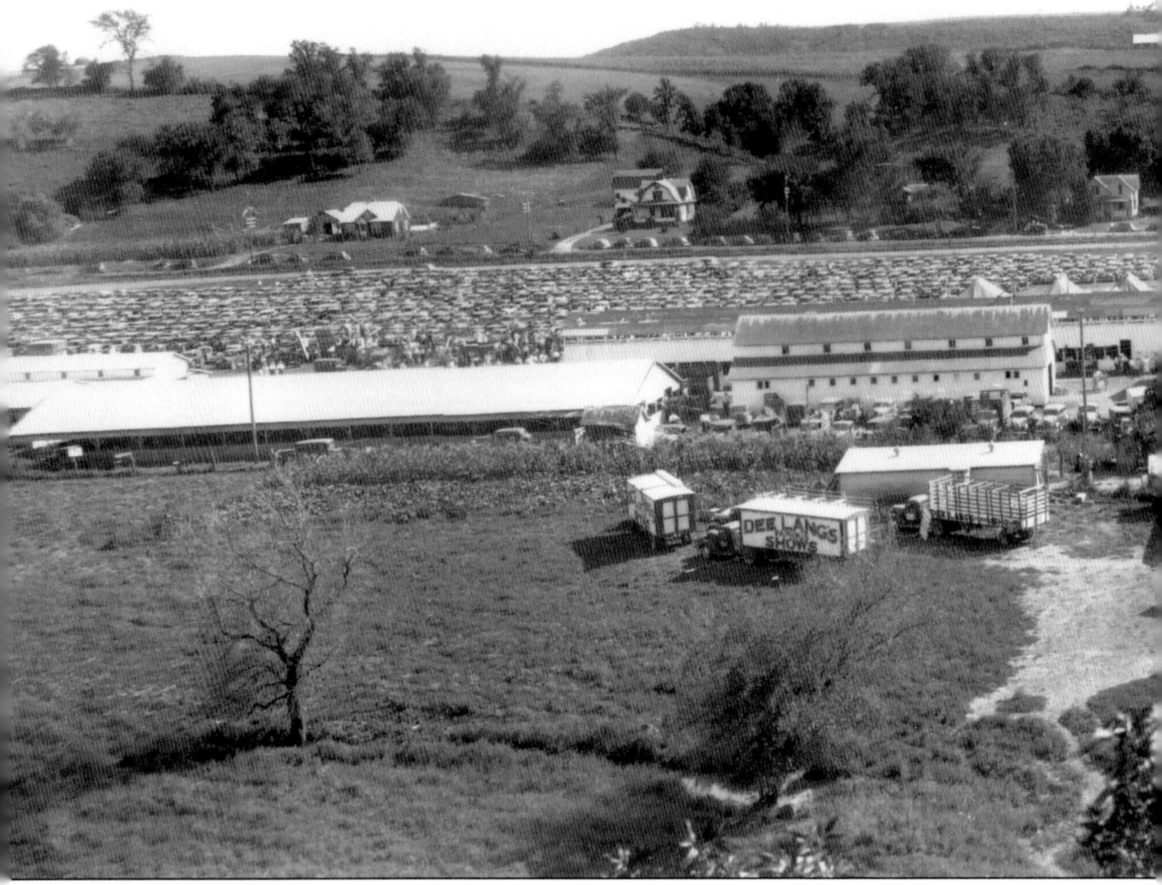


Matt Bue took this panoramic shot during the 1938 County Fair from the scenic overlook on the highway above the fairgrounds. On Sunday August 29, 1938, more people attended the Fillmore County Fair in a single day than any other in its then 79-year history. Fifteen thousand

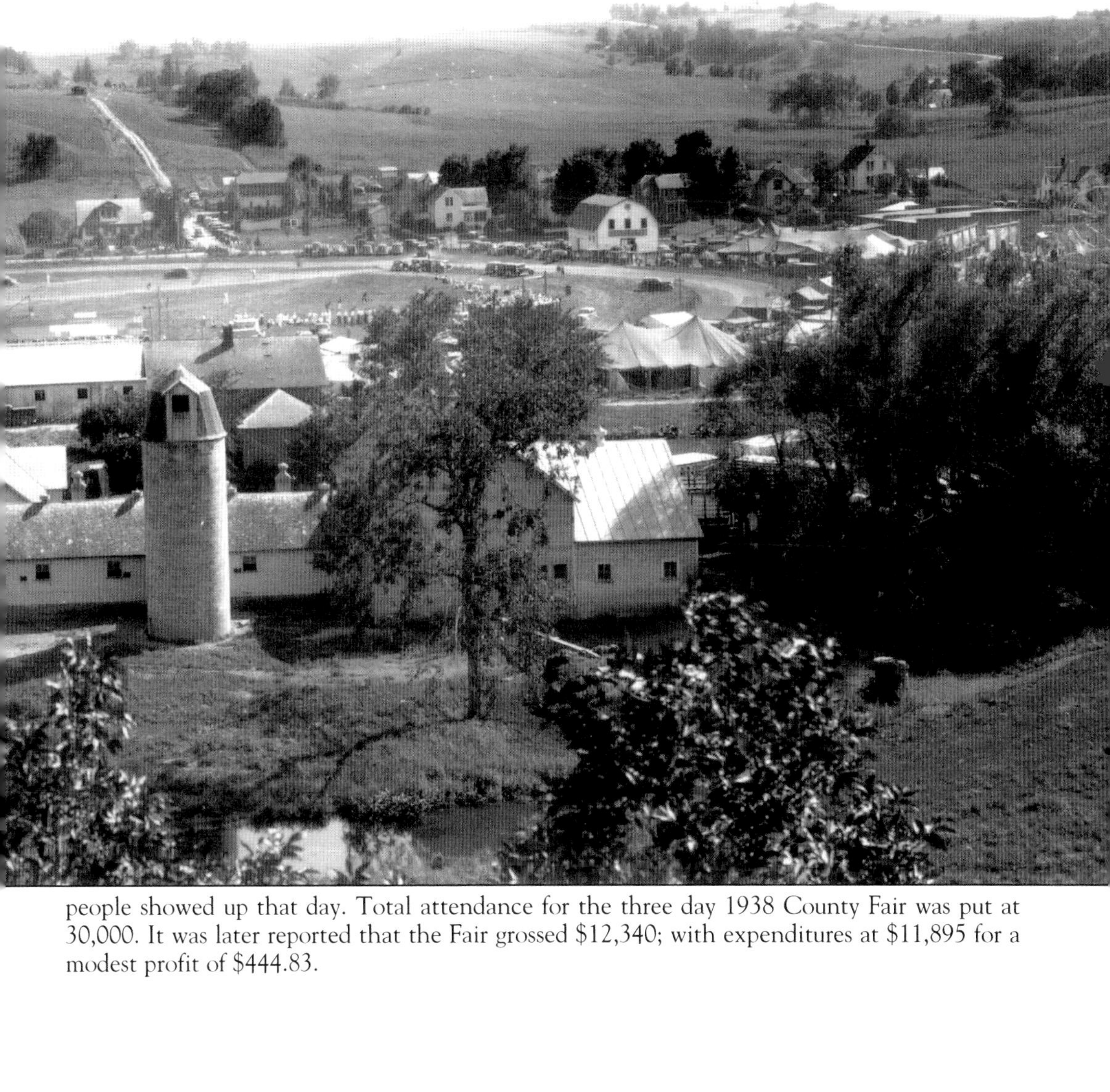

people showed up that day. Total attendance for the three day 1938 County Fair was put at 30,000. It was later reported that the Fair grossed $12,340; with expenditures at $11,895 for a modest profit of $444.83.

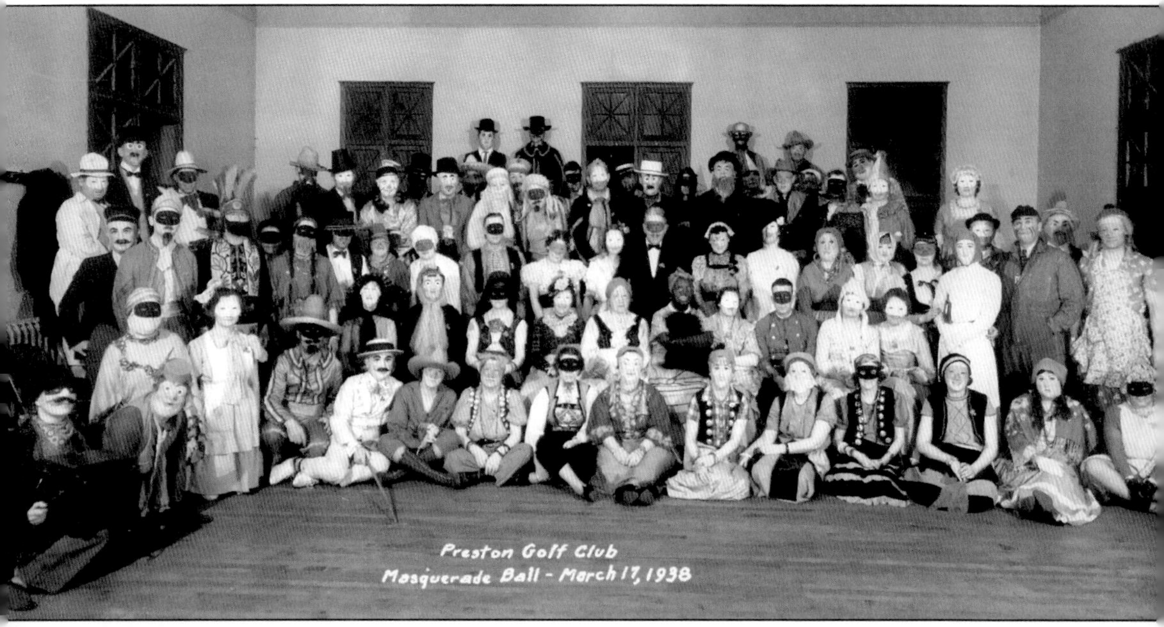


In spite of the lingering effects of the Great Depression and the sounding of distant war drums in Europe, people still liked to dress up and have a good time. This Masquerade Ball and Dance was held at the Town Hall by the Preston Golf Club on St. Patrick's Day, 1938. First prize for the best-dressed man was awarded to Doc Nehring, who dressed in an Arab costume. Mrs. Moppy Anderson won the best-dressed prize for women by dressing in a costume of the Gay Nineties.

Pictured from left to right are the following: (front row) Mrs. Jay Galvin, Jay Galvin, Mrs. E.A. Vischer, Mrs. L.K. Austin, Roy Flattum, Moppy Anderson, Mrs. B.E. Rosvold, Mrs. C.M. Quanrud, Mrs. Earl Kidd, Mrs. A.P. Nelson, Mrs. M.C. Munson, Mrs. Chris Evenrud, Mrs. Tim Grebin, Mrs. J.P. Nehring, Mrs. W.A. Heitner, and Mrs. Art Stegner; (second row) Mrs. Joe Christenson, Mrs. C.F. Lewis, Mrs. Art Ehrman, Mrs. Moppy Anderson, Mrs. Oscar Ause, Mildred Sailor, Eldora Driscoll, Ralph Fairbairn, Mrs. Wm. Ott, and Mrs. Al Krause; (third row) Art Noel, Earl Kidd, Chris Evenrud, Mrs. Chas. Keehn, Mrs. Roy Flattum, George Soffa, Mrs. M.N. Langum, Mrs. H. Becker, Michael Shanahan, Ruby Nelson, Mrs. J.F. Anderson, J.F. Anderson, Miss Sahrada, Mrs. F. Arny, Mrs. M.E. Love, Mrs. Art Noel, Mrs. A.M. Chilson, Mrs. C. Numedahl, Lyle Austin, Bill Thompson, Glen Gleason, and Art Stegner; (fourth row) Joe Christenson, A.P. Nelson, A.C. Krause, E.A. Vischer, Oscar Ause, M.N. Langum, Tim Grebin, Clarence Numedahl, M.E. Love, Mrs. Geo. Soffa, M.C. Munson, Dr. J.P. Nehring, Dr. F. Arny, Wm. Heitner, Moline, Don Nagle, Wm. Ott, Kirkibie, C.F. Lewis, Orace Hanson, Mrs. Wm. Klein, Joye Kruegel, Bill Klein, Bob Keehn, and Mrs. Glen Gleason; (fifth row) Edgar Klepper, Art Ehrman, Dr. C.M. Quanrud, and Ben Rosvold.

# *Six*

# Unfortunate Events

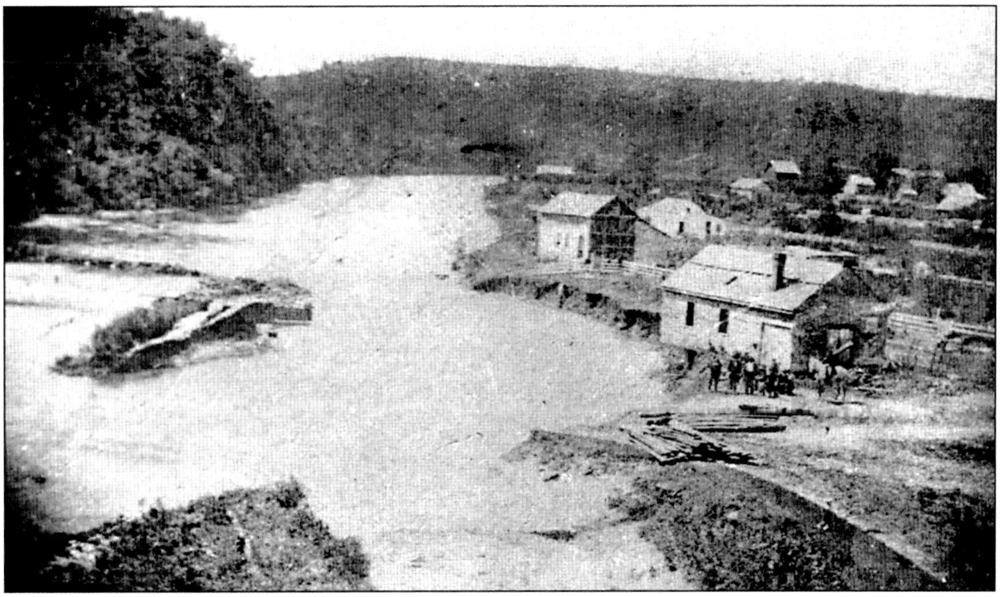

This photo was taken in 1865, showing the primitive village of Preston at flood time near today's south bridge. In late February of that year, two men attempted to ford the flood-swollen Root River, when they discovered that massive ice chunks had broken up the planks on the bridge. Once in the water, the horses spooked and the men's buggy overturned. While one of the men made it to shore, the other one was swept downstream and drowned. The less fortunate man's name was Archibald Donald of Newburg, a settlement in southeastern Fillmore County. After he was pulled from the river it was discovered that Mr. Donald had $900 in his pockets. The two men had been on their way to Rochester in order for Mr. Donald to "obtain a substitute to enter the military service in place of his son." (Photograph courtesy of Minnesota Historical Society.)

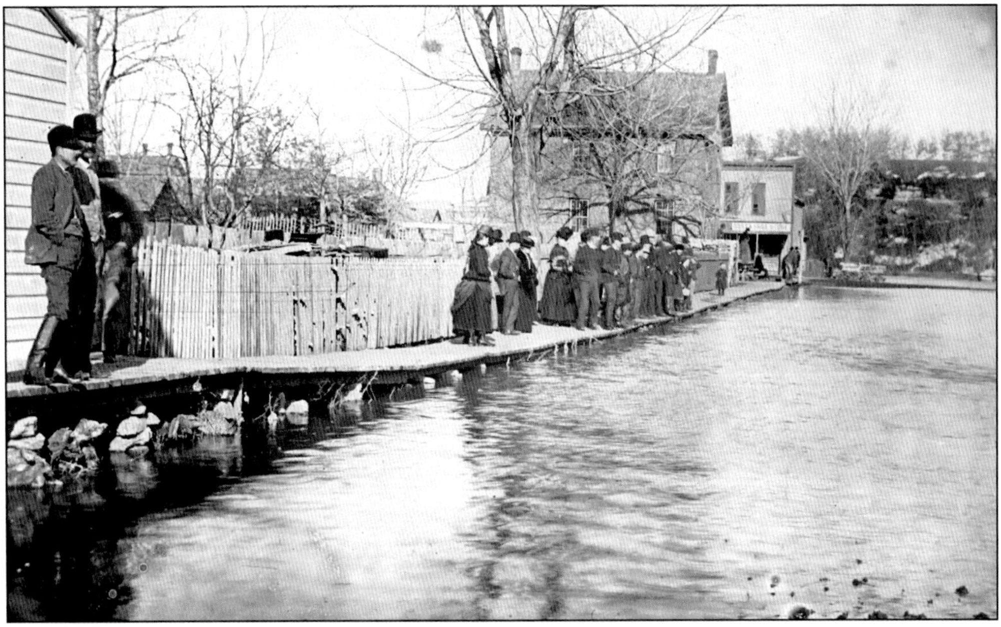

This photograph taken by A.L. Sleyster shows the effects of an early spring rain along with melting snow that caused the South Branch to swell out of its banks in April of 1888. It was reported that the wagon bridge at Carimona and a large part of the Mill Dam there were carried away by the waters. In Preston, the lower streets filled with water, evidenced here as locals survey the flood along River Street. The Conkey Brothers Mill, originally the Kaercher mill, sustained around $200 damage, a hefty amount of money in those days. The railroad station and tracks also sustained heavy damage, as is shown in the photograph below.

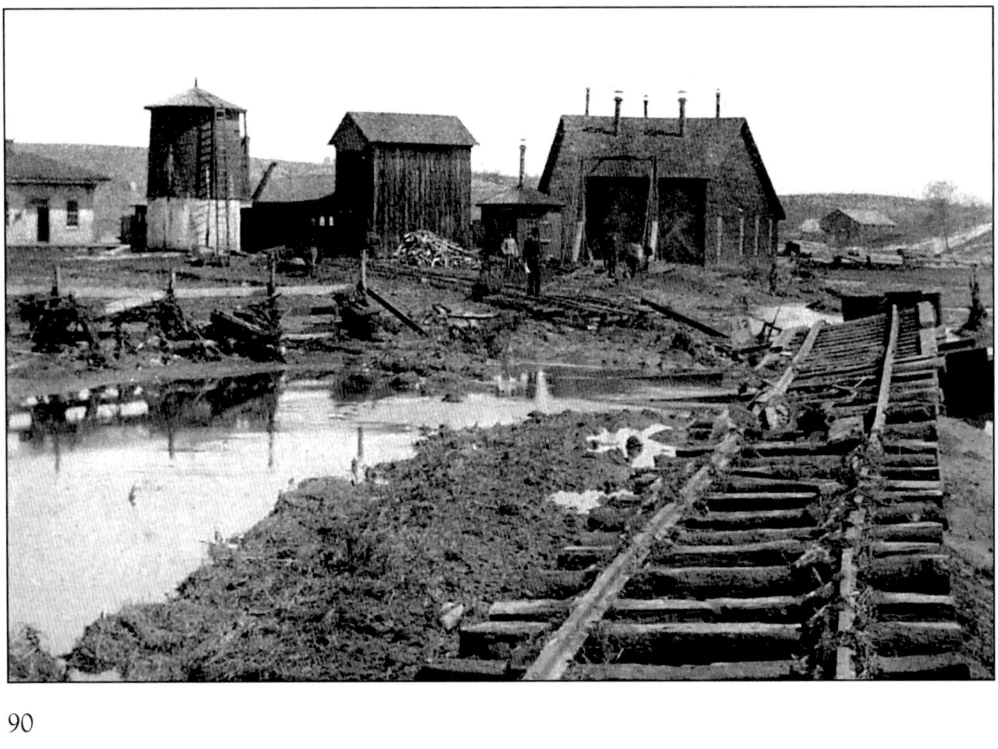

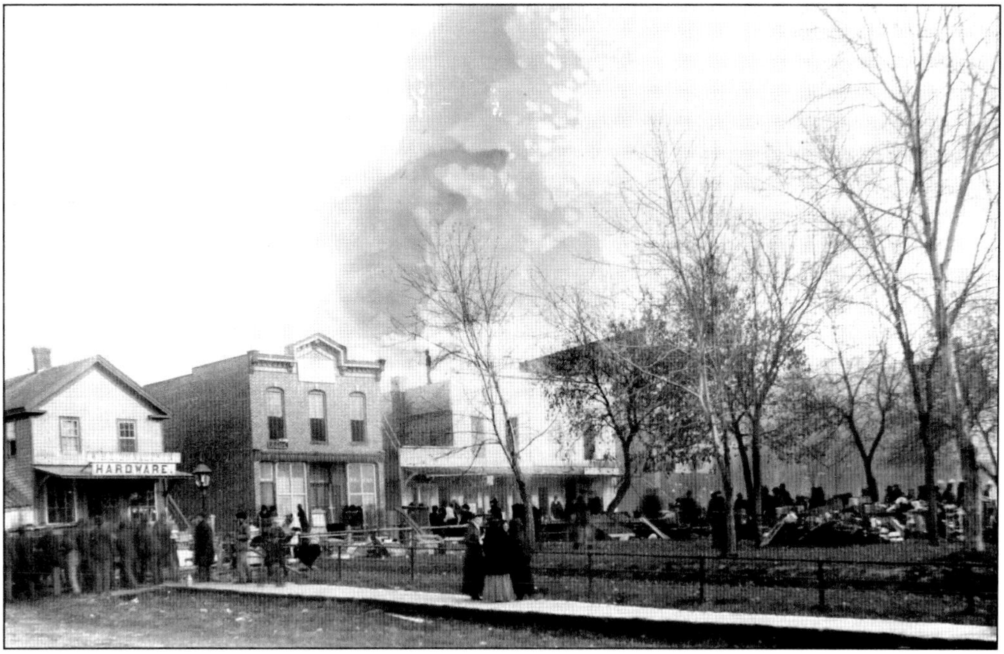


This fire took place on Fillmore Street in 1894. There was little written in the local papers about the origins or the damage, though the presence of smoke appeared to draw quite a crowd around the courthouse park.

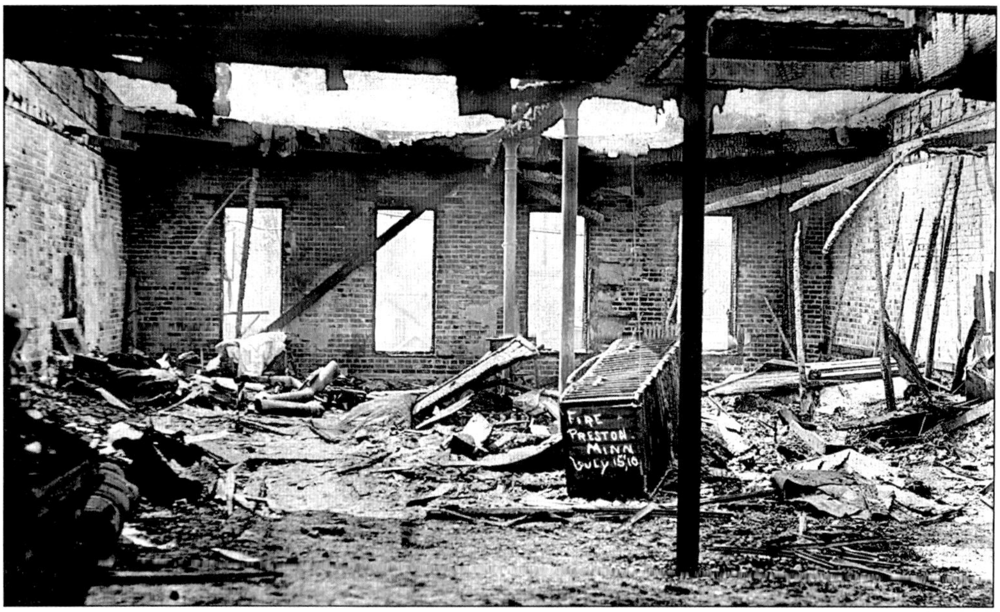


Another fire on Fillmore Street was discovered at midnight on July 15, 1910. The *Preston Republican* reported that "The fire boys did great work after they began throwing water," but their efforts were hampered when the two nearest hydrants malfunctioned. The loss was estimated at $9,000 for the undertaking parlor and the dress shop that shared the building. "The fact that there was no wind at all is the only thing that saved the entire business portion of town from being burned."

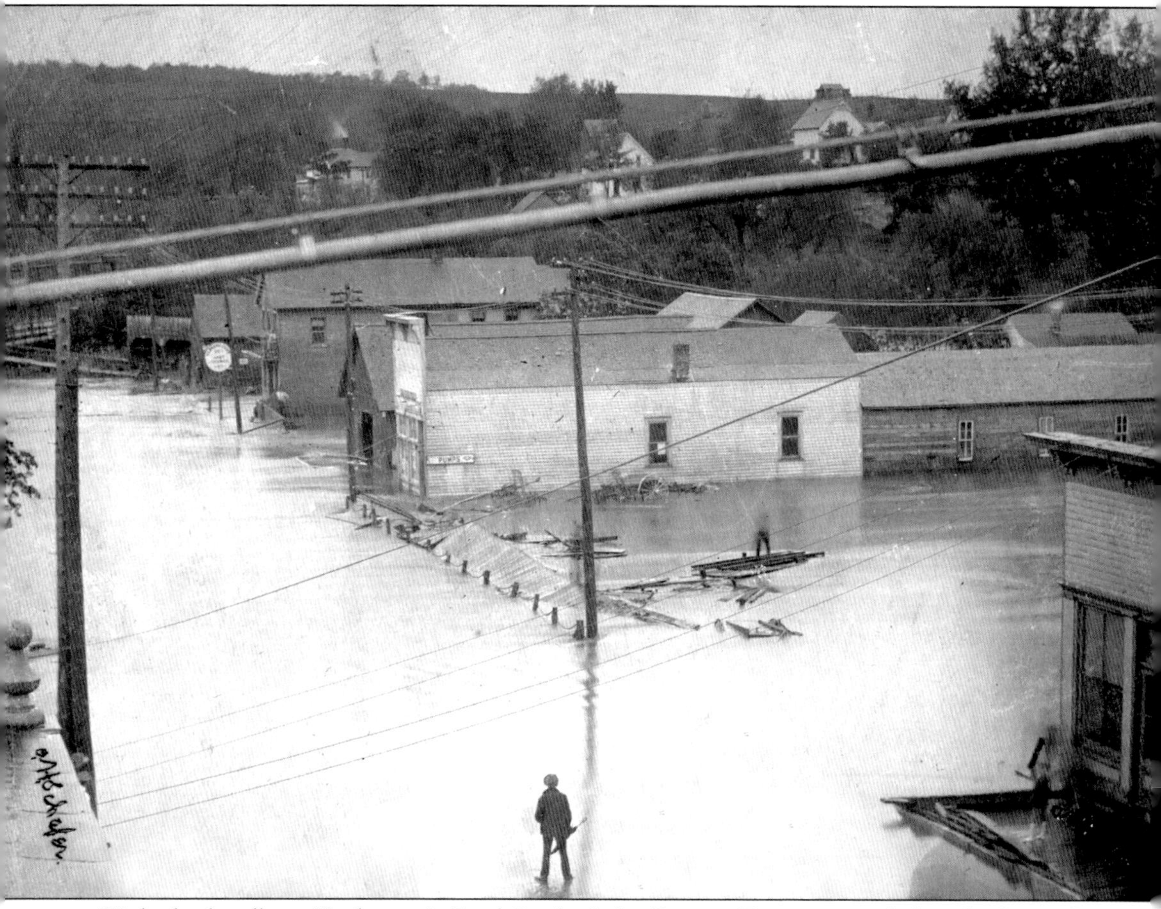

With the headline, "Lightning's Fatal Stroke," the *Preston Times* reported that the May 17, 1902 storm was the "worst in the history of this vicinity." The *Times* claimed, "The oldest inhabitant in Preston does not remember such high water. The flooding led to substantial financial losses, as is evidenced by this photograph of lower St. Paul Street." There were human tragedies as well, including when 34-year-old Preston businessman Henry Conkey was killed by lightning near the fairgrounds. Conkey was known as a born horseman and had won many horse races across southern Minnesota and northern Iowa. During the storm he had gone out to retrieve a valuable colt when he was struck by the lightning. A dozen miles or so to the west of Preston, near Forestville, the Herman Willbright family's buggy capsized while attempting to cross the swollen river for safety, which led to their three young children being washed away and drowned.

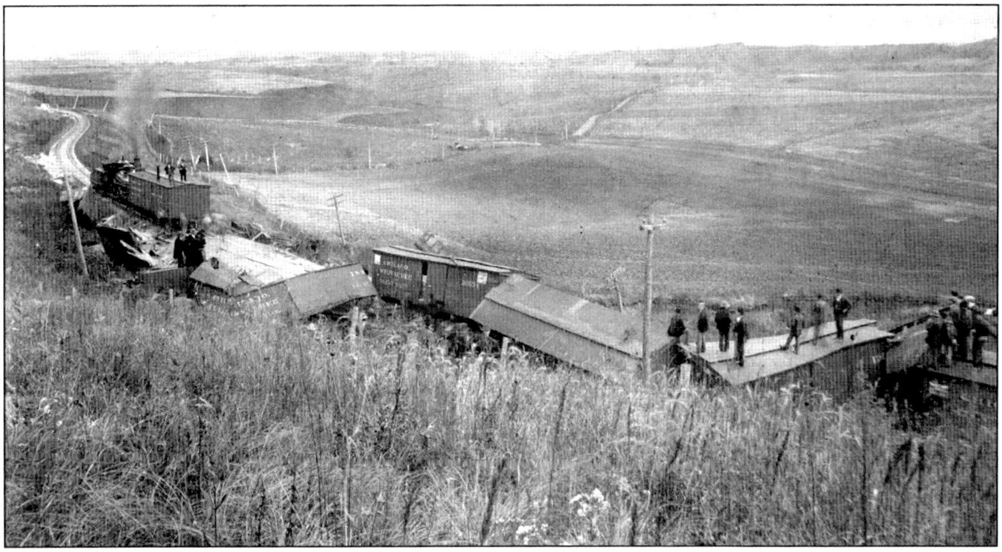

On Saturday afternoon, September 25, 1902, the eastbound freight from Fountain, heavily loaded with merchandise and grain, was headed down the steep hill towards Isinours when one of the cars jumped the track. Within moments ten other cars out of the middle of the train "were but a mass of wreckage, piled in indescribable confusion." It was reported that the following day, thousands visited the scene, "driving there for miles in all directions." The railroad's brakeman, 24-year-old Lloyd Case of Fountain, was killed in the accident

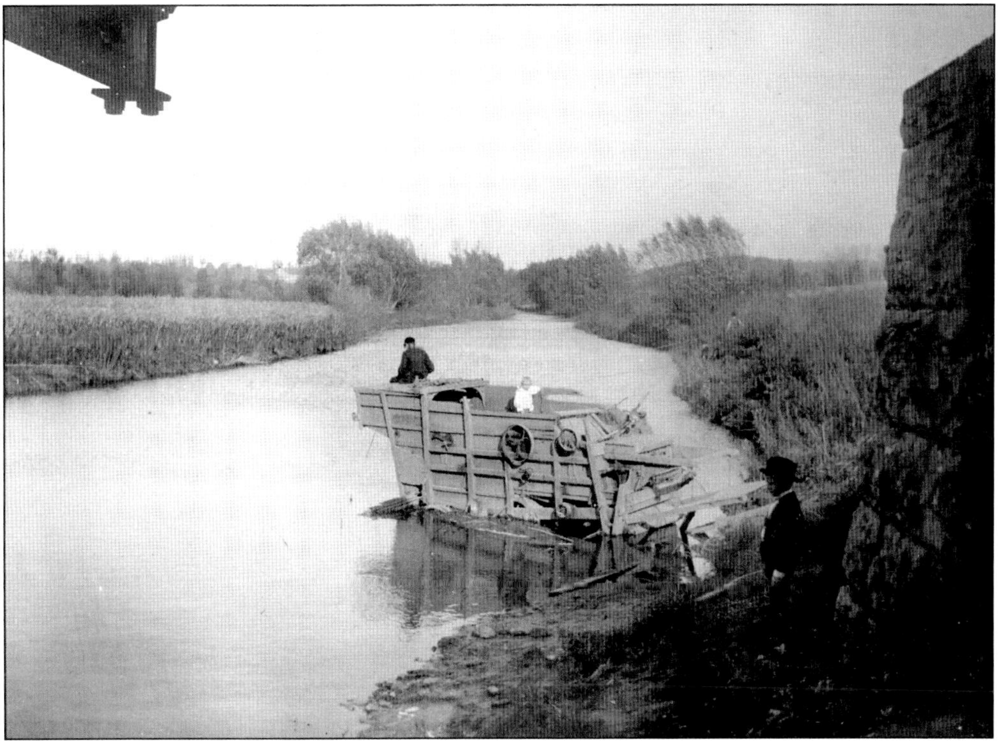

In this undated photograph, a thresher lies in the Root River beside a bridge on the east side of Preston, while a fisherman tries his luck from a new vantage point.

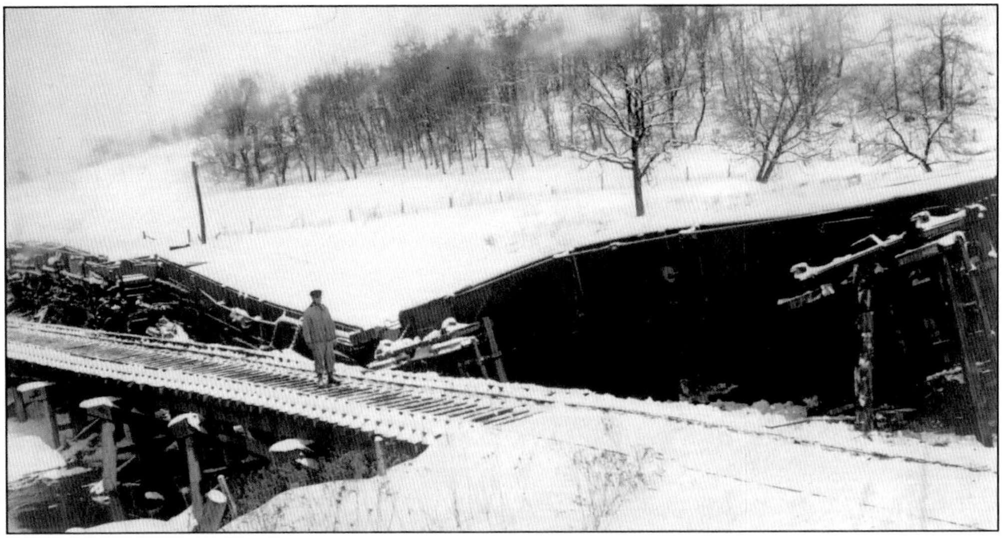

The passenger train from La Crosse over the Preston Reno Branch was wrecked about four miles east of town, near the Matt Simonson place on March 13, 1917. As the *Preston Times* reported: "There were a large number of passengers aboard and these noticed nothing unusual until the train suddenly commenced to bump along on the ties, flowed almost instantly by being thrown on their sides, the smoker falling into Camp Creek from an elevation of six feet, the ladies' coach remaining partly upright, the baggage car flat on its side just across the creek, all more or less wrenched and damaged. When the excitement of the wreck had partly subsided it was found that a considerable number had been more or less injured. It was seen at once that M. R. Cluss of Brownsville had been dangerously hurt. He was unconscious and bleeding profusely. He was taken to Preston and carried to the office of Dr. George Love. A cursory examination gave no hopes and he died about an hour later without regaining consciousness." A former resident of Preston, Mr. Cluss was traveling to attend a board meeting of the Farmers and Merchants State Bank and to visit his two daughters living in Preston: Mrs. Herb Vickerman and Mrs. Virgil Vickerman.

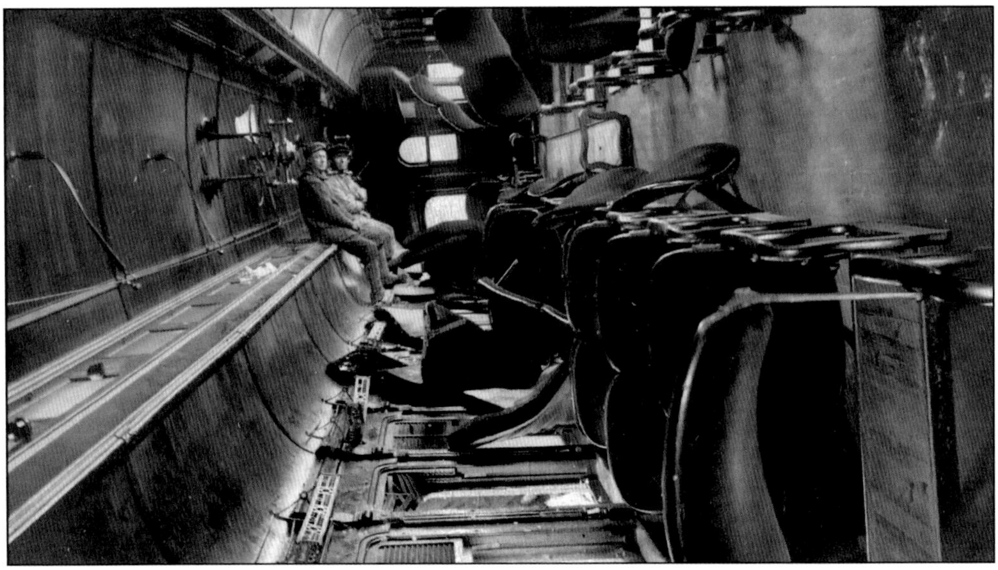

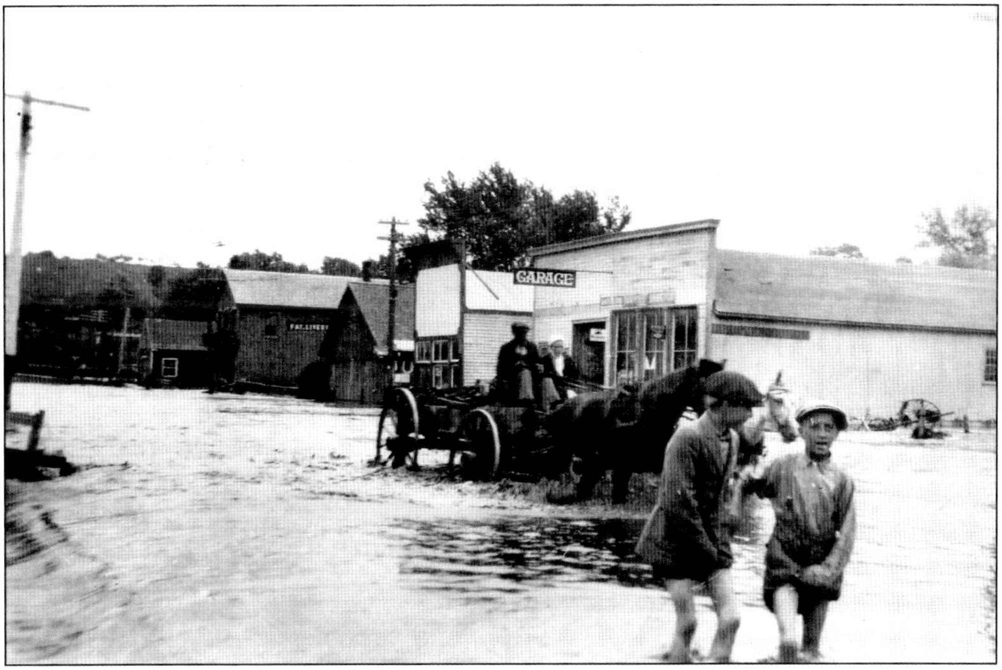


Yet another flood swept through Preston during the third week of June in 1917, when the Root River went on "a rampage," according to the *Lanesboro Leader* which ran the headline, "Furious Storms Sweep Fillmore County." After a brutal winter with heavy snowstorms, Preston was braced for a higher degree of spring flooding than usual. But the real flood came on June 23, when a "succession of violent electrical, wind, rain and hail storms swept over Fillmore County. The storm came from all directions as the wind shifted from quarter to quarter." Two days later another heavy rainstorm soaked the area, and with the damage to the tracks it was impossible for trains to run out of Preston.

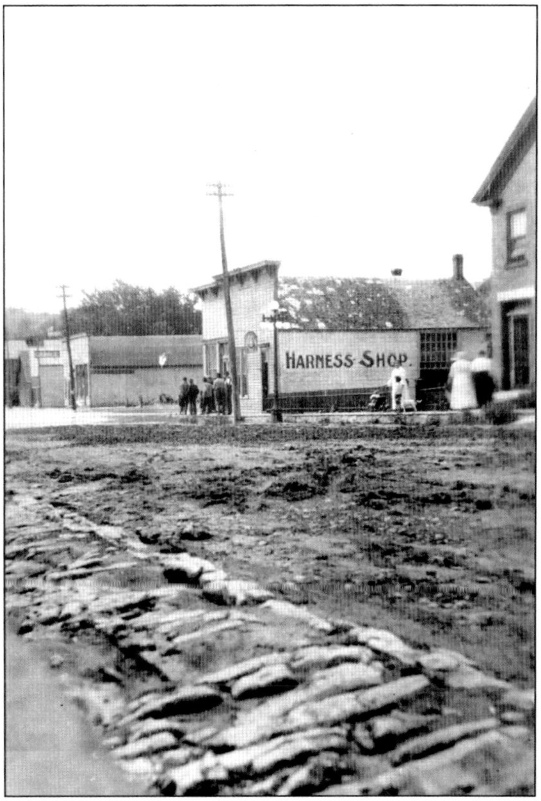

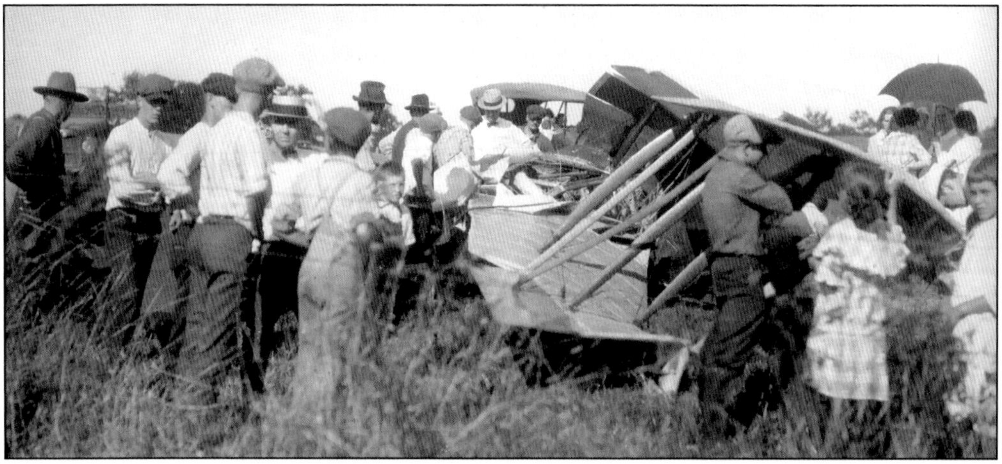

An adventure turned tragic on August 19, 1921, when Herbert Riebe, a barnstorming pilot affiliated with the Rochester Aircraft Co. showed up in Preston to give rides. The second passenger to go for a ride was a 21-year-old man named Ross Bright, who had recently moved to Preston, taking over the Gem Theater, which he had renamed Bright's Star. According to reports, Bright talked the pilot into doing a nose spin from 2,000 feet. In front of a crowd of onlookers the plane never righted itself and crashed some "40 rods south of the Crown Hill cemetery."

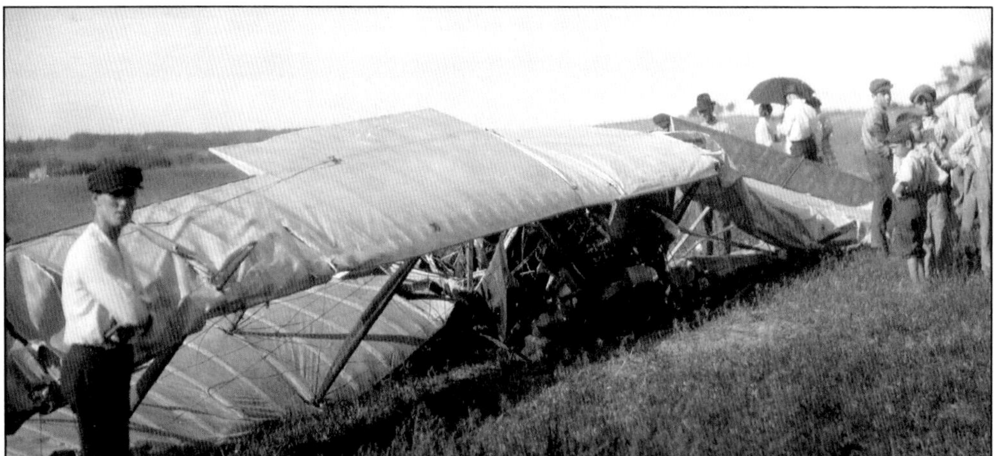

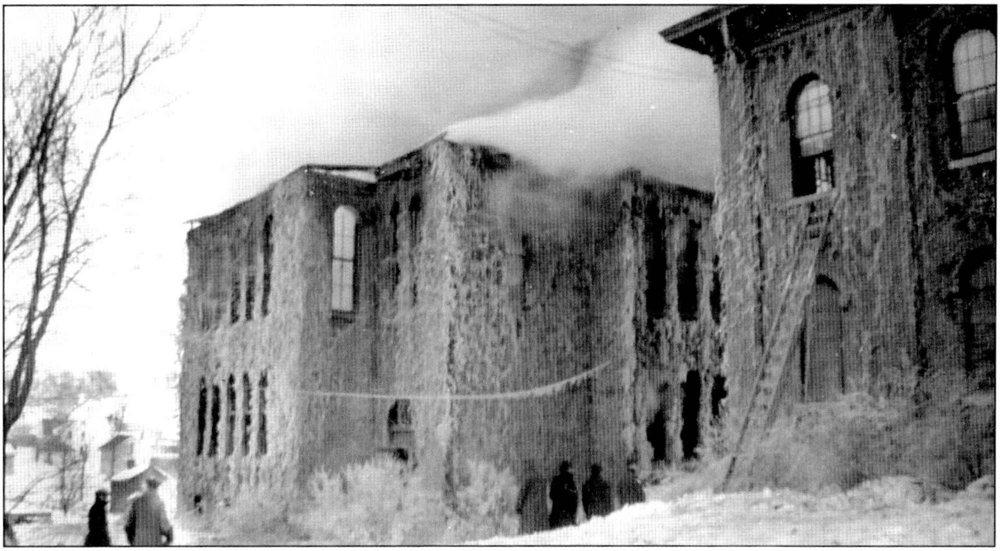

The high school burned down on the bitterly cold morning of January 23, 1922. Some reports said it was as low as 33 degrees below zero. The fire was first seen by a man coming out the creamery just down the hill from the school. Three of his children were in the school and he called the fire hall immediately to sound the alarm. By the time the students got outside the entire roof was up in flames, and in a few more minutes the assembly hall roof caved in, the spot where most of the students had been gathering just before the fire alarm was sounded. An investigation determined that the school janitor had caused the fire when he had burned papers that morning through the chimney. The resulting sparks from the hot paper fire ignited the roof.

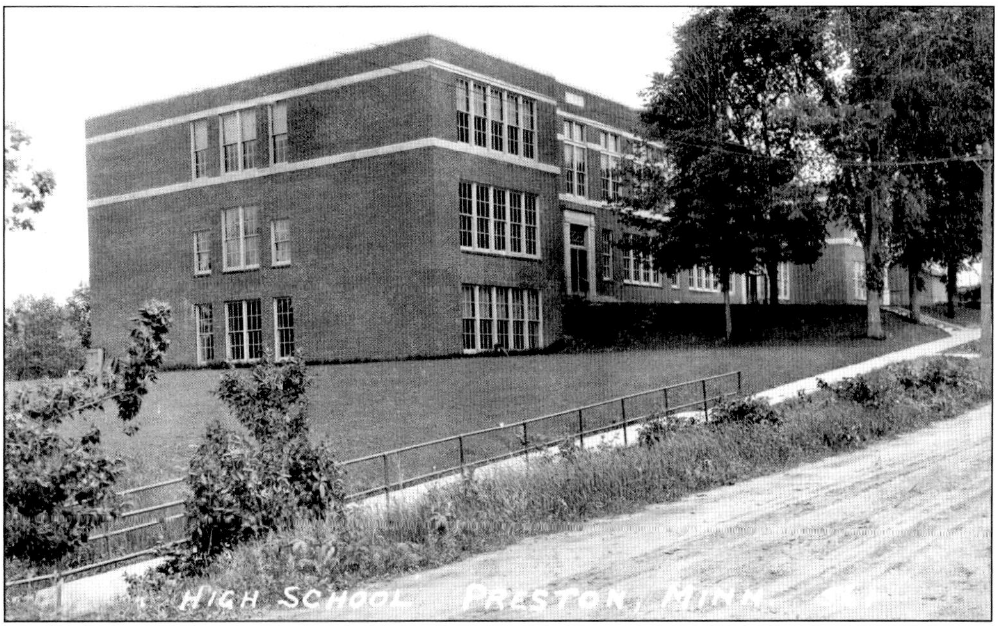


With the high school totally destroyed and the adjoining grade school called a fire trap, the town's citizens voted overwhelmingly in favor of replacing the entire school. The new school building housed all of Preston's schoolchildren, including junior and senior high. The building cost around $150,000 to build and was completed in March of 1923.

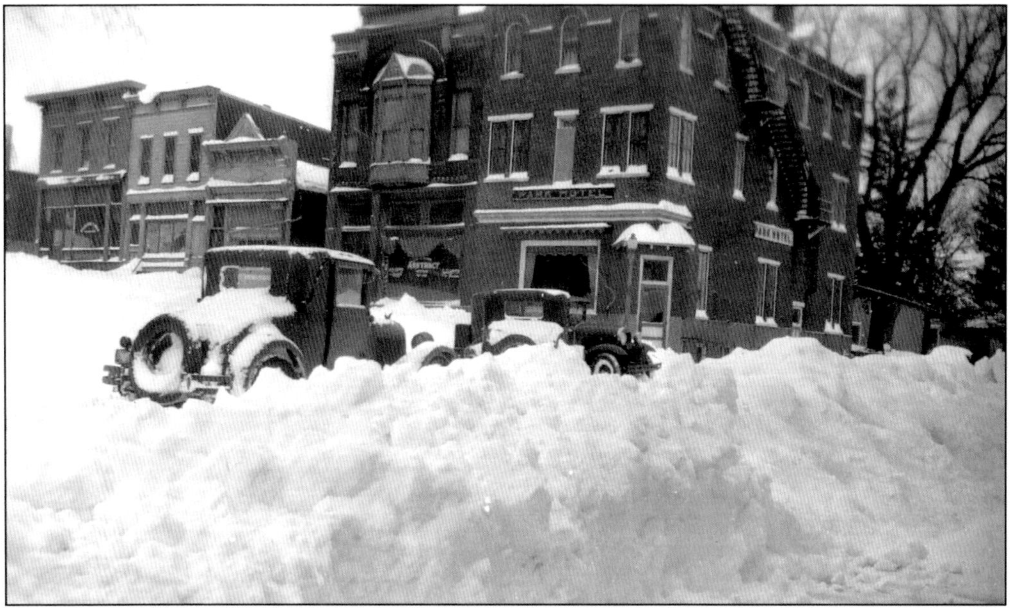

A late March blizzard in 1933 paralyzed much of the county, including these two cars on Main Street. The storm started on a Friday night with rain and sleet and then "the weatherman decided to give us a taste of real Minnesota weather," the *Preston Times* reported. By Saturday evening, over two feet of snow lay on the ground. "Had as much snow come in November it would have been with us all winter but this is Spring and it will be headed for the Mississippi," the *Times* stated.

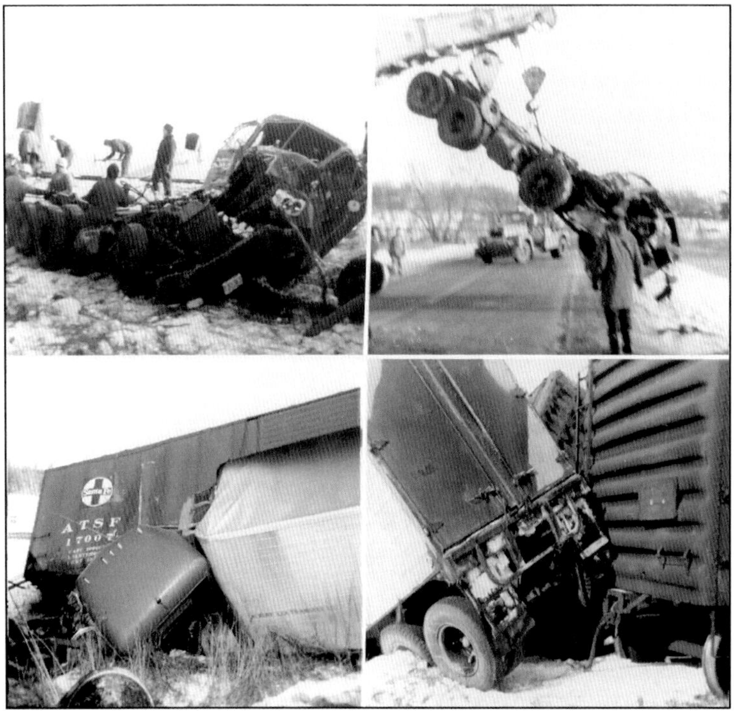

This collage shows a truck/train accident in January of 1966, just east of Preston where Highways 52 and 16 crossed the Preston-Isinours train track. The semi truck, loaded with grain and coming down the hill from the south, was unable to stop where the train was crossing the road. The driver and his relief driver, both from Albert Lea, were not seriously injured. Just six weeks earlier a similar accident occurred when a semi-flatbed truck collided with a train at the same location. The driver in that instance was seriously injured. The semis in both accidents were completely wrecked with extensive damages to the trains as well.

# *Seven*

# SCENES AROUND TOWN

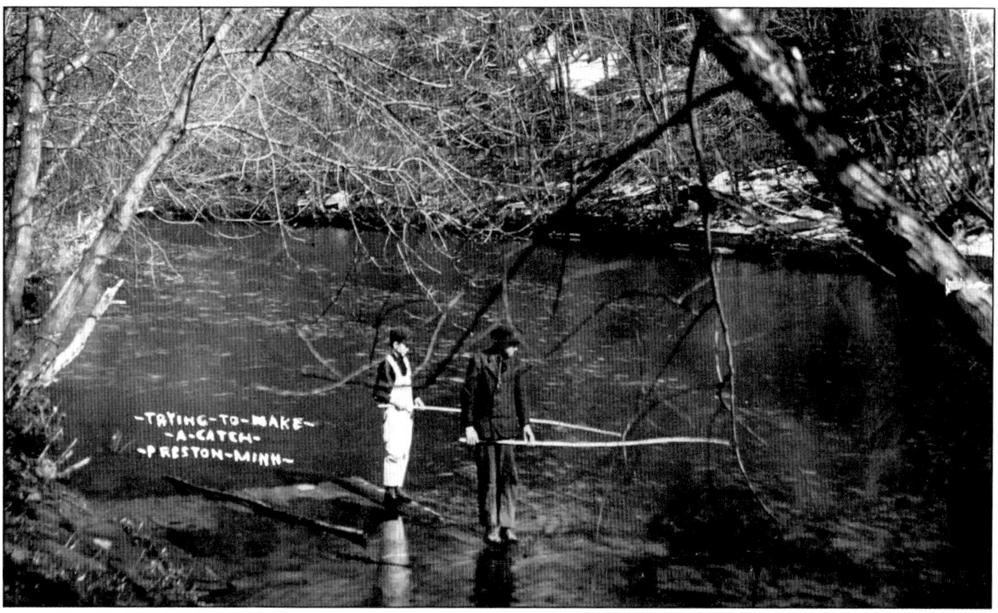


The *National Republican* reported in 1896: "Few villages can equal Preston for the beauty of her natural surroundings. But strange to say our citizens do not appreciate or enjoy the exquisite scenes that charm every stranger who visits Preston. Of late, however a little interest is shown in the boating and almost any evening the dip of oars and of merry voices can be heard on the river. Let the good work go on until a score of boats adorn the bosom of River Root and let our charming valley ring with song and laughter."

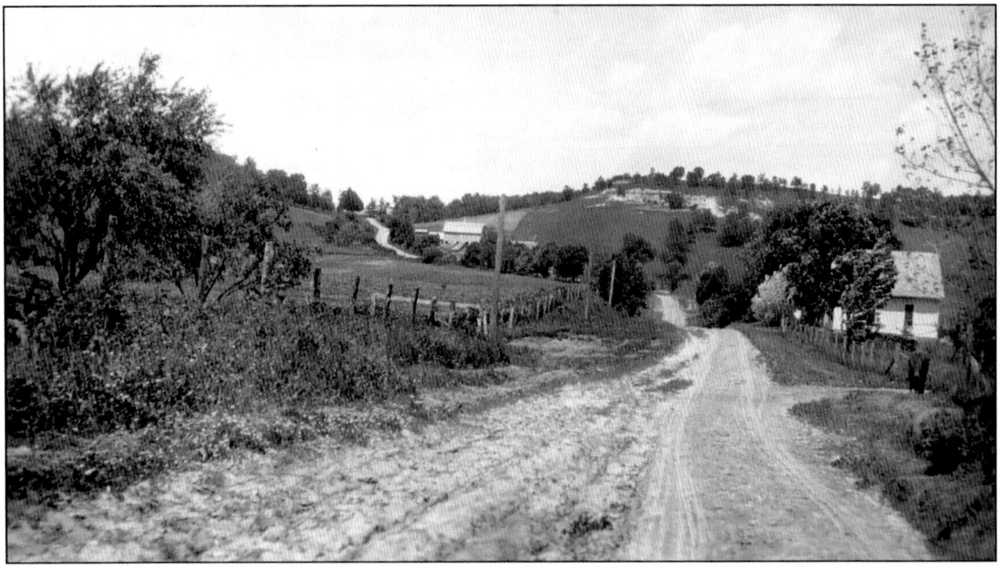

In the plat book of 1896, when much of Preston consisted of country fields and dirt roads, this by-way was called Gap Lane. The picture was taken near today's Middle and Elementary schools, looking straight north. Other parts of town closer to the courthouse had sidewalks, though they were "rickety and old" as the *Preston Times* wrote in 1894. "There are sidewalks in this town which should shame a heathen and yet we are compelled to stumble over them day after day and unless something is done somebody will be injured."

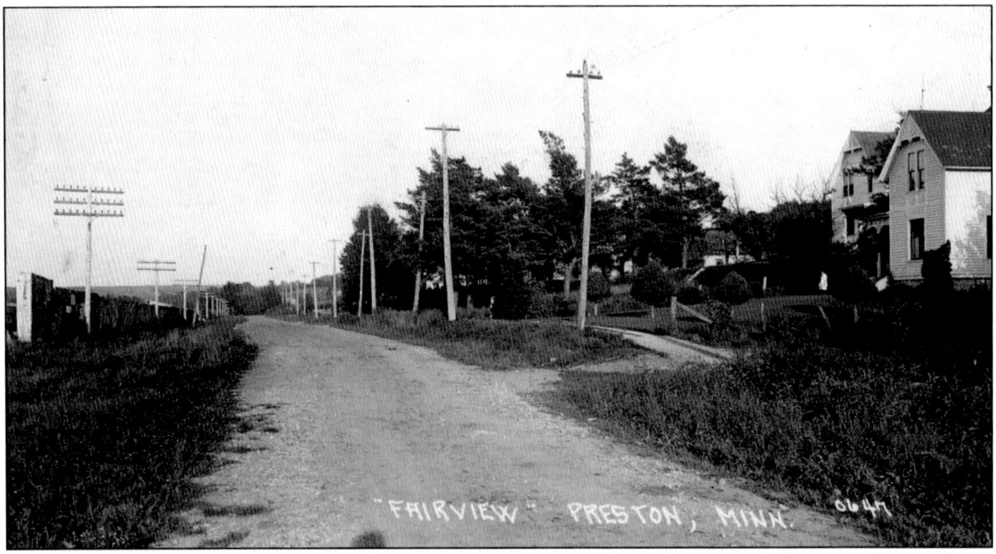


Automobile traffic was still sparse in 1917, but the *Preston Times* reported that residents of Fair View, where this picture was taken, were complaining bitterly about autos speeding along their stretch of road. "Unfortunately the 'fool at the wheel' does not confine his speeding to any particular locality," the editor wrote. "We see him or her up town almost every day, and we cannot help but wonder what speed ordinances are for when there is absolutely no effort being made to enforce them. If the speed maniacs were only endangering their own necks we would not care, but the decent car driver and the peaceable pedestrian are constantly exposed to danger from these road hogs."

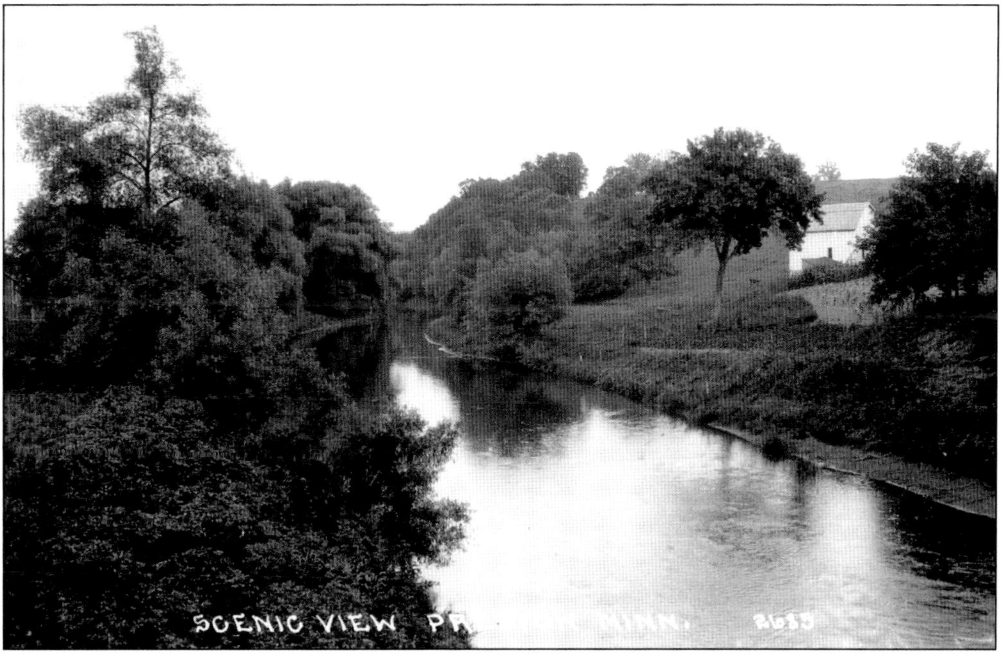


This tranquil scene along the Root River in Preston belies the fact that there were strange and untidy events going on, as the editor of the *Preston Times* made known to his readers in March, 1899, when he wrote that the area around the river at the Preston fairgrounds had been "converted into a rowdy's resort. Prize fights, drunken brawls and gambling are common and some of the frequenters of the grounds are in female garb whatever their gender. How much of the Village Marshall's time is devoted to sleep?"

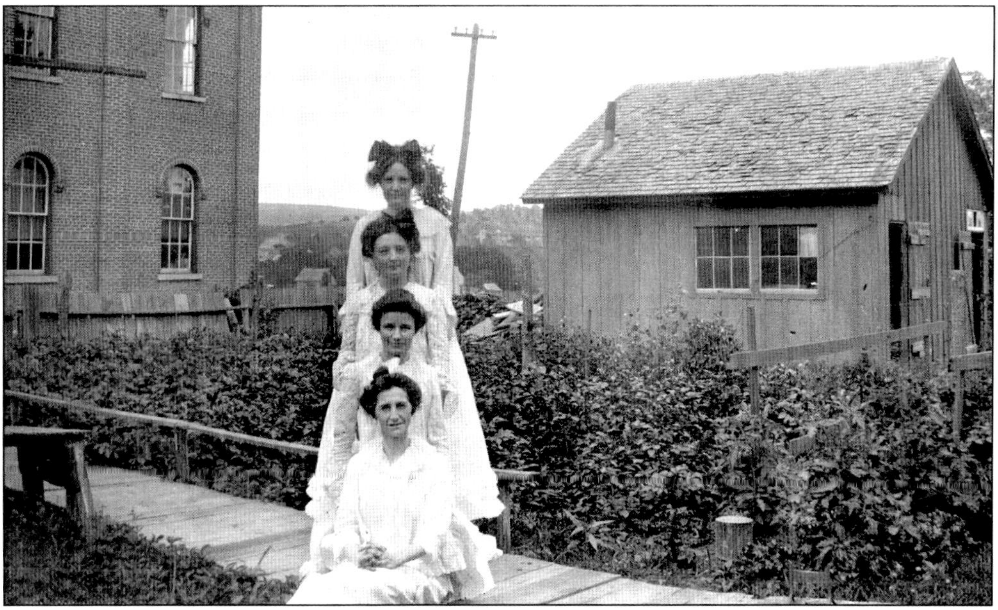

The 1915 Preston schoolteachers posed for a shot in the William Kruppenbacher garden next to the school. Pictured from bottom are Cora Bigelow, unidentified, Mrs. Read, and May (Gartner) Pretsch.

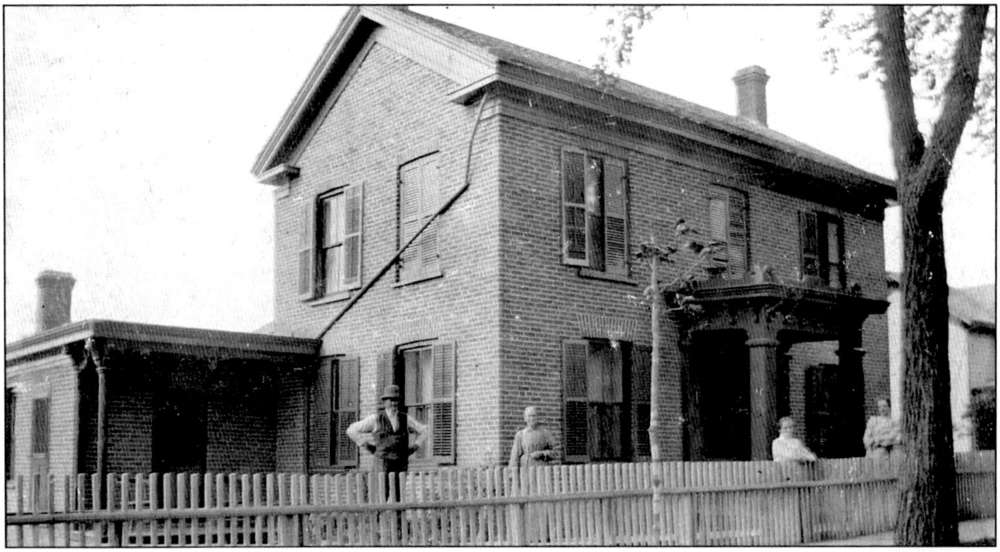

The August and Frederika (Schultz) Schoenbaum house on Fillmore Street was built with local brick and is pictured c. 1900. It still stands as a fine-looking house in the 21st century. Born in Germany in 1827, August arrived in Preston in 1857. He died in 1906. His obituary said that he was a man of "sterling integrity, (who) never wronged man, woman or child." Pictured from left to right are August and Fredricka Schoenbaum, with their daughters Bertha and Louisa Schoenbaum.

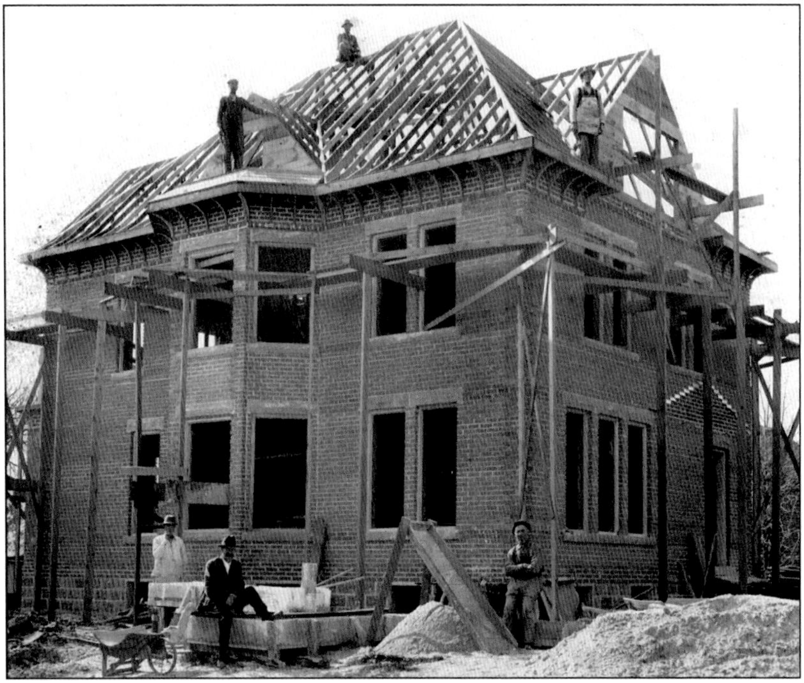

Mike Long, a livestock buyer, erected this house in 1918 "on his fine lots on Oak Ridge," as the *Preston Republican* reported. "He will erect a handsome two story structure 28 by 36 feet, using pressed brick, somewhat similar to the brick in the library and city hall. These improvements will materially add to the beauty of the west part of the town." The house was later purchased by Dr. J.P. Nehring, who opened it as the Preston Hospital, in January of 1944. In 1950 there were 207 births at the hospital, a large percentage of the county's births, as the county's births totaled 392. The first seven years showed a total of 1,585 patients and 1,034 births in the hospital. Nehring ran the hospital until 1958 when he sold the building, which was then used as a boarding house.

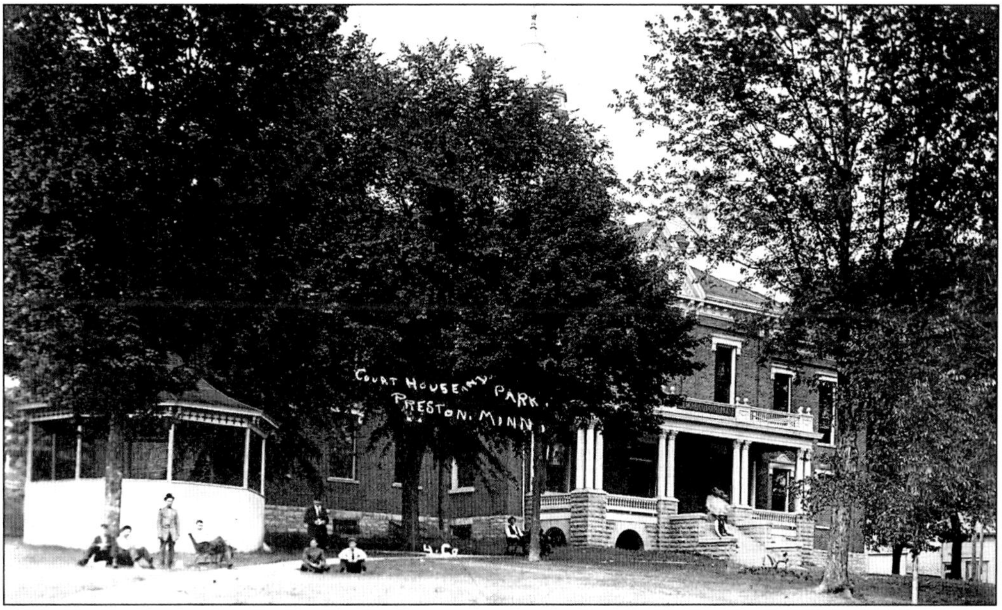

The bandstand on the southwest lawn of the courthouse was used for many events, including outdoor high school graduations. In 1907 the *Preston Times* reported, "The band stand is receiving a new coat of paint. Just a bit of evidence that there is still a spark of civic pride." By 1915, though, the bandstand was in bad shape, as reported by the *Times*: "The old unsightly and badly rotted band stand is to be taken out of the park and future band concerts will be given from the porticoes."

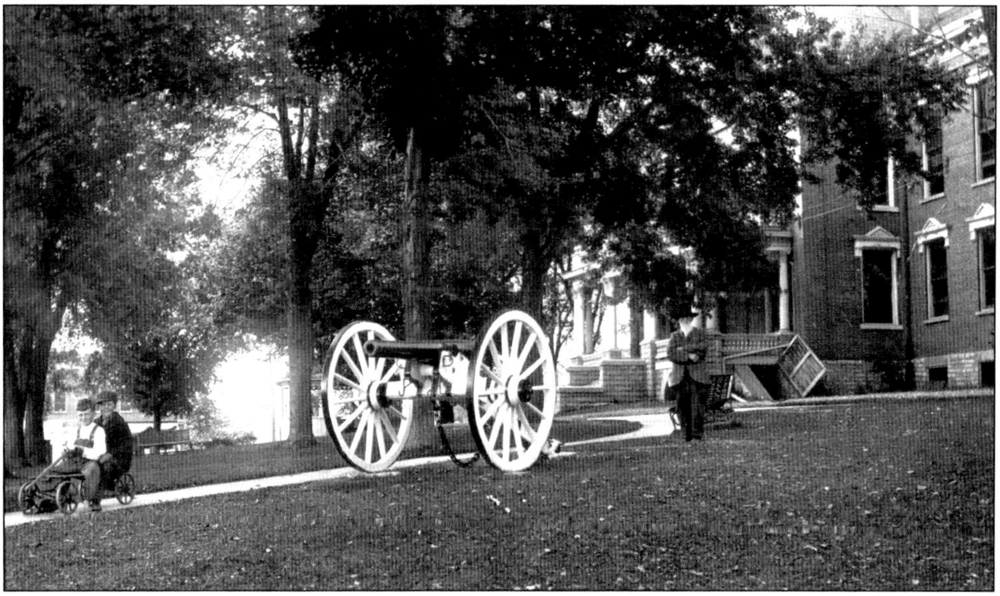

This cannon was from the Civil War era and sat in the courthouse park for many years until it was melted down for metal during World War II, with the promise that it would be replaced with another weapon following the end of the war. It wasn't until 1994 that Preston got its "war memorial" weapon with the acquisition of an M-60-A tank, which is now parked at the Trail Head of the Root River Trail.

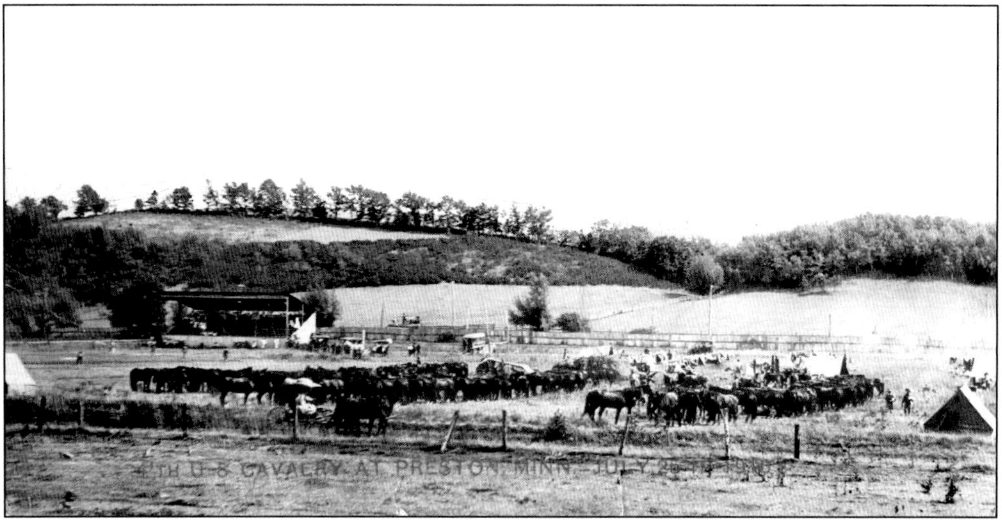


During the summer of 1910, the 4th Cavalry from Fort Snelling, camped at the fairgrounds in Preston while on route to Sparta, Wisconsin. Before arriving, the cavalry requested a campground with four acres, preferably with blue grass sod, and adjacent water for 200 animals. They were met outside of town by Preston's mayor, G.E. Love, and the Preston band. The locals found the soldiers to be "an orderly bunch and well behaved lot of fellows." A baseball game that evening between the soldiers and the Preston team drew a large crowd with Preston winning 11-9.

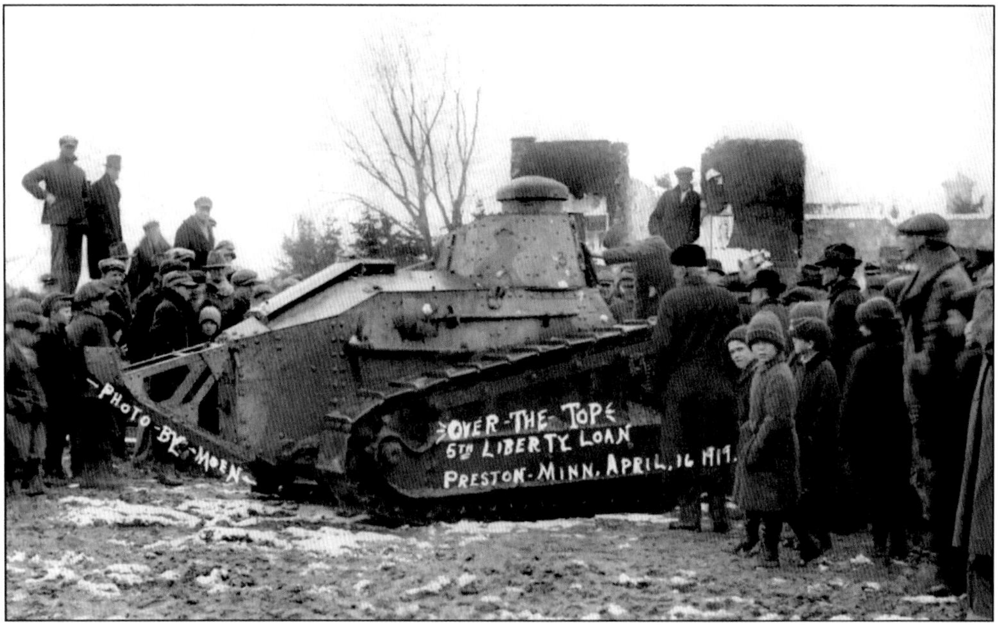


Even though the Great War had been over for several months, the U.S. government still had to pay for it. So they sent out a "real war tank showing the scars of German bullets" to towns across the country to solicit funds for the Fifth Victory Liberty Loan program. In April of 1919, the 16-foot-long, 7-ton tank paraded the streets and then demolished the old livery barn of the Tibbetts House. The weather was bad and the roads were reported almost impassable but crowds still showed up from all across the county to see the unique instrument of modern warfare.

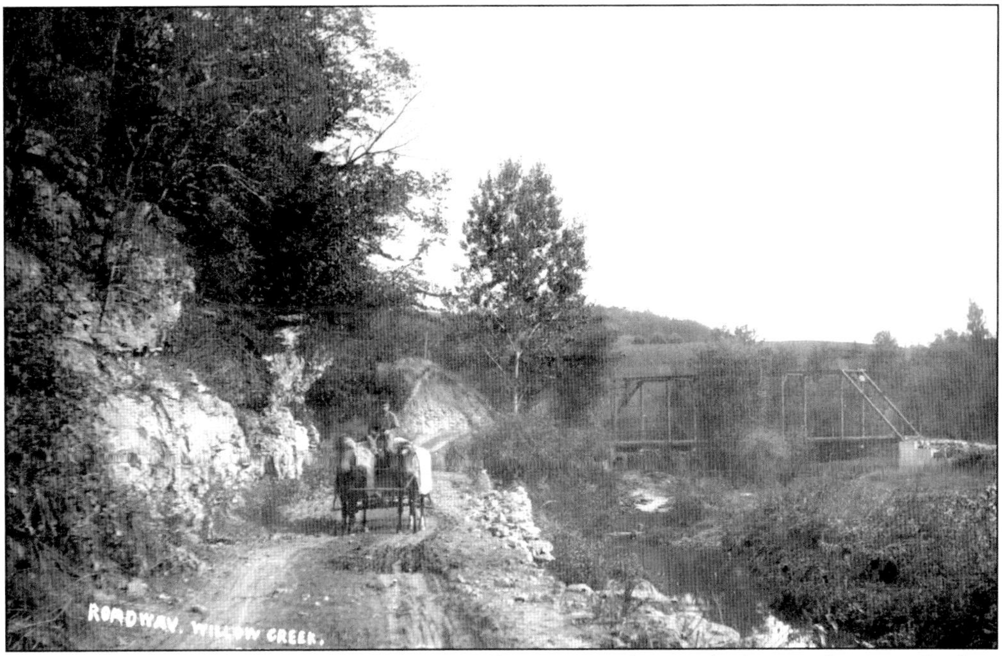


Carimona, the township bordering Preston to the west, was known for having the "most bridges and most difficult roads to keep in repair of any town in the county," according to a newspaper article in 1912. Here a team and wagon makes its way along the bluff by the Willow Creek Bridge less than a mile from town.

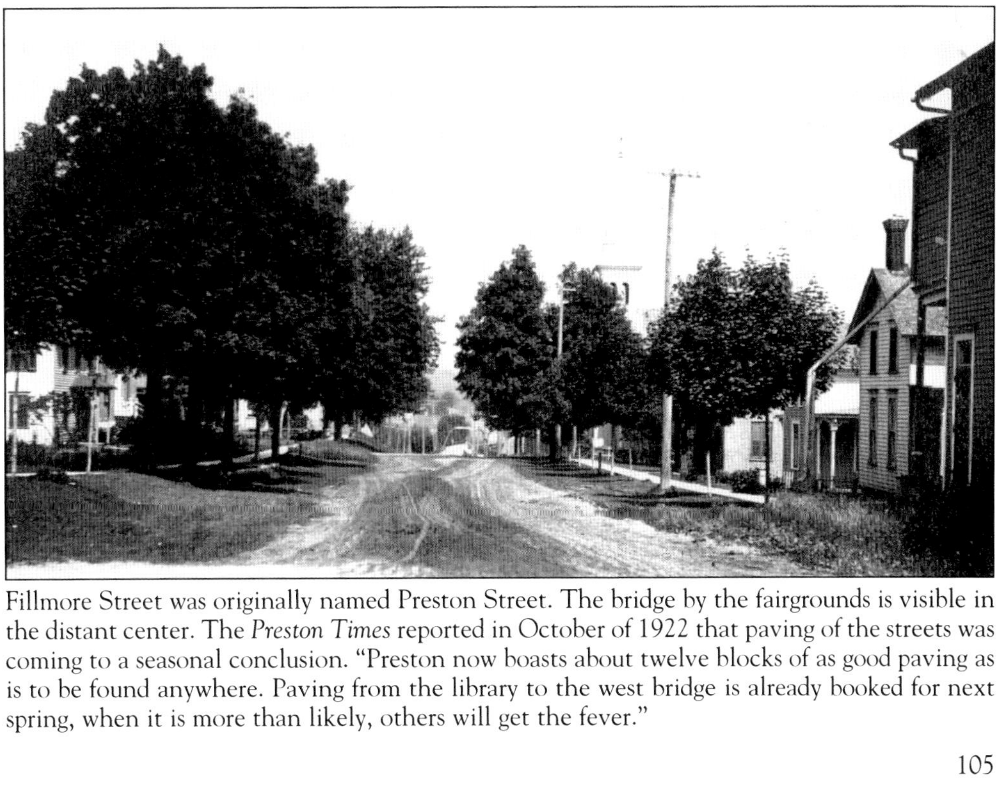

Fillmore Street was originally named Preston Street. The bridge by the fairgrounds is visible in the distant center. The *Preston Times* reported in October of 1922 that paving of the streets was coming to a seasonal conclusion. "Preston now boasts about twelve blocks of as good paving as is to be found anywhere. Paving from the library to the west bridge is already booked for next spring, when it is more than likely, others will get the fever."

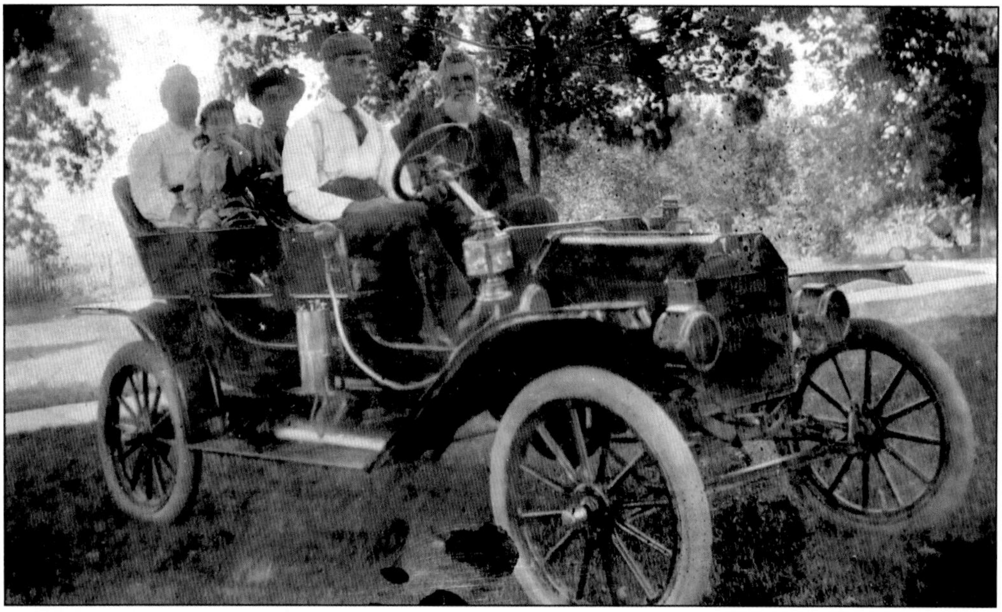

Here, the aged Civil War veteran Jerome Utley of Preston gets a ride in a "horseless carriage" around 1912. Charles Utley is behind the wheel and in the back are George and Louisa Utley with an unidentified child. Jerome Utley (1835–1928) homesteaded near Carimona in the late 1850s. He enlisted in the Second Minnesota Volunteer Infantry in 1864 and served until the close of the war the following year. He was a Fillmore County Commissioner for six years and was president of the Fair Board for many more years.

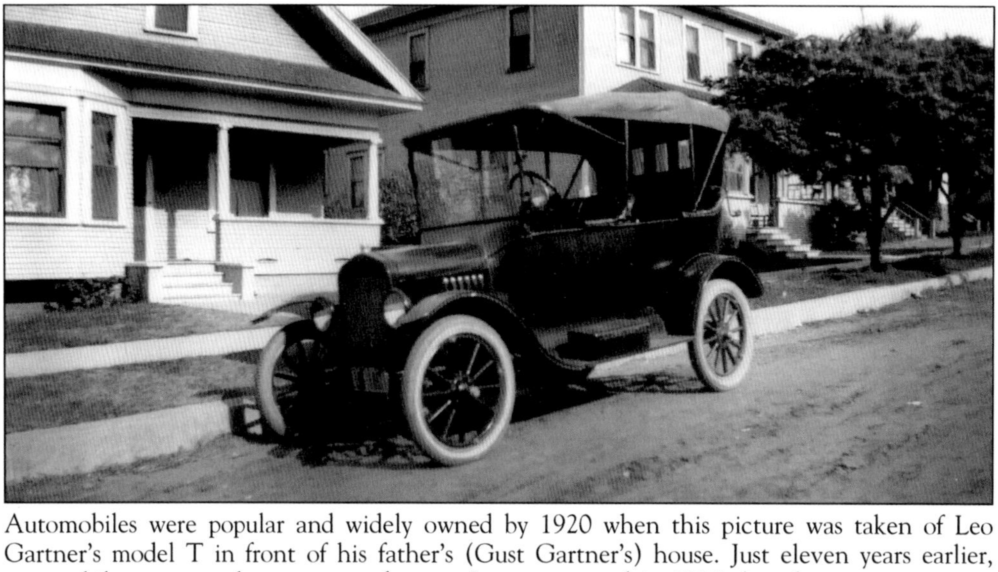

Automobiles were popular and widely owned by 1920 when this picture was taken of Leo Gartner's model T in front of his father's (Gust Gartner's) house. Just eleven years earlier, automobiles were rarely seen around town. It was reported in 1909 that there were just two automobiles owners in Preston. After a "joy ride" that same year "into the Greenleafton country, one of Fillmore County's favored spots," the editor of the *Preston Times* was overwhelmed with "auto fever." "Did you ever ride in a swiftly moving powerful automobile on a beautiful June day, literally annihilating distance and drinking in the beauties of nature as you viewed the fast moving scenery continually unfolded before you? A train ride seems tame by comparison."

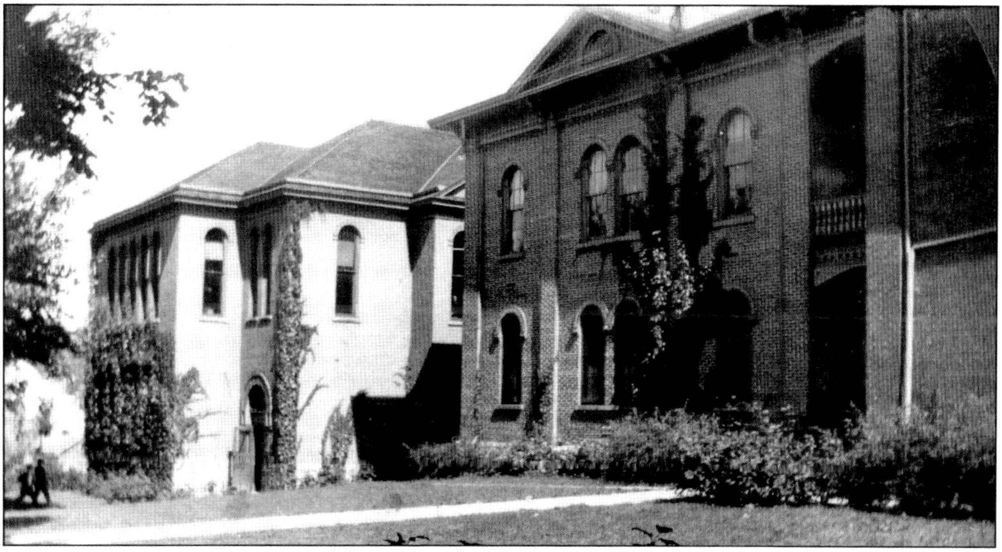

Preston's first school was a log house built on Main Street in 1856. A larger grade school building was built on Pleasant Street in 1868 at a cost of $10,000. By 1895, an addition with assembly hall, office and laboratory were added. There were eight teachers for the 12 grades. In 1901, a new high school was erected north of the grade school building at a cost of $13,500. The total enrollment at that time was 409, with 51 high school students.

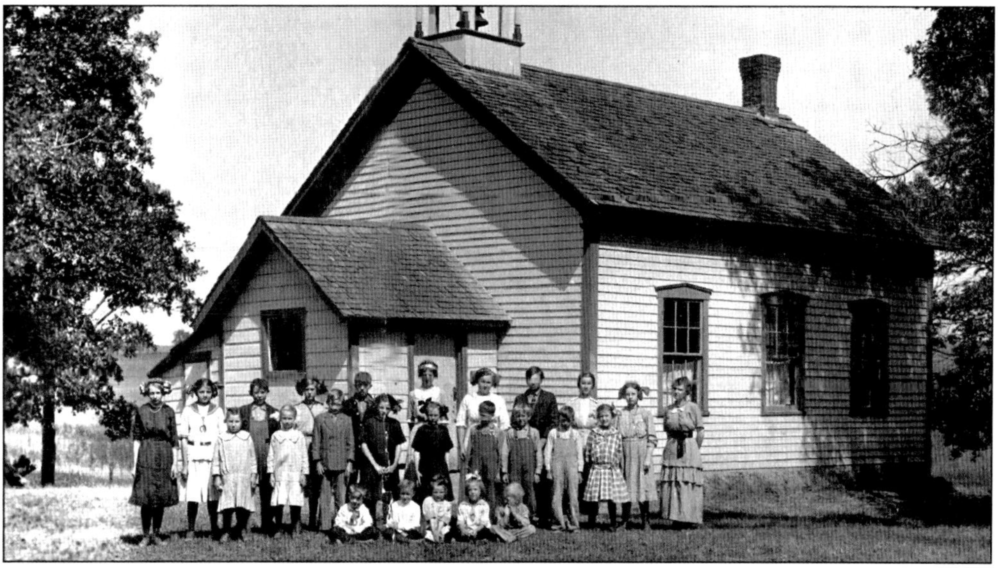

Children in the rural areas typically went to one-room country schools for the first eight grades. After eighth grade, many of the boys began farming, in effect ending their formal educations. Others and most of the girls would find a room with board in Preston while they attended high school. The Flying Cloud School, pictured above in 1917, was located 11 miles southwest of Preston near Greenleafton. From left to right are the following: (front row) Winton Gluen, Meril Vrieze, unidentified, Evangeline Grooters, and unidentified; (second row) Rachel Leutink, LaVina Ruesink, Earl Ruesink, Mary Crowe, Margaret Crowe, Ervin Dornink, Joel Miller, unidentified, Zella Vanderbie, and unidentified; (back row) Alice Miller, Laurena Gluen, Howard Miller, Dena Prinsen, Ernest Wubbels, Pearl Dornink, and Martha Roberta Parry (teacher).

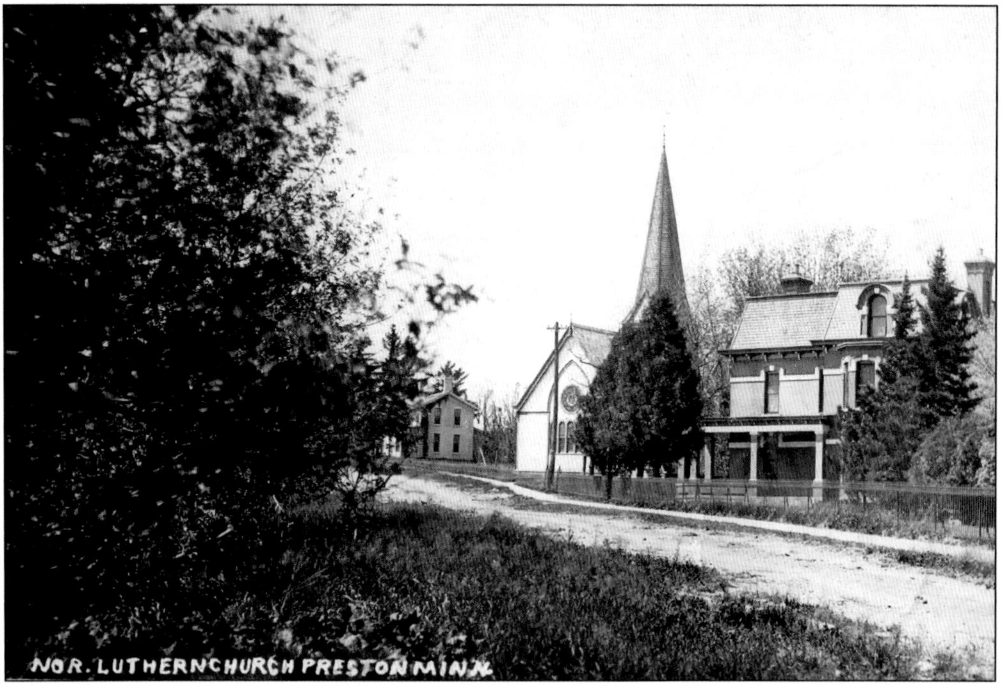


When this church was built in 1895 it was called St. Paul's Norwegian Lutheran Church due to its many Norwegian members. Church services were held in both English and Norwegian, until 1916, when the members voted to make English the official language. The church was then known as St. Paul's English Lutheran Church. Many people called it St. Paul's On-the-Hill to avoid confusion with the town's other Lutheran church, which was named St. Paul's German Lutheran Church. In 1949, the congregation officially changed its name to Grace Lutheran Church.

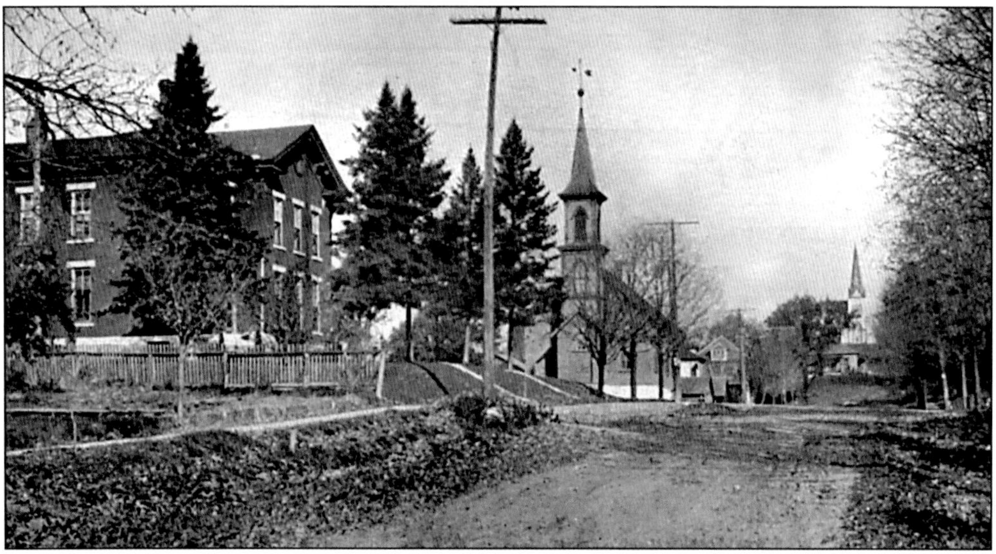

With the county jail on the left, the Evangelical United Brethren Church was located on the corner by the county jail. It was built in 1875 and for many years was called the Methodist Episcopal Church. The building was demolished in 1964, due to the merging of the E.U.B. congregation with the First Methodist Church of Preston.

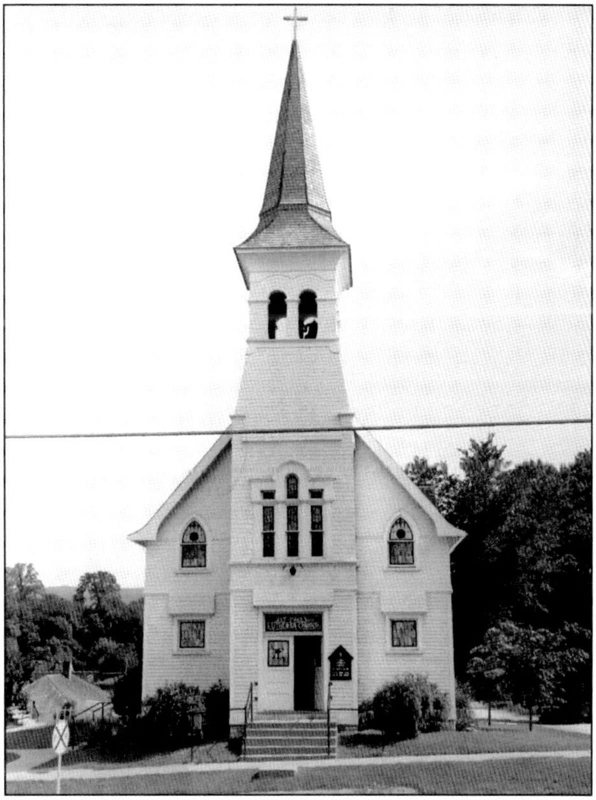

While noting that Preston was "sadly deficient of places of worship," the *Preston Republican* declared in an 1865 editorial that "if it were true that church buildings and civilization go together, the people of Preston might be considered as being in at least a semi-barbarous condition." At the time several efforts had been made to build churches but only the German Evangelical Society had a "small but neat church." The other denominations that existed met in the schoolhouse and after the courthouse was built, they occasionally met there. Pictured above is the St. Paul's German Lutheran Church, which was built in 1873. The lower picture shows the interior of the church as it appeared in 1923 when the congregation celebrated its 50th Golden Jubilee. In 1873, the church started with 14 charter members. It was reported that in 1923 the congregation consisted of "90 homes, 250 communicants and 325 souls." In 1958 the two Lutheran churches in town merged to form the Christ Lutheran Church.

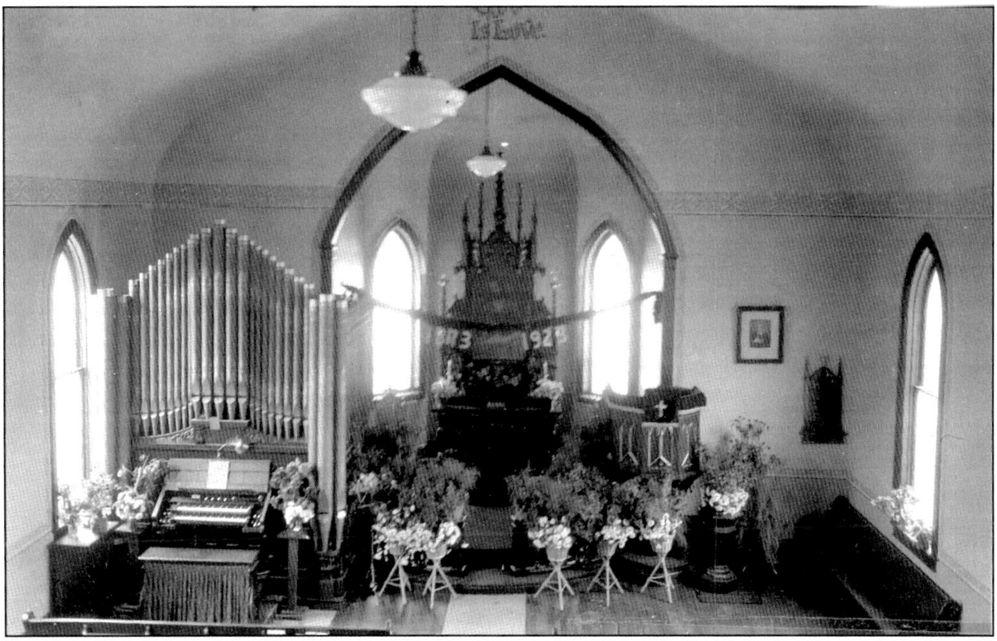

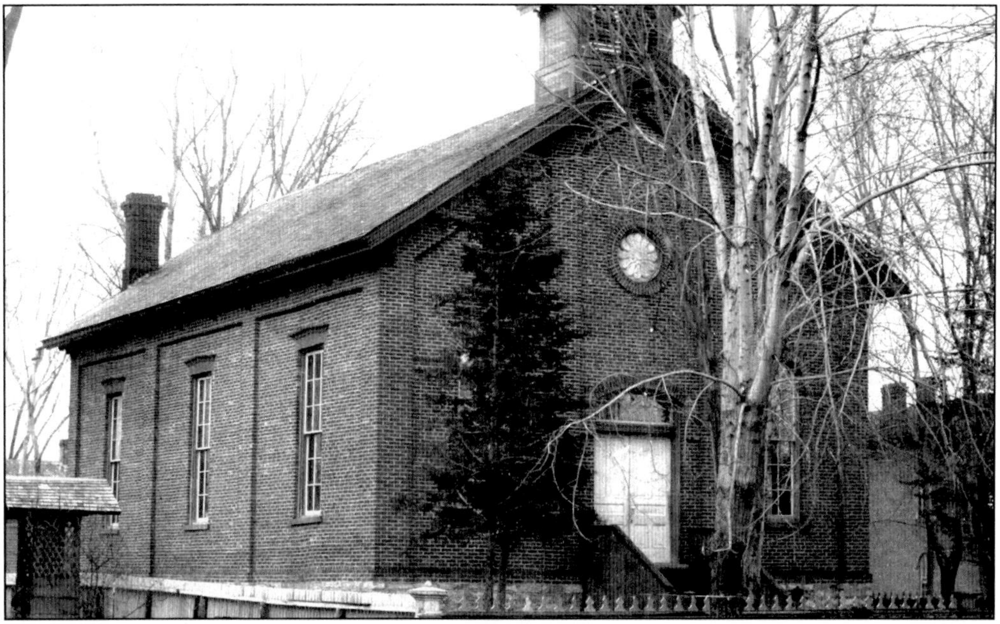

This is a photo of the Presbyterian Church, built in 1868 on the southeast corner of Pleasant and Fillmore streets. Church operations ceased around the 1950s. The basement was then used as a lunchroom for the nearby elementary school. Chuck Knies later used it for his aluminum window business, before the building was demolished.

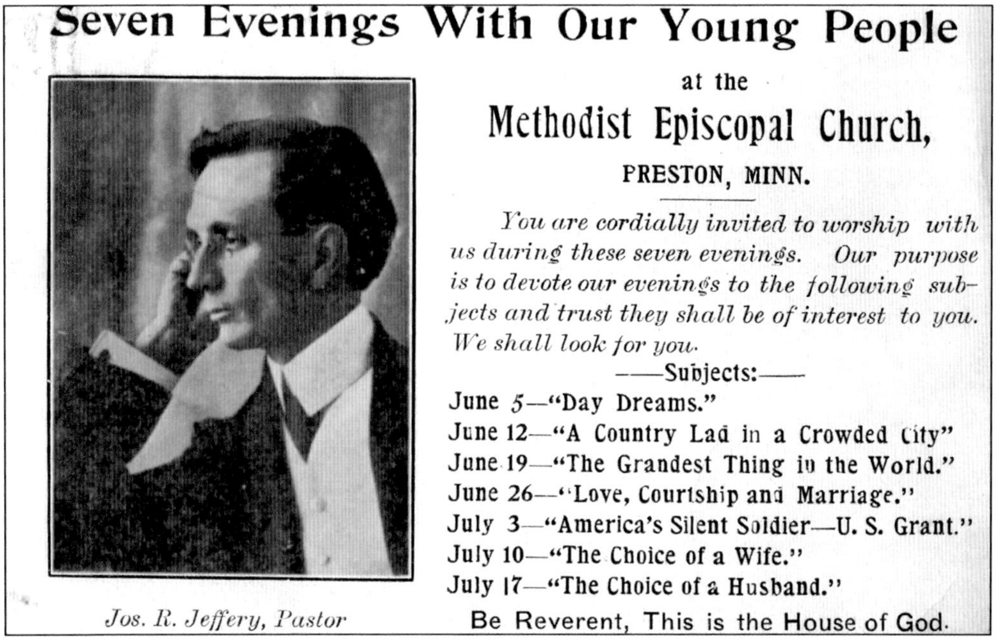


As always, the parents of Preston were concerned for the correct and appropriate behavior of their children. With that in mind, Reverend Joseph Jeffery of the Methodist Episcopal Church (he served in Preston the years 1909–1910) organized a series of special sermons dealing with issues of the day. A local newspaper reported around that time that, "There are signs of improvement among some of the young people of Preston. They do not fish, hunt, or play ball on Sunday."

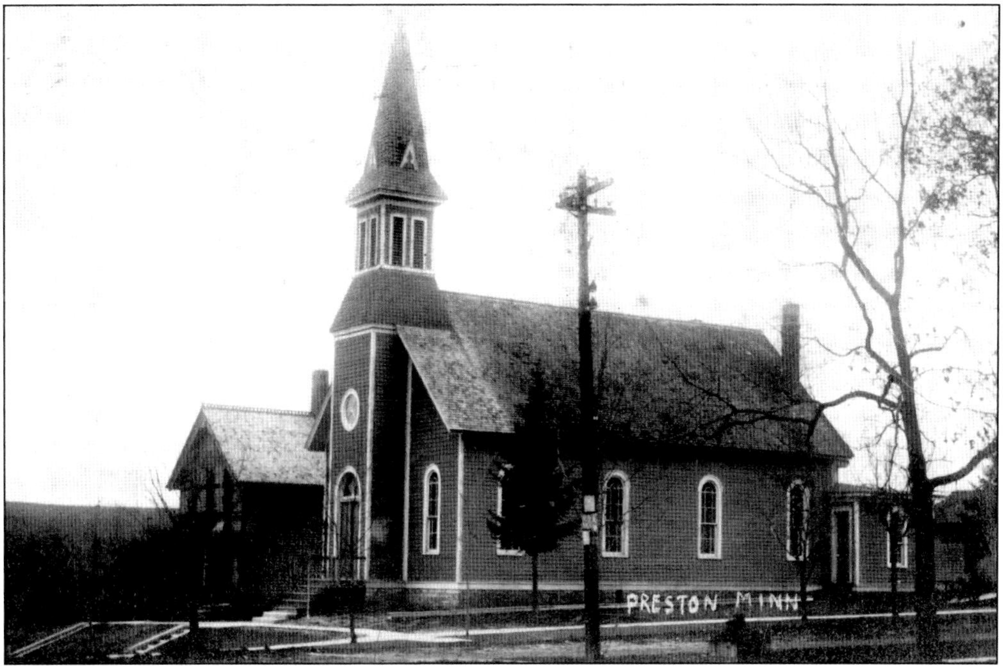


The first Catholic service in Preston was held in the J. O'Brien home in 1857. St. Joseph's Catholic Church, shown above, was completed in 1878 at a cost of $2,000. There were 10 church members at the time. A new church was built on the same site as this one in 1929 at a cost of $35,000. It was named St. Columban's Catholic Church and still bears that name today.

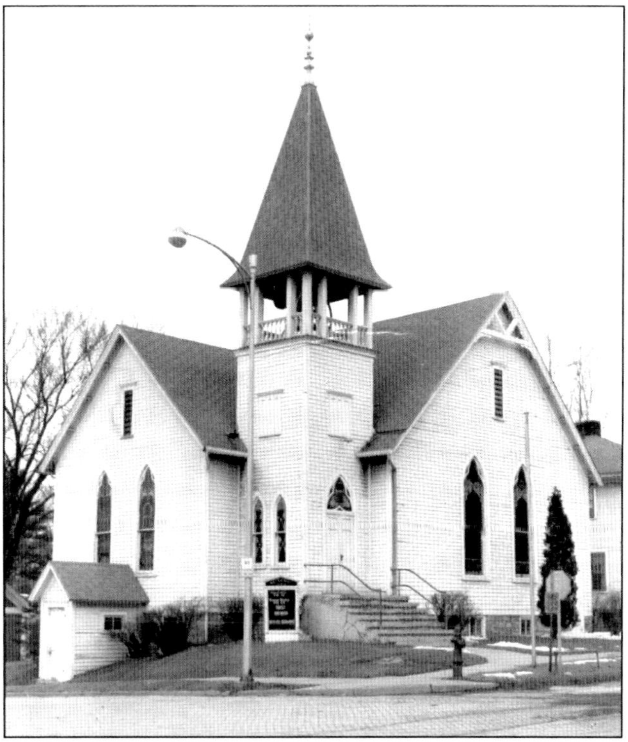

The Methodist congregation in Preston met in a refitted brick school house for nearly thirty years before building this church on the northwest corner of Fillmore and St. Paul Streets (the present location of the Rustad Building). The church as built at a cost of $1,627, not counting the windows, and it was dedicated on May 5, 1895 with over 500 people in attendance. The church building was in use until the new United Methodist Church was built in 1967.

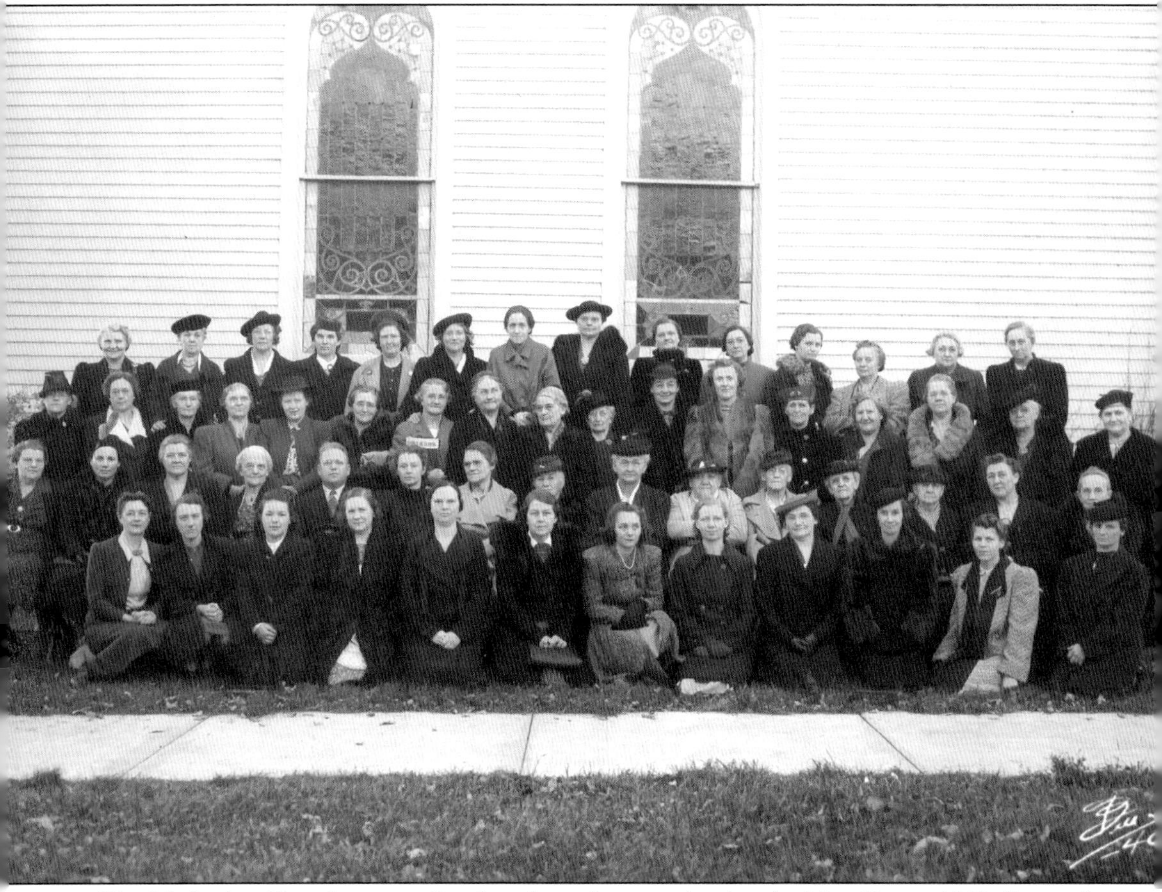

The Methodist Church women lined up for a photograph taken by Matt Bue in 1940. Pictured from left to right are as follows: (front row) Mesdames E. Love, R. Sutton, A. Ashton, A. Stegner, C. Cutler, M.R. Anderson, V. Moss, F. Ashton, J.G. Dean, L. Richards, J. Webster, and W.E. Neuman; (second row) Mesdames J.D. Utley, C. Michener, F Lindsay, Rev. and Mrs. Tannehill, J. Hahn, F. Sutton, C.J. Spies, and G. Dovenberg; (third row) Mesdames E. Klein, D. Wimmer, H. Engle, A.M. Levy, G. Simpson, Miss Hannah Hutton, C. Utley, P. Wilson, Miss Laura Read , Miss Mildred Chalfant, C. Lewis, G. Martz, R. Thacher, H. Miller, B.F. Fowler, E. Gaser, and H. Long; (back row) Mesdames Wm. Confare, J. Bixby, E. Reitz, R Barnes, W. Ferrian, E. Cummings, T. Hahn, A. Vatthauer, F. Pickett, J. Forthun, C. Maust, L. Berry, C. Barnes, and Wm. Holton.

# *Eight*
# THE 1930S AND ON

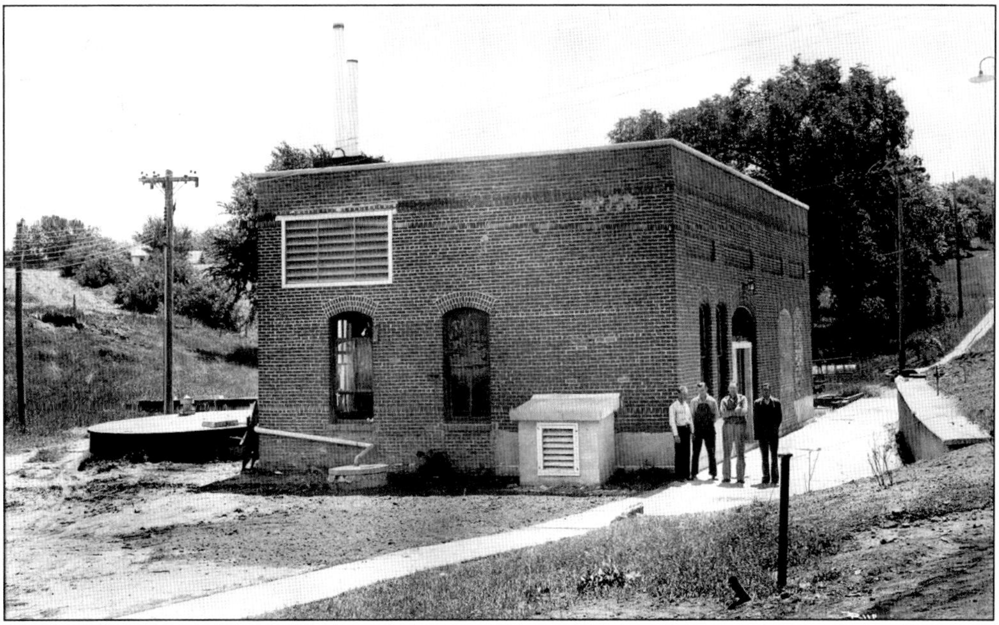

New equipment was installed in the Municipal Power Plant in 1935. Since 1915, Preston had received its electricity from the Brightdale Power Plant on the north branch of the Root River near Lanesboro and this building had served as a distribution center. The city council determined that they wanted Preston to generate its own electricity and the distribution system was replaced with two Fairbanks-Morse diesel engines. One had the delivery capacity of 150 horsepower or 97 kilowatts; the other a capacity of 300 horsepower or 200 kilowatts. Pictured from left are Plant Superintendent F.H. Stebbins and operators Howard Magdlin, Guy Perceuq, and Carrol Kaump.

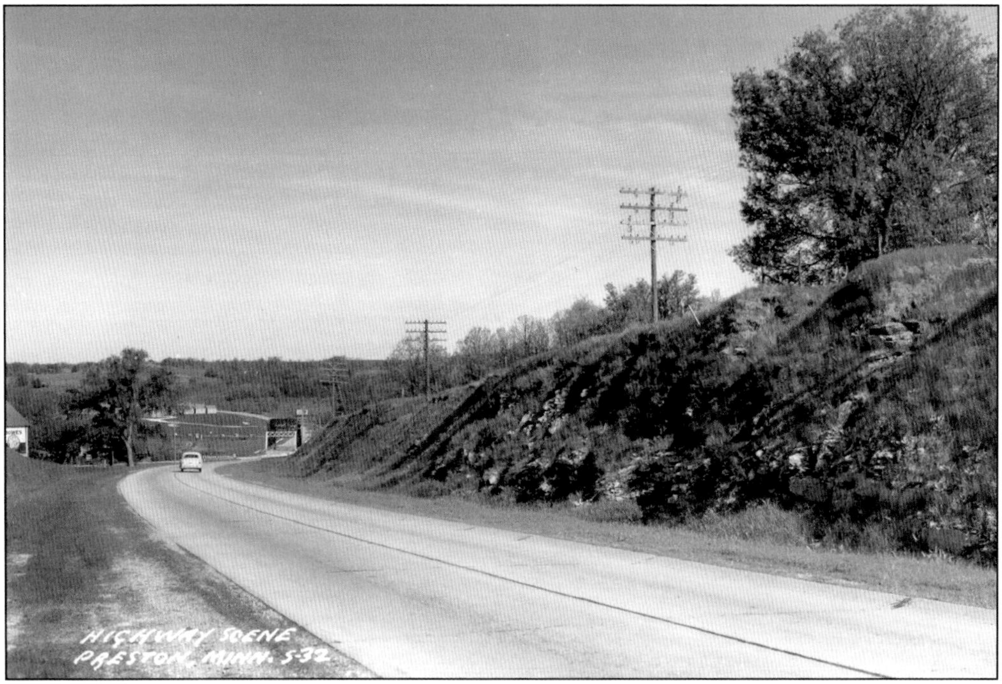


In September of 1932, the paving from Chatfield to Fountain and Preston and on south to Prosper was completed. There was now an all-paved route from the Twin Cities to Chicago and it went right through Preston. In pioneer days, this route was known as the Dubuque Trail. A huge celebration was held in Prosper, on the Minnesota/Iowa border, where a granite marker was placed. The improvements, as well as other road projects throughout the state, were made possible by a $20 million bond issue, authorized by the state legislature.

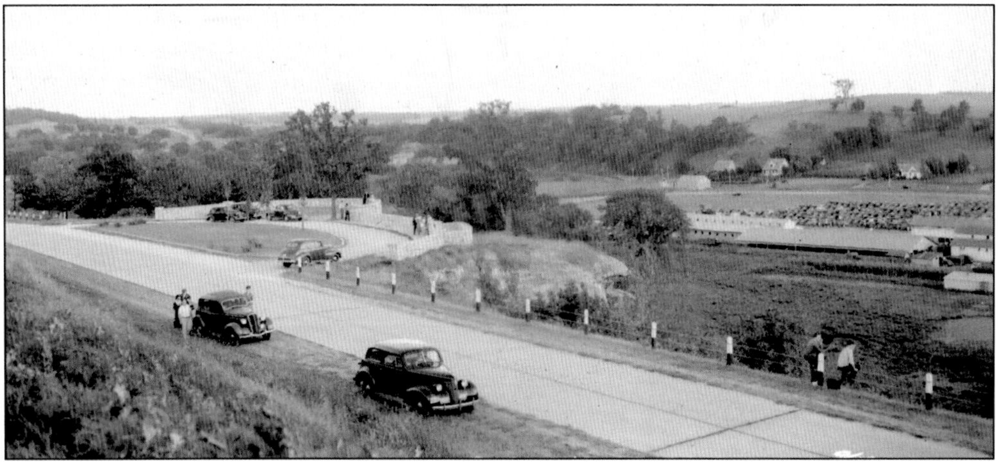

The Civilian Conservation Corps (CCC) was established by President Franklin Delano Roosevelt in 1933 during the Great Depression. Its stated purposes were to reduce unemployment and to preserve the nation's natural resources. One of the local projects assigned to the CCC was the construction of the Preston Overlook during the years 1937–1938. The overlook provided long views of the Root River Valley, the Fillmore County Fairgrounds, the town of Preston, and the hills and farmland to the south. The wall was built of random rubble gray or buff-colored limestone on a stone footing.

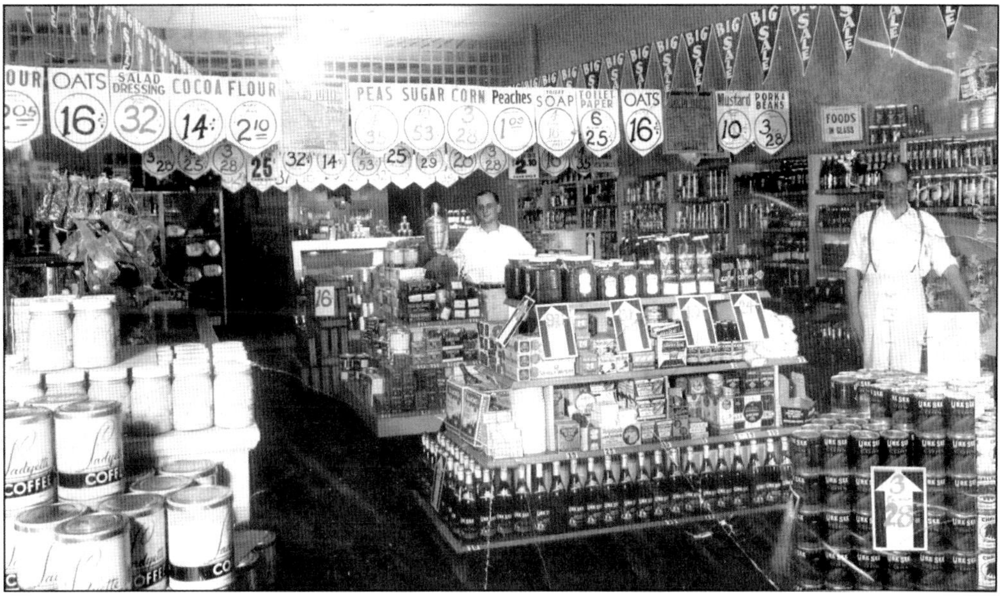


Pictured are Howard Gartner (left) and Leo Gartner (right) in 1937 shortly after they moved into their new store, which they named the Gartner Cash Store. Their father, Gust, first started in the grocery business along the same street in 1889. The first gasoline pump in Preston was out front of the Gartner Mercantile Store.

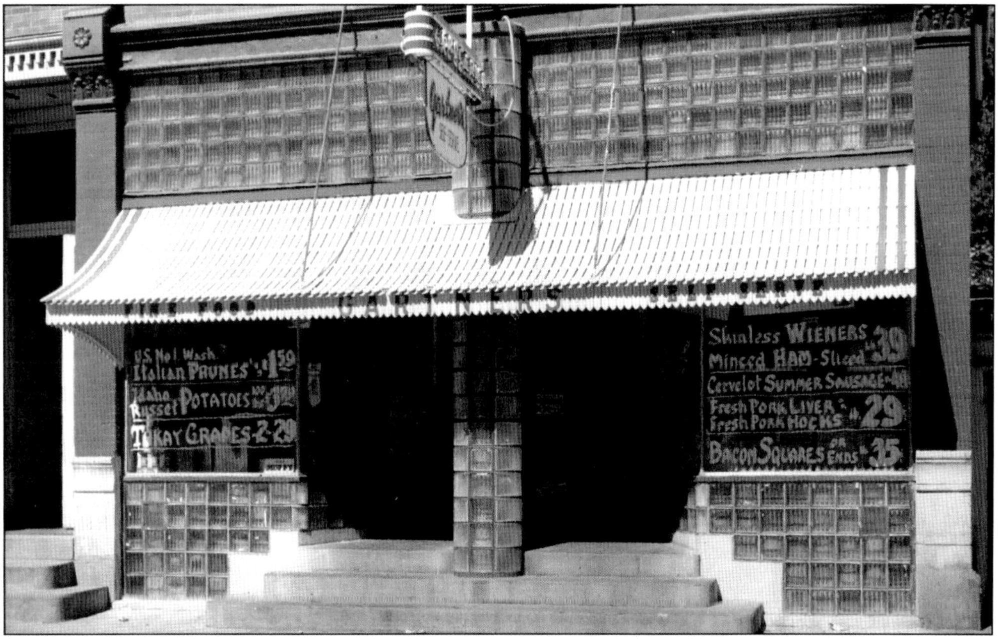


This is the front of the Gartner Cash Store when it opened in the newly remodeled Harold Hopp building in 1937. The use of glass brick, then an innovation in modern storefronts, had brought nationwide publicity in grocery trade magazines. Harold Hopp, a former Preston boy, was an executive during the 1930s of the Owens-Illinois Glass Company, which manufactured the bricks. This same building housed the Victory Café for many years after the Gartners moved their grocery business into the building to the east.

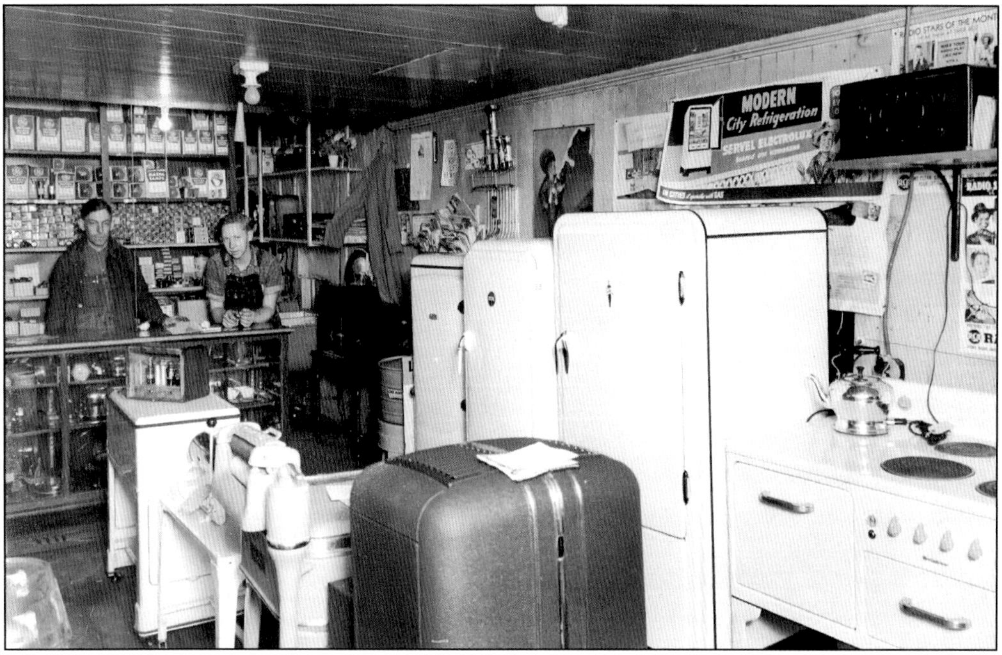


Duxbury Electric opened in 1931, renting a room next to the Rosvold barbershop on Main Street. This business handled new and old motors, electric appliances of all sorts, washing machines, refrigerators, and radios. Pictured from left are Lee Duxbury and Floyd Scheevel. Floyd recalls that his Uncle Lee paid him $2 a week, plus room and board.

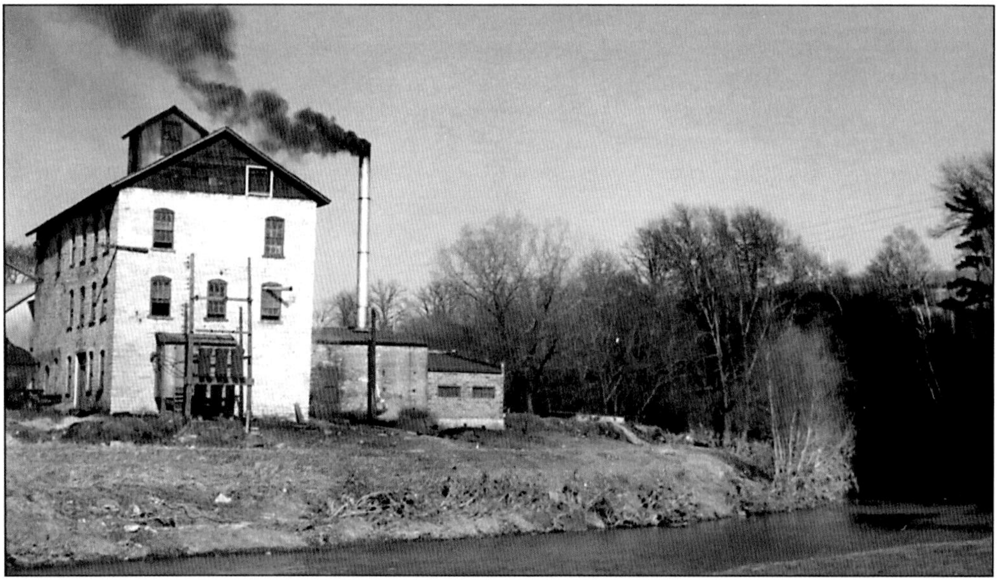

By the 1940s, the old Kaercher Mill was still operating using diesel power. Owner Herb Spies served as Preston's mayor from 1931–1945 and then again from 1948–1951. Spies liked to tell farmers that he packaged everything but the noise in his feed manufacturing plant in Preston. Spies also converted corncobs, which had always been considered a waste product, into poultry litter. Another business venture Spies was involved in was a chicken hatchery that produced 80,000 chicks every year.

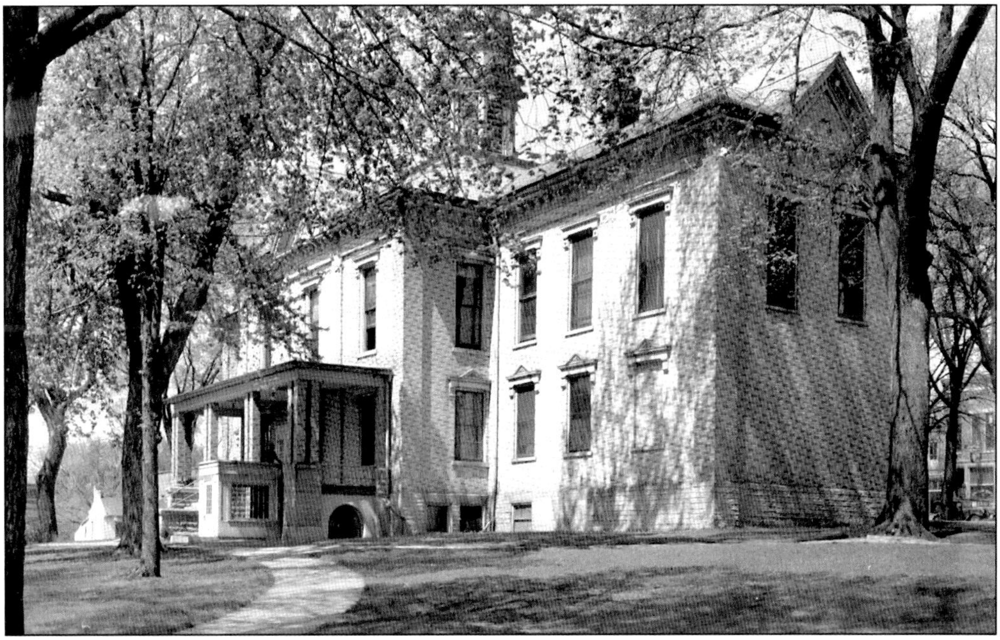

This shows the stately old courthouse in the early 1940s which once again served as the headquarters of the Fillmore County Draft Board. In the picture below, taken in March of 1943, a group of draftees line up just before they were bussed to Fort Snelling in Minneapolis for examinations and physicals. According to the "Service Record book of Men and Women of Preston and Vicinity" sponsored by the V.F.W. Auxiliary, nine Preston area men died during the World War II. They were: Joseph Berland, Michael Doherty Jr., William Drogemuller, Raymond Halsey, Lloyd Magdlin, Richard Numedahl, Robert Reishus, Aubrey Serfling, and Milo Stevens.

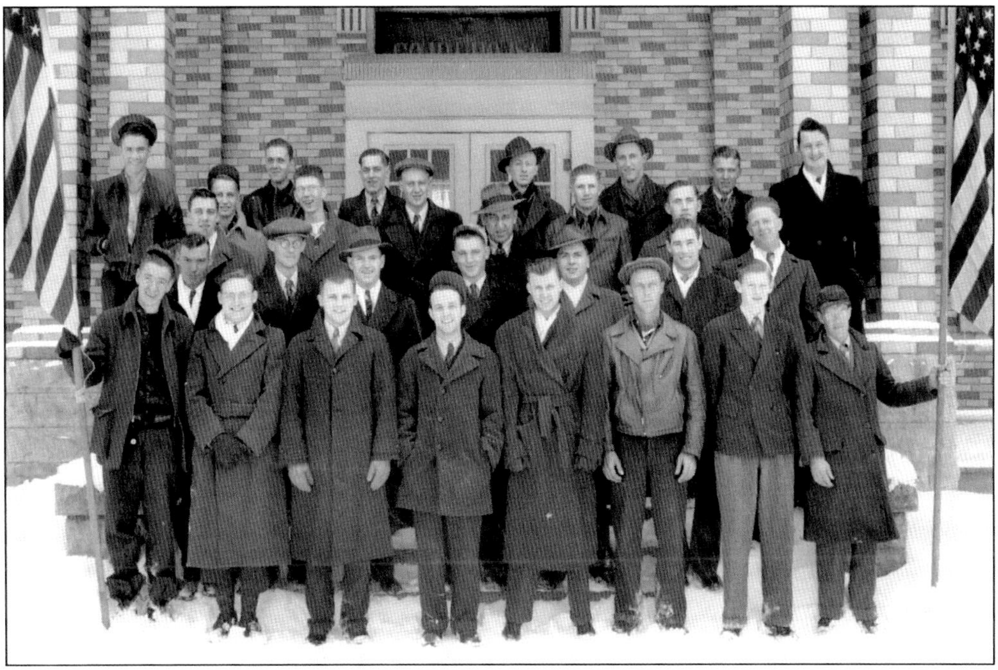

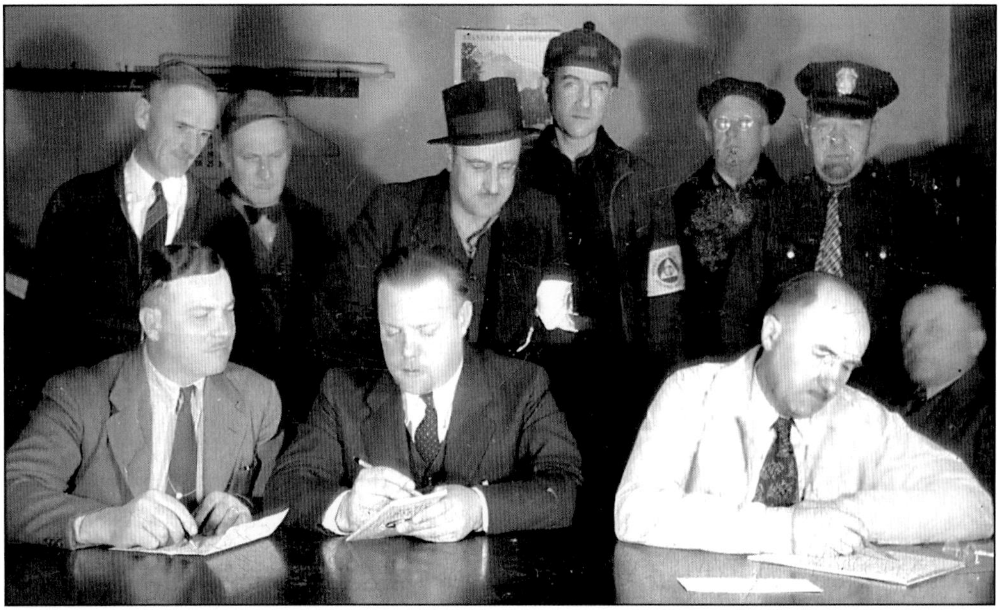

In May of 1941, President Franklin Roosevelt described America as being in "a state of unlimited emergency" and advised each city to organize its own Civil Defense System to plan and prepare for the dangers looming on the horizon. After Japan's attack on Pearl Harbor later that year, the concept of Civil Defense took on a new reality. Preston's Civil Defense officials during the mid-1940s were, from left to right (front row) Bill Heitner, Doc Nehring, and Jay Lough; (back row) Tim Grebin, Walt Dreier, George Soffa, Wils Garratt, unidentified, Ed Vischer, and unidentified.

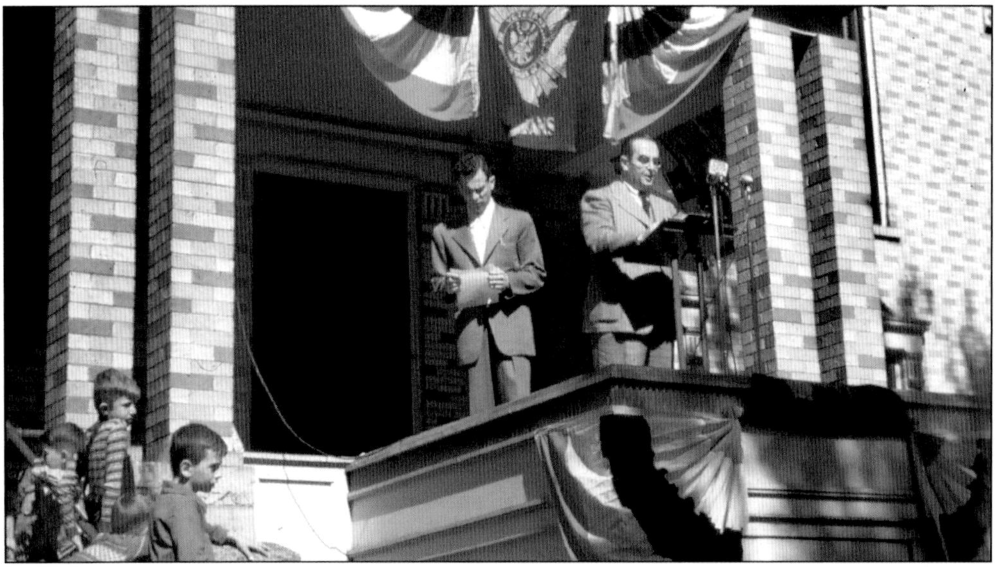

Cedric Adams (1902–1961) was said to have the best-known voice in the Upper Midwest. From 1934 until his death in 1961, he was a fixture on WCCO radio. He did 20 radio shows each week, including the noontime news. He also wrote a daily newspaper column for many years. Here he is shown giving a talk from the south courthouse porch in Preston during a town celebration in 1948.

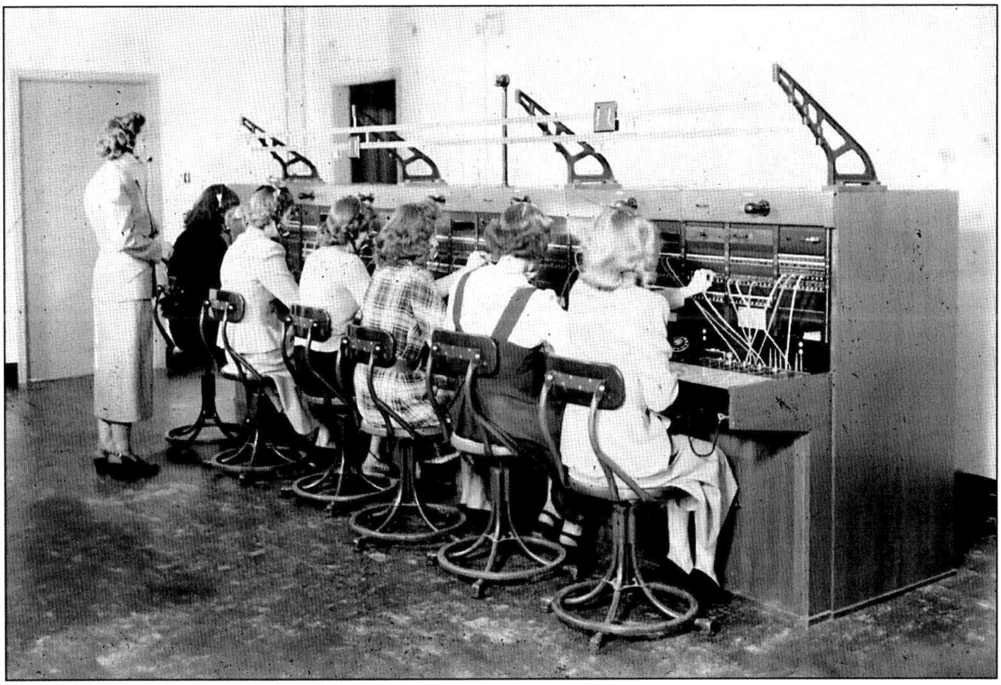

Pictured are six operators at the new Northwestern Bell building while chief operator, Margaret McDonough, looks on. The facility was built in 1949 at a cost of approximately $185,000, when Preston was converted to a new dial telephone system service. The Preston operators handled long-distance calls and provided other assistance such as telephone number information, repair service, and the like.

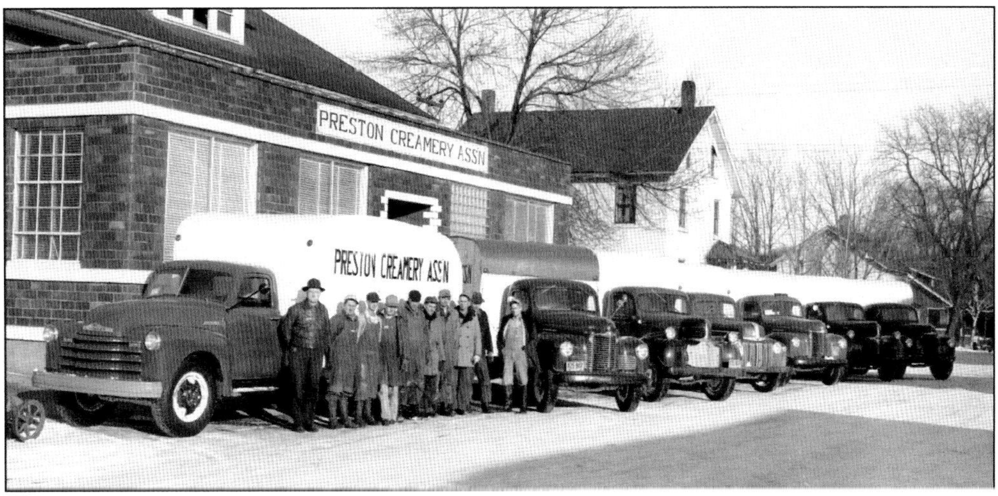


The Preston Creamery Association was organized in 1910 by 57 Preston-area farmers. They bought an existing creamery located near the fairgrounds, which had had been run by A.G. Olson. After a devastating fire in 1924, the creamery moved to its present location on River Street. This photo, showing a lineup of employees and trucks, was taken in 1948. Pictured from left to right are Ed Van Sande (secretary), Francis Shanahan, Vernon Shanahan, Vincent Shanahan, Fowler Stevens, Ronald Thacher, Jerome Simonson, Max Cutler, Paul Miller, and Chester Maust (manager-buttermaker).

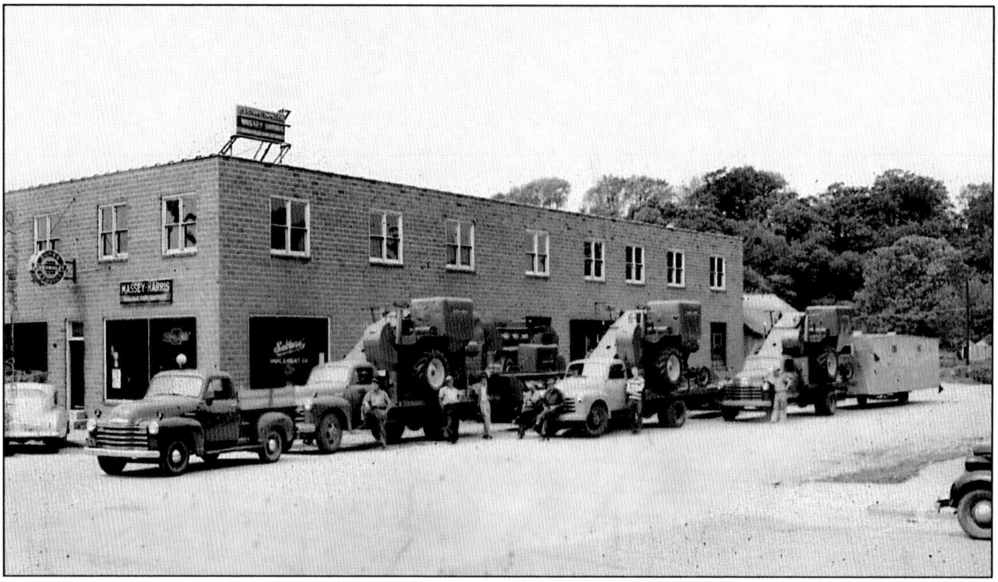


Loaded on trucks and ready to head south for the summer wheat harvest are three No. 27 Massey-Harris 14-foot cut self-propelled combines. Sold by the Sethre Implement Company of Preston for $5,000 a piece, they were purchased by Jack Adams of Predmore and Joe L. Kennedy of Rochester. The caravan left Preston on June, 15, 1950, headed for Altus, Oklahoma. The plan was for the three machines to start harvesting in the Oklahoma wheat fields, then travel over to the Texas panhandle before heading north through Kansas, Nebraska, and the Dakotas.

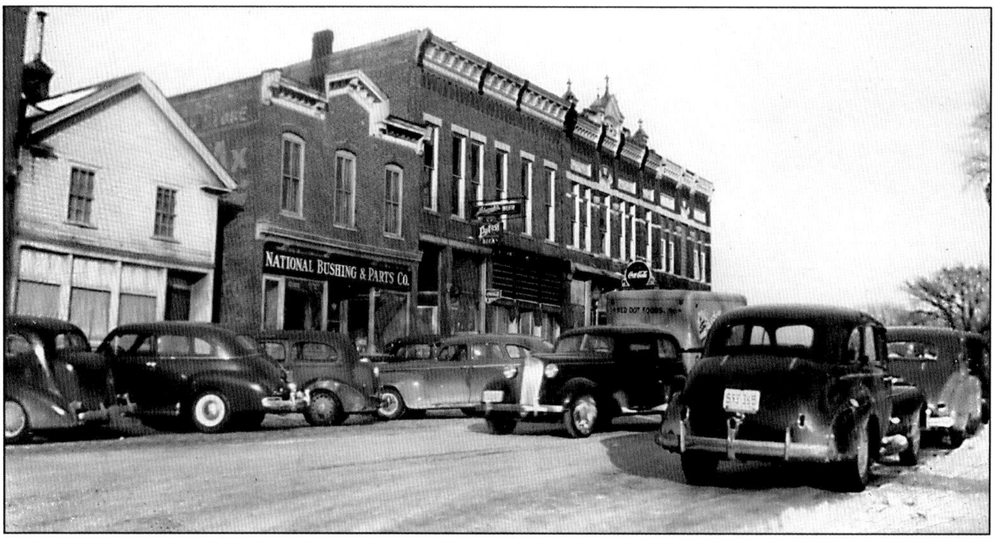


By March of 1949, the Grand Opera House disappeared from the Preston scene when it was converted into two apartments. The Grand Opera House was located on the second floor of the Gartner Building (just above the Coca-Cola sign in this photograph from the late 1940s). News Editor Lud Gartner recalled the days of glory of the Opera House in the *Preston Republican*: "Many were the road shows, traveling movies, musical attractions, home talent plays, political meetings, athletic events, commencements, class plays, wrestling matches and other dances galore held there. I can vividly remember seeing my first moving picture show there, the never to be forgotten. 'Birth of a Nation': What an impression it made!"

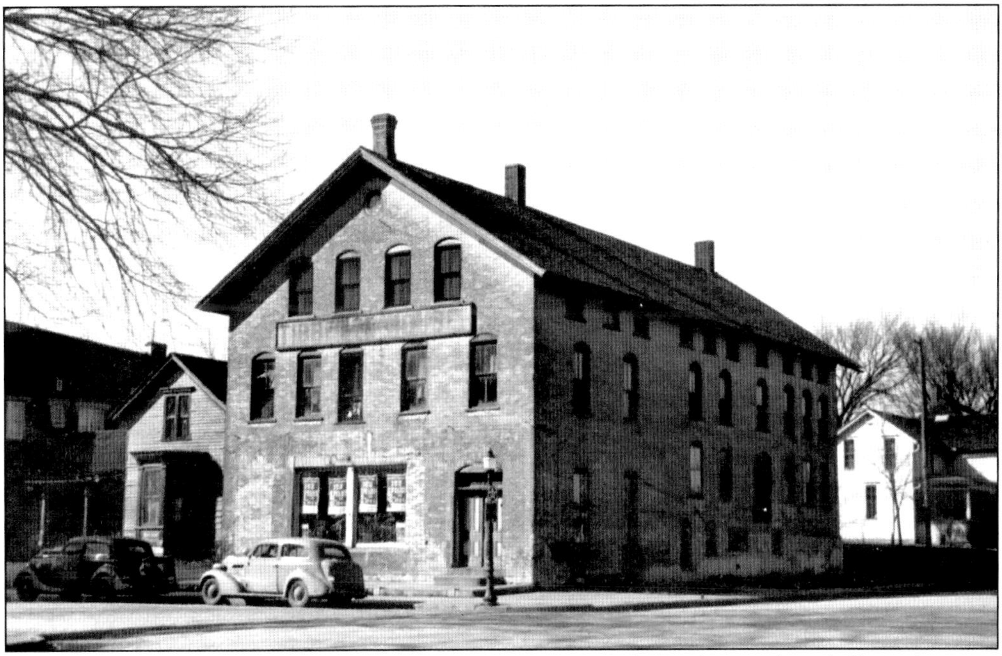

By the mid-1940s, the venerable old Tibbetts building was ready for the wrecking ball. At the time, the building was owned by Dr. Wendell Grinnell, who had once planned to turn the hotel into a hospital. Though his dream was never entirely realized, he did keep an office in the house just to the west of the Tibbetts building. Grinnell practiced medicine for 54 years in Preston. In 1946 he sold the building to a Minneapolis salvage company for demolition and later sold its furnishings at auction, which included over 40 bed and dresser sets, tables, chairs, mirrors, and lobby furniture.

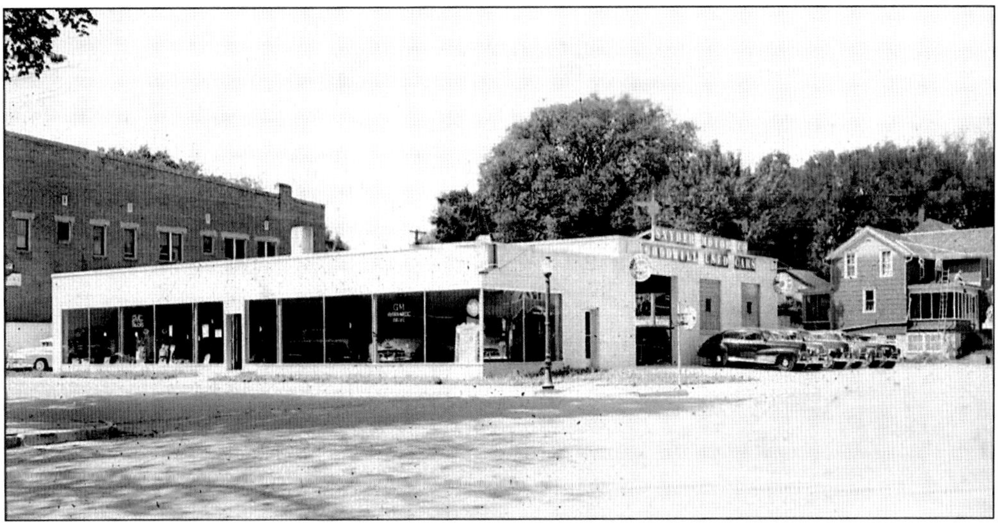

The Snyder Motor Company, representing Pontiac and Cadillac cars, built their garage on the site of the old Tibbetts House. The building was constructed of cement blocks and measured 80 by 80 feet. "The new building will be a beauty and will do an awful lot toward improving the appearance of Preston's business district," the *Preston Republican* wrote in 1950. The Snyder Motor Company would vacate the building in 1957, selling it to Howard and Leo Gartner, who, after extensive remodeling, opened it as the Gartner Brothers Foodland.

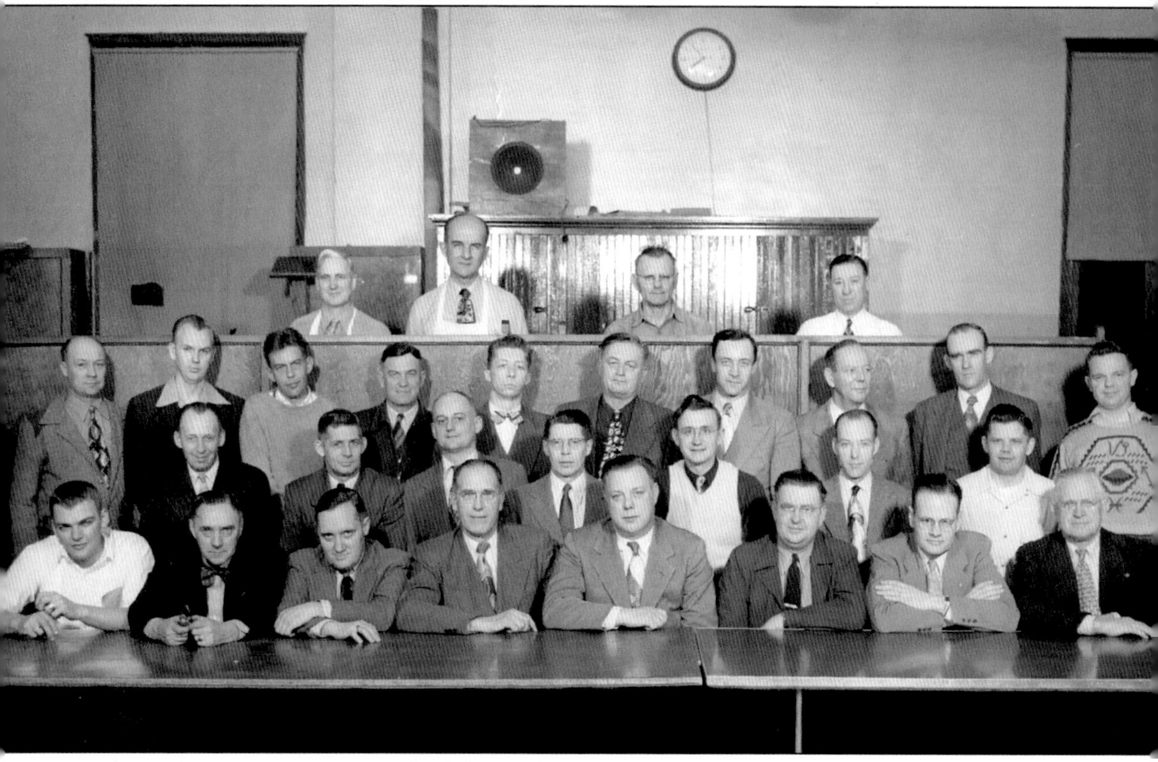

The 1950 Preston Commercial Club posed for a photo in the Town Hall. Pictured from left to right are the following: (front row) Mickey Myers, Porter Remington, Dean McKnight, Walter Barlow, Dr. J.P. Nehring, Paul Berges, Rev. Richard Vordale, and John A. Johnson; (second row) Art Schibursky, Chester Maust, Howard Gartner, Phil Gartner, Buster Heitner, unidentified, and Byron Ingvalson; (third row) unidentified, Ken Kline, Herman Ebert, Bill Heitner, Elmer DeVries, Kelly Tessum, unidentified, Pete Gilbertson, Judge Joseph Murray, and Bob Keehn; (fourth row) Doc Quanrud, Wils Garratt, Lyle Austin, and Russ Sutton.

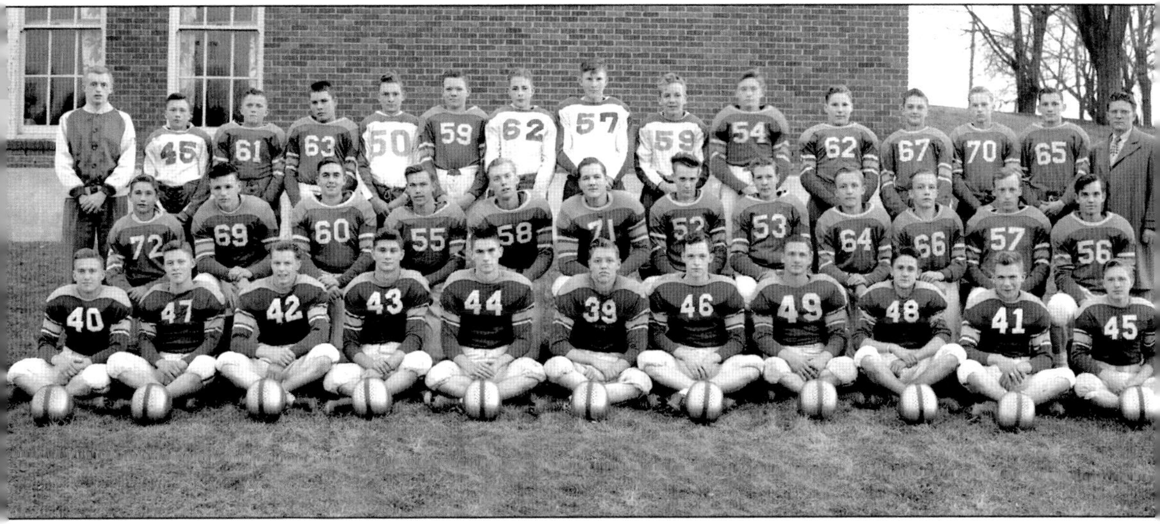

For many, Preston's most memorable football team is undoubtedly the 1950 team. The Blue Jays won all seven of their games by a wide margin. They racked up 308 points during the season and went unscored upon until the last quarter of the final game of the season. Co-captain and left halfback Buzz Meighen was the leading scorer in the entire state. His statistics included 22 touchdowns for a total of 132 points and he passed for five more touchdowns. He averaged 15 yards every time he carried the ball and averaged one touchdown every third time he carried the ball. Pictured from left to right are as follows. (front row) Clarence Quanrud, Arden Gillund, Richard Aug, Larry Hunt, Phil McElroy, Arden Madson, Buzz Meighen, Keith Krogstad, Jerry Grebin, Chuck Mandelko; (second row) Allen Mandelko, Bill Walsh, David Drury, Richard Cutler, Harold Strand, James Mathison, Chuck Strand, Wendell Anstett, Wiley Vrieze, Frank Riehl, Jerry Pickett; (back row) B. Hansen, (manager) ,Richard Hellickson, C. Jacobson, Glenn Ullom, Kenneth Hahn, Warren Madson, Bradley Schwieger, Richard Behnke, Richard Prinsen, Joe Walsh, Roger Eskra, Conrad Aug, Robert Michener, Coach Norman Larsen.

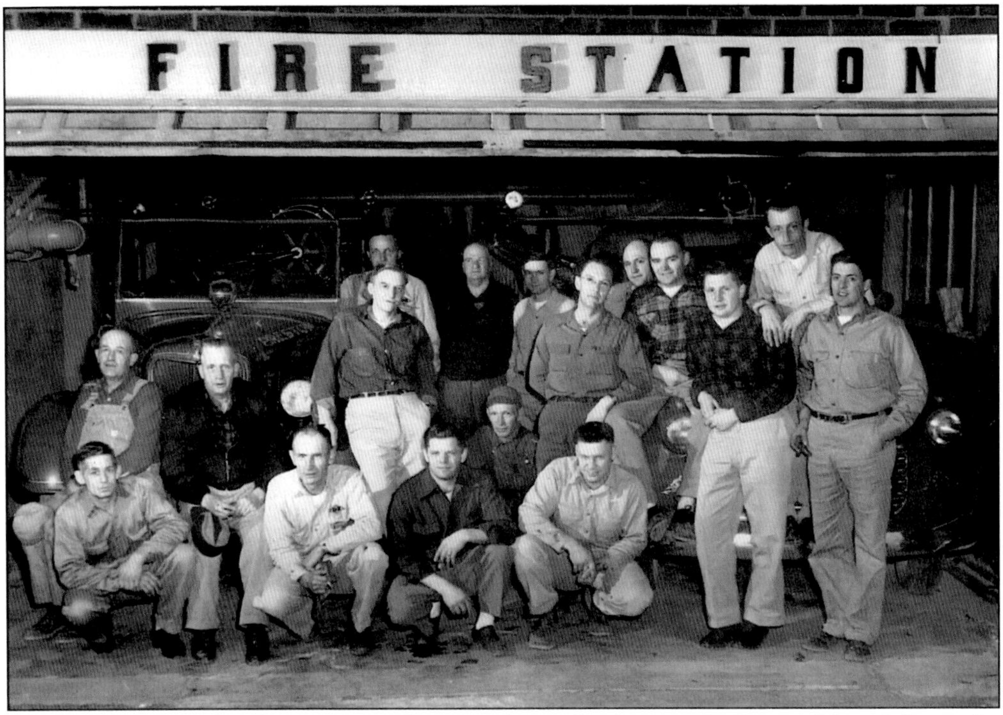


Preston's volunteer fire department is shown in this 1954 photograph. Pictured from left to right are the firefighters: (front row) Chester Maust, Walter Dreier, Byron Ingvalson, and Einar Jorgensen; (second row) Gus Gartner, Howard Miller, and Herman Dreier (kneeling); (third row) Norman Jorgensen, Russ Vischer, Lyle Simonson, Lyle Miller, Bud Bastian, and Robert Lyngen; (fourth row) Clarence Leutink, Ernie Schwartz, Bud Rathke, and Verle Vrieze.

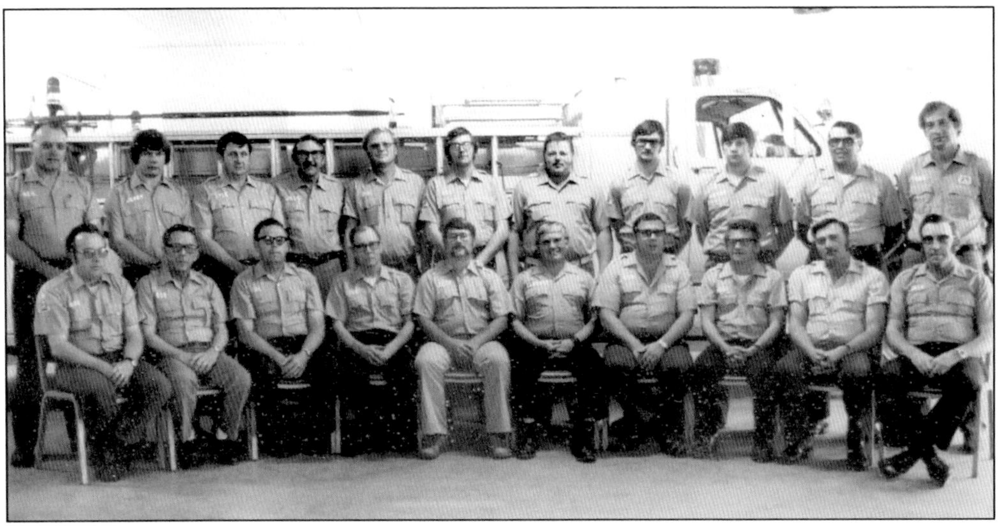

Twenty years later, the volunteer firemen of the 1970s sat for a group portrait. Pictured from left to right are as follows: (front row) Don Hagedorn, Robert Sethre, Al Christianson, Don Trende, Steve Trende, Clarence Quanrud, Vern Dahl, Robert Hanson, Richard Hellickson, and Loren Woellert; (back row) Neil Bremseth, Jerry Hampel, Lyle Miller, Willis Hampel, Phil Milne, Bob Benson, Larry Severson, Larry Ristau, Dawson Grabau, Lavern Knoepke, and Mike Gartner.

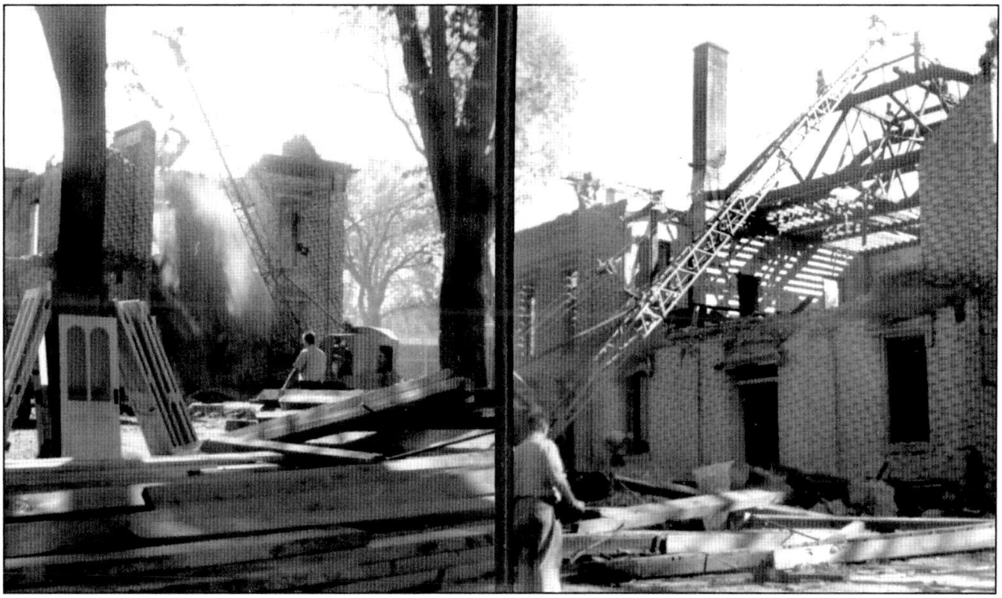

A special county election was held in February of 1956 on the proposal that Fillmore County issue a $250,000 bond for building a new county courthouse. The bond was issued, carried by a mere 90 votes with over 3,300 people voting. The old courthouse was not taken down until the south portion of the new courthouse was built, in order to allow county business to continue without interruption. In September of 1957, the county employees moved into their new offices and the demolition of the 93-year-old courthouse began in early October. The judicial branch was then built on the north side and the cornerstone was laid on December 10, 1957.

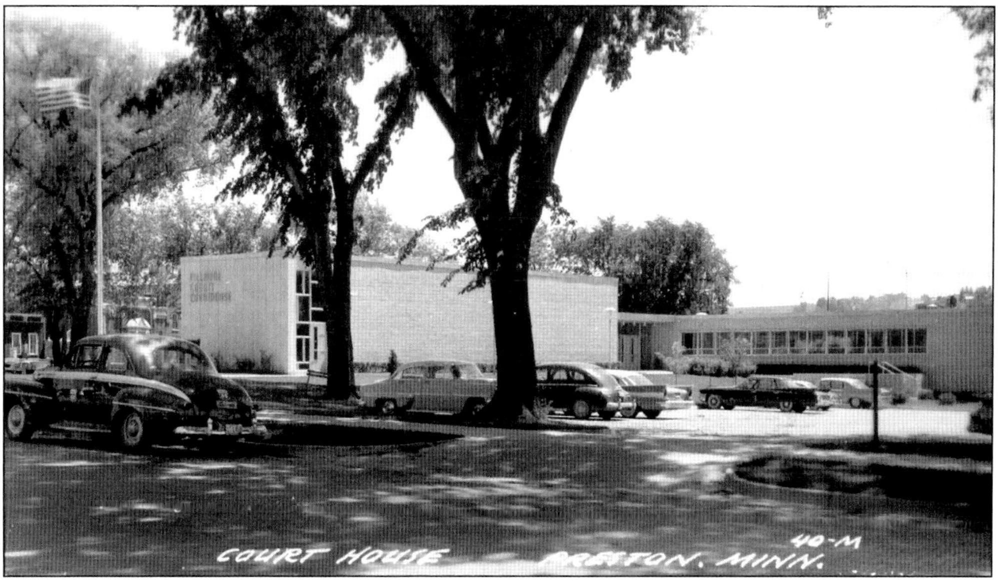


"The new building is a beauty, one that Fillmore County can well be proud of," the *Preston Republican* wrote in September of 1957. The flat roof was designed so that the building could receive an additional floor if expansion was ever deemed necessary. There were two parking lots with space for 56 cars, which relieved parking congestion on the streets. The total cost of the project, which was constructed from 1956 through 1958, was $475,000 with a $250,000 bond issue.

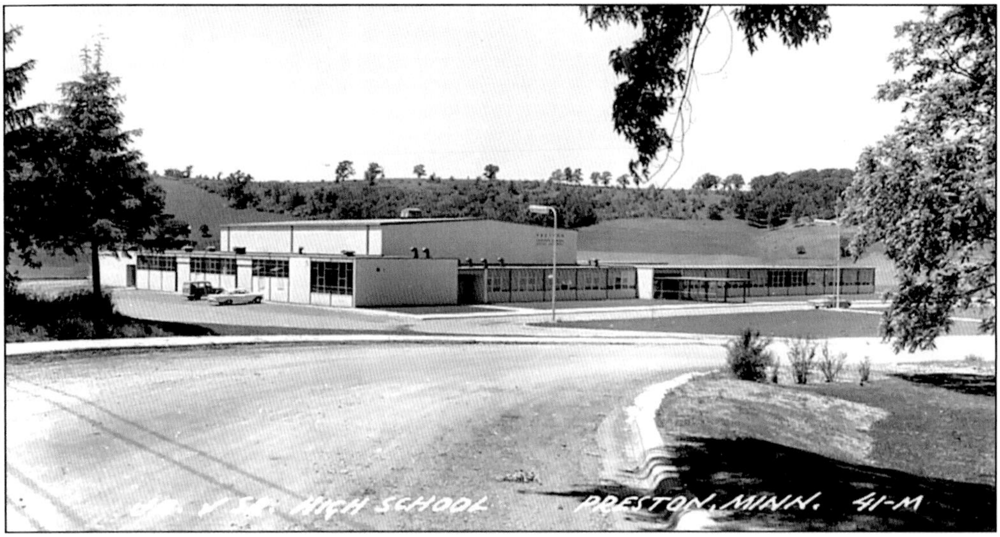


In the mid-1950s, 18 common and rural school districts voted for dissolution and consolidation into the Preston School District. This brought 610 students into the Preston School District for grades K–12. A school bond issue for $940,000 was passed in September of 1957 to build a new school. The vote was 388 in favor and 263 opposed. The project included a $100,000 elementary unit in Fountain and a $725,000 high school in Preston. The remaining $115,000 was used for purchase of the site, equipment, and architect fees. The new junior/senior high school was built and dedicated on November 15, 1959. Total cost of the building project was $822,000.

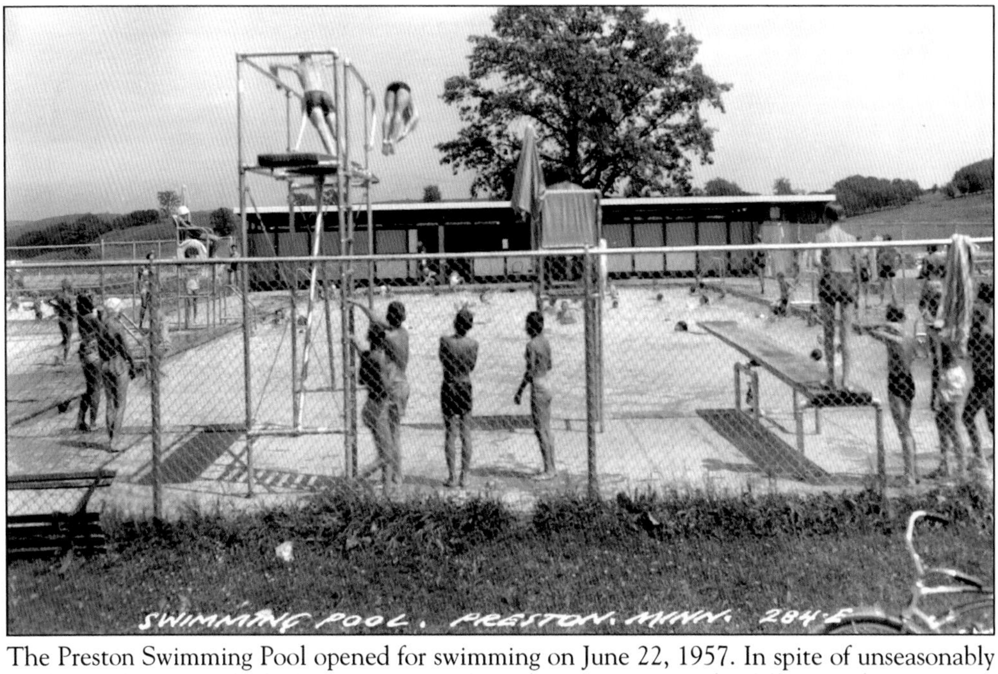


The Preston Swimming Pool opened for swimming on June 22, 1957. In spite of unseasonably chilly weather, a total of 250 swimmers took to the new waters. The following day was even colder, and just 50 "polar bears" turned out. The large pool measured 42 by 84 feet and the wading pool measured 20 by 30 feet. The cost of the construction was $32,720, not including the bathhouse and fencing.

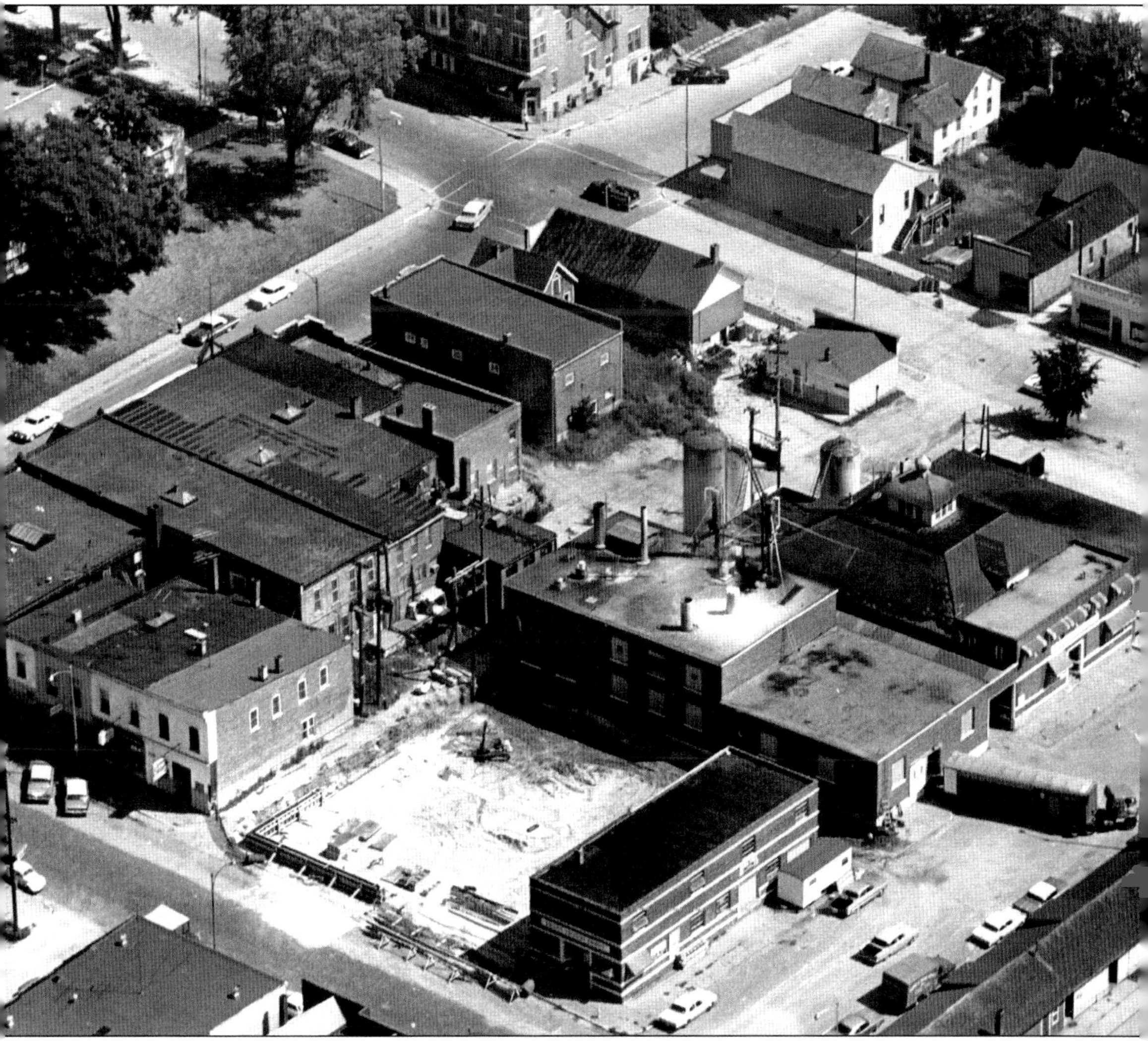

The Preston Creamery Association started construction on a drying plant and warehouse addition to their existing building in August of 1966. The new building was constructed on the site of the former Schibursky Shoe Store and Bud Olson buildings. The large building measured over 10,000 square feet and boosted the milk drying capacity of the plant by some 30 percent.

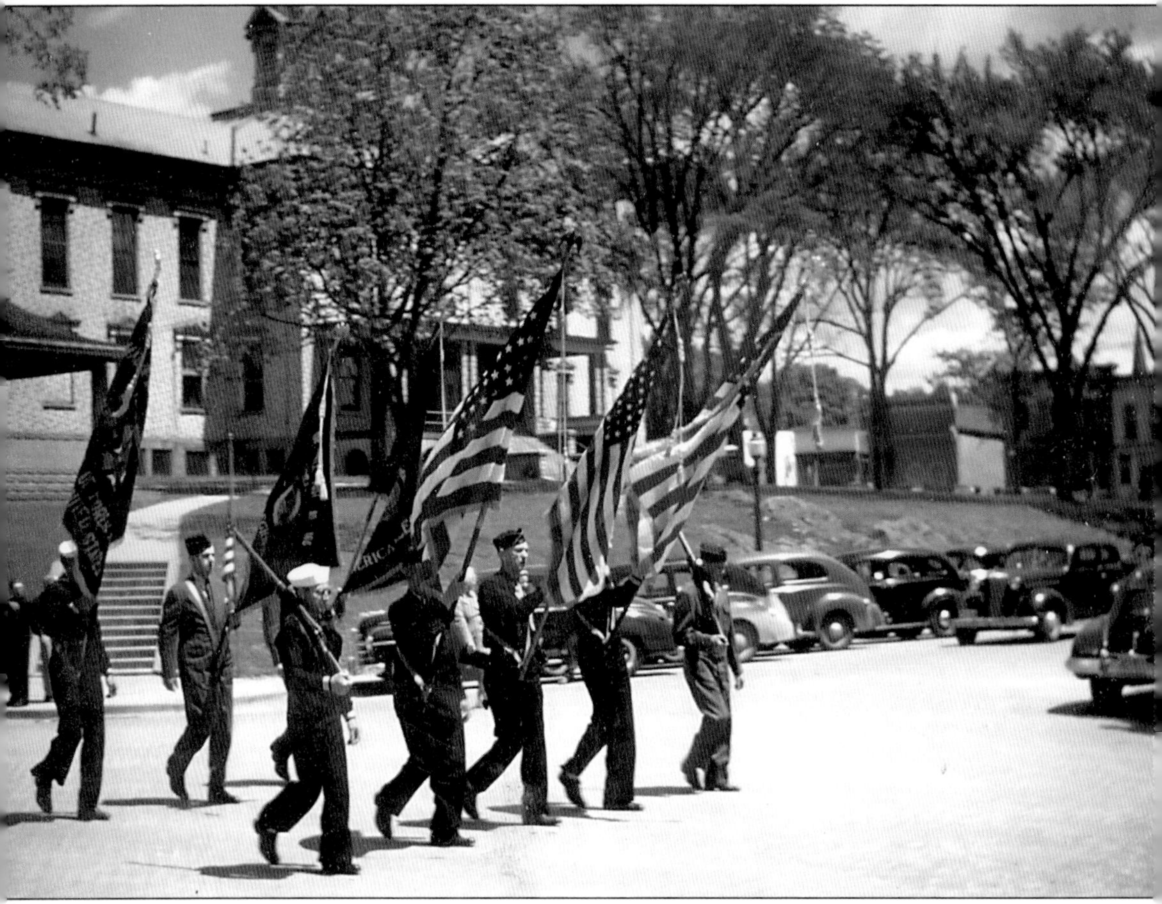

Veterans of World War II proudly march in the color guard for a late 1940s Memorial Day parade. Tommy Carlin is pictured on the left in the front row, and Ray LaFreniere is on the far right in the front row. The Veterans of Foreign Wars Post was formed in Preston on April 6, 1946. There were 37 charter members of the new Post, all veterans who had served on foreign lands in some branch of the military.